T0301012

2nd Edition

Yves Balasko
University of York, UK

2nd Edition

 **World Scientific**

EW JERSEY · LONDON · SINGAPORE · BEIJING · SHANGHAI · HONG KONG · TAIPEI · CHENNAI · TOKYO

Published by

World Scientific Publishing Co. Pte. Ltd.

5 Toh Tuck Link, Singapore 596224

USA office: 27 Warren Street, Suite 401-402, Hackensack, NJ 07601

UK office: 57 Shelton Street, Covent Garden, London WC2H 9HE

Library of Congress Cataloging-in-Publication Data

Names: Balasko, Yves, author.

Title: Foundations of the theory of general equilibrium / Yves Balasko (University of York, UK).

Description: 2nd edition. | New Jersey : World Scientific, [2016] | Includes bibliographical references.

Identifiers: LCCN 2015041027 | ISBN 9789814651707 (hc : alk. paper)

Subjects: LCSH: Equilibrium (Economics)

Classification: LCC HB145 .B32 2016 | DDC 339.5--dc23

LC record available at http://lccn.loc.gov/2015041027

British Library Cataloguing-in-Publication Data

A catalogue record for this book is available from the British Library.

Desk Editors: Nisha Rahul/Karimah Samsudin

Typeset by Stallion Press
Email: enquiries@stallionpress.com

Printed in Singapore

Contents

Chapter 1

The Exchange Model

1.1. Introduction

The theory of general economic equilibrium consists of a collection of mathematical models whose goal is to represent the main determinants and forms of economic activity. Unlike the so-called partial equilibrium models, general equilibrium models do not assume away the many complex interactions that are typical of modern economies. The first general equilibrium model is due to Walras and appeared in the *Eléments d'Economie Politique Pure* whose first edition was published in 1874 [41]. This model went through some evolution in the subsequent works of Pareto, von Neumann, Hicks, McKenzie, Arrow, Debreu and a few others to culminate in Debreu's *Theory of Value* [12]. The formulation adopted by Debreu and the emphasis placed on work made by Arrow and Debreu in particular made such a big impression that this model quickly became known as the Arrow–Debreu model. More complex models that explicitly addressed time and uncertainty in particular, the big absentees of the Arrow–Debreu model, were then developed to fill in some gaps appearing in the Arrow–Debreu model.

The exchange model is the simplest model of all general equilibrium models because there is no specific structure in this model on the commodity space and there is no production. There is in particular no time nor uncertainty. Only exchange is considered.

Despite the relative simplicity of exchange in that model, its study quickly becomes quite challenging.

The more complex models include production, public goods, externalities, financial assets, time and uncertainty. All these models are built on the simpler exchange model. This evidently reflects the economic importance of markets in modern economies that affect all forms of economic activity. This therefore explains that the properties of the exchange model are going to play a decisive role in the study of those more complex general equilibrium models. The exchange model plays in economics a role that is similar in many respects to the role played by linear algebra, calculus and point-set topology in mathematics. This reason alone would amply justify a full book devoted to the study of the exchange model.

The study of a general equilibrium model is essentially a study of the properties of the equation defined by the equality of supply and demand in that model, an equation known as the equilibrium equation. There is more than one way to skin a cat and, unsurprisingly, to study an equation. Algebra is one of them and may seem to many to be the most appropriate. But geometry can also be helpful because many properties can have nice geometric formulations. For example, squaring the circle is a question about the nature of the non-trivial roots of the equation $\sin x = 0$. The study of equations that are differentiable in the sense that it is possible to compute their derivatives can take advantage of the global perspective and tools that have been developed in Differential Topology [1, 19, 20, 29, 35]. Of particular interest is Morse Theory that relates singularities of smooth mappings and global properties of smooth manifolds [28]. It is even more remarkable that the study of the equilibrium equation can be rephrased as the study of the natural projection, a smooth mapping between two smooth manifolds introduced by Balasko in [8]. The natural projection provides the exact setup for the application of the Arnold–Thom–Zeeman theory of singularities of smooth mappings, a theory also known under the flashy name of Catastrophe Theory [2, 3, 18], to the study of the properties of the equilibrium equation of the exchange model.

In this book, three different approaches are developed. This introductory chapter is devoted to a minimalist but very general presentation of the exchange model, and Chapter 2 looks at the study of the equilibrium equation from an algebraic perspective. The model is general in the sense that the number of consumers and goods are arbitrary or, in other words, larger than or equal to two. Nevertheless, the exchange model considered in this chapter is not the most general one because consumers' preferences are assumed to be represented by log-linear utility functions. Under this restrictive assumption, solving the equilibrium equation is equivalent to finding the eigenvector associated with the Perron–Frobenius root (or eigenvalue) of some positive matrix, in other words a linear algebra problem. Chapter 3 is devoted to the special case of an exchange model with two consumers, two goods and fixed total resources. These assumptions simplify the model to such an extent that it is possible to study many of its properties with the tools of elementary analysis without compromising rigor. Geometry also plays an important role in this chapter. Incidentally, the material in the first part of that chapter is standard fare and can be found in almost every graduate textbook. This systematic treatment of the exchange model first appeared in Bowley's remarkable little book [11] and is recalled here mainly for reader's convenience.[1] A third-dimension, the price dimension, is added to the Edgeworth–Bowley box in order to "see" what the equilibrium manifold looks like in a three-dimensional space. Several important properties of the natural projection, the map from the equilibrium manifold into the parameter space, can then be established by just adopting this perspective. These properties are general in the sense that they remain true for an arbitrary number of goods and consumers as will be seen in later chapters. This part has no textbook equivalent. Chapter 4 prepares the study in full generality of the exchange model by developing consumer theory for an arbitrary number of goods. In this chapter, consumers are equipped with preference relations that

---

[1]The first presentation of the Edgeworth–Bowley box diagram with application to the equilibrium prices associated with a given economy is due to Pareto [31].

can be represented by smooth, smoothly monotone and smoothly quasi-concave utility functions. Under these assumptions, consumers' demand functions satisfy a number of properties that go from the Weak Axiom of Revealed Preferences (WARP) to the properties of the Slutsky matrix that involves the first-order derivatives of individual demand functions. Again, the material in this chapter is well known and can be found in any graduate textbook. It is included in this book for reader's convenience.

From Chapter 5 on, the stage is set for the study of the equilibrium equation through the equilibrium manifold and the natural projection with the help of the concepts and tools developed in Differential Topology for the study of smooth mappings and their singularities. Chapter 5 is devoted to the study of the equilibrium manifold, the domain of the natural projection. Total resources are assumed to be variable in this chapter and the following one. The main result in this chapter is the diffeomorphism of the equilibrium manifold with a Euclidean space. Chapter 6 follows with the study of the natural projection, a map that can be identified to a smooth proper map from a Euclidean space into itself. Chapter 7 extends the properties proved in the two previous chapters to the case of a smaller parameter space when total resources are fixed. Results obtained in Chapters 5 and 6 do extend to the cases considered in Chapter 7, but they require in general much stronger assumptions. These assumptions are satisfied in the setup considered in this book, but one can think very easily of environments where they would not be satisfied anymore. Chapter 8 goes deeper into the analysis of the natural projection by relating its singularities to Thom's general formulation of envelope theory. Chapter 9 develops a dual version of the envelope theoretic approach to the natural projection. In this setup, the equilibrium equation is shown to be equivalent to the equation describing the intersection of smooth submanifolds. This perspective lends itself more easily to the analysis of the general case of an arbitrary number of goods and consumers under fixed total resources than the direct approach to the equilibrium manifold and its natural projection. Applications are given to the characterization of economies with multiple equilibria, to the characterization of economies with a unique equilibrium and also to the study of the smooth selections of equilibrium prices. Chapter 10 ends this book by briefly discussing various extensions of the exchange model to sunspot equilibria and production in particular. A mathematical appendix that contains the main mathematical properties used in the book is included for reader's convenience.

1.2. Goods, Prices and Consumers

The exchange model is the simplest of all general equilibrium models because there is only one kind of economic agents, the consumers and exchange is the only economic activity. This model offers no representation of financial instruments nor money. Time and uncertainty do not appear explicitly. Nevertheless and despite its relative simplicity, this model has enough structure to capture many important features of price-decentralized economies.

The exchange model requires the definition of the following three elements: (1) The goods that are traded; (2) Consumers' individual endowments; (3) Consumers' demand functions reflecting consumers' preferences.

1.2.1. Goods

Number of goods

Exchange can take place only with at least two goods. (There is no money in the model.) The number of goods $\ell \geq 2$ is assumed to be finite.

Measurability

The words 'goods' and 'commodities' are considered as synonymous and used interchangeably. It is implicit that each good traded in a market is measurable, by which one means that the equality and the sum of two quantities of that good are defined. In Physics, mass is measurable while ordinary temperature is not. (It suffices to add temperatures measured on the Celsius and Fahrenheit scales respectively to see that the sum of two temperatures depends on the choice of a temperature scale and, therefore, is not intrinsically defined.) In consumer theory, ordinal utility is another example of a non-measurable concept. For a presentation of modern measurement theory, see for example [30] where the "sum of two quantities" is defined as the "concatenation operator."

National Defense is an economic good to the extent that its production requires resources that are not available for alternative uses. But, there is no obvious way of defining the equality of two quantities of national defense or, even harder, of their sum. Non-measurability is a characteristic of many public goods. Goods traded in markets have to be measurable.

Divisibility

In addition to being measurable, goods are assumed to be divisible. Not many commodity, if any, are perfectly divisible. The divisibility assumption is at best an approximation whose relevance depends on the size of the smallest indivisible marketable quantity of a good.

Units

It is always possible to define a unitary quantity or unit of any measurable good. Unless explicitly specified otherwise, units of divisible goods are chosen arbitrarily. For indivisible goods, units must be multiples of the smallest indivisible quantities. Once units have been defined, the number x^j, a real number for a divisible good and an integer for an indivisible good, represents a well-defined quantity of that good j. This quantity can be either positive or negative. One interprets positive quantities as actually owned (by some consumer who is usually specified by the notation or the context) while negative ones correspond to debts. The Euclidean space $\mathbb{R}^\ell$ is known as the commodity space.

Commodity bundles

The vector $x = (x^j) = (x^1, x^2, \ldots, x^\ell) \in \mathbb{R}^\ell$ describes quantities of goods as the coordinates of a vector of the commodity space $\mathbb{R}^\ell$. These quantities can be positive or negative. The vector $x \in \mathbb{R}^\ell$ is known as a commodity bundle.

1.2.2. Prices

Once a unit has been defined for good j, the price of one unit of that good is a strictly positive number $p_j > 0$. It is more simply known as the price of good j. The prices of the ℓ goods define the price vector $p = (p_1, p_2, \ldots, p_\ell) \in \mathbb{R}^\ell_{++}$.

Numeraire

The price vector $p = (p_1, p_2, \ldots, p_\ell)$ is normalized by the convention $p_\ell = 1$. One then says that the ℓth commodity is the numeraire. The numeraire is a commodity used as a standard of reference to express the prices of the other commodities. The numeraire can be viewed as a form of commodity money. An example of numeraire would be gold in ancient economies. Setting the price of good ℓ to $p_\ell = 1$ is known as the numeraire convention. Other normalizations exist for the price vector $p = (p_1, p_2, \ldots, p_\ell)$. The numeraire convention lends itself most easily to computations and is therefore the one used by default in this book.

The set of (numeraire normalized) price vectors is the set,

$$S = \{p = (p_1, p_2, \ldots, p_{\ell-1}, p_\ell) \in \mathbb{R}^\ell \mid p_j > 0 \text{ for all } j \text{ and } p_\ell = 1\}.$$

Value of a commodity bundle

By definition, the value of the quantity x^j of commodity j given the price p_j (of the unit of commodity j) is equal to the product $p_j\, x^j$. The value of the commodity bundle $x = (x^j)$ given the price vector p is simply the inner product,

$$p \cdot x = \sum_{j=1}^{\ell} p_j\, x^j.$$

1.2.3. Consumers

There is only one kind of economic agent in the exchange model. These agents exchange goods between themselves. They are customarily called consumers in order not to be confused with producers, another category of economic agents considered in economic theory. Since a consumer can exchange goods only with another consumer, the number m of consumers in an economy is finite and at least equal to 2.

Consumption space

The consumption space X of a given consumer is a subset of the commodity space $\mathbb{R}^{\ell}$. The idea of the consumption space is to express the idea that not all commodity bundles can be consumed. For example, a standard interpretation considers that only non-negative quantities of goods can be consumed, in which case the consumption space is the non-negative orthant $\mathbb{R}^{\ell}_+ = \{x = (x^1, \dots, x^{\ell}) \in \mathbb{R}^{\ell} \mid x^j \geq 0\}$. If one wants to allow buying and selling agents to be more than just consumers who consume the goods that they have bought on the market, it is natural to allow for the "negative" consumption of some goods. These negative quantities must then be delivered to the market by those consumers when the market closes.

In this book, we will consider that the consumption space is the full commodity space except in Chapters 2 and 3.

Demand functions

The main goal of consumer theory is to express a consumer's buying and selling activities as a function of market prices and consumer's wealth from the preferences that the consumer has for goods. The goal of equilibrium theory is then to derive the properties that are satisfied by markets made of such consumers. This approach will be developed in the next chapters. In the meantime, a minimalist version of consumer's behavior suffices for the definition of the main characteristics of the exchange model up to the definition of an equilibrium concept. This minimalist version will not be sufficient, however, for a general study of the properties of the exchange model.

Consumer's behavior is modeled by way of a function or mapping defined on the space of prices and wealth and taking its values in the consumption space X.

Definition 1.1. Consumer i's demand function is a mapping f_i: $S \times \mathbb{R} \to X$.

The vector $f_i(p, w_i) \in X$ represents the bundle of goods that is demanded by consumer i given the price vector $p \in S$ and wealth $w_i \in \mathbb{R}$.

The following properties are assumed to be satisfied by demand functions:

Definition 1.2.

(i) Walras law (W) is the identity $p \cdot f_i(p, w_i) = w_i$ for all $(p, w_i) \in S \times \mathbb{R}$.

(ii) Smoothness (S) is differentiability of f_i up to any order.

Endowments

Definition 1.3. Consumer i's endowments are represented by a vector $\omega_i \in X$.

The commodity bundle $\omega_i \in X$ represents the goods owned by consumer i before the market opens. These goods can also be thought of goods that are brought to the market by consumer i. Again, note that there are no sign restrictions on the endowment vector $\omega_i \in X$ if the consumption space is the full commodity space $X = \mathbb{R}^\ell$.

The endowment vector $\omega_i \in X$ is a commodity bundle, a vector in the commodity space, and is not to be confused with the argument of consumer i's demand function, namely the wealth w_i that is only a real number.

Given the price vector $p \in S$, consumer i's wealth w_i is then equal to the value $p \cdot \omega_i$ of the endowment vector ω_i for the price vector $p \in S$.

1.3. The Exchange Model

1.3.1. The endowment m-tuple

The endowment m-tuple $\omega = (\omega_1, \omega_2, \ldots, \omega_m) \in X^m$ represents the endowments of every consumer in the economy. The set of endowment m-tuples is denoted by Ω and is known as the endowment or parameter set.

1.3.2. The exchange model

From now on, the demand functions f_i are fixed for $1 \leq i \leq m$. The exchange model is defined by the ℓ goods, the consumption space X and the parameter space Ω. The only variable parameter is the endowment m-tuple $\omega = (\omega_i) \in \Omega$. An economy is identified to its endowment m-tuple $\omega \in \Omega$.

1.3.3. Individual excess demand

Given the price vector $p \in S$ and endowment vector $\omega_i \in X$, consumer i's demand is equal to $f_i(p, p \cdot \omega_i)$. Consumer i's excess demand is then equal to

$$z_i(p, \omega_i) = f_i(p, p \cdot \omega_i) - \omega_i.$$

Consumer i's excess demand function is the partial map $z_i(\,.\,, \omega_i) : S \to \mathbb{R}^\ell$ that associates with $p \in S$ the excess demand $z_i(p, \omega_i)$.

1.3.4. Aggregate excess demand

The aggregate excess demand for the pair $(p, \omega) \in S \times \Omega$ is the sum over all consumers in the economy of their individual excess demands. Aggregate excess demand is then equal to

$$z(p, \omega) = \sum_{i=1}^{m} z_i(p, \omega_i).$$

The aggregate excess demand function for the economy $\omega \in \Omega$ is defined as the partial function $z(.,\omega) : S \to \mathbb{R}^\ell$.

1.4. Equilibrium

Definition 1.4. The pair $(p, \omega) \in S \times \Omega$ is an equilibrium if and only if the associated aggregate excess demand $z(p, \omega)$ is equal to 0.

The equilibrium $(p, \omega) \in S \times \Omega$ is then a zero of the equilibrium equation,

$$z(p, \omega) = 0. \tag{1}$$

The equilibrium equation (1) expresses the equality of total demand and supply. Indeed, at $(p, \omega) \in S \times \Omega$, total demand is the sum of individual demands and is equal to $\sum_i f_i(p, p \cdot \omega_i)$. Total supply is the sum of individual resources or endowments and is equal to $\sum_i \omega_i$. Then, $z(p, \omega) = 0$ is equivalent to

$$\sum_i f_i(p, p \cdot \omega_i) = \sum_i \omega_i. \tag{2}$$

Definition 1.5. The price vector $p \in S$ is an equilibrium (price vector) for the economy $\omega = (\omega_1, \omega_2, \ldots, \omega_m) \in \Omega$ if and only if the pair $(p, \omega) \in S \times \Omega$ is an equilibrium.

An equilibrium price vector $p \in S$ for the economy $\omega \in \Omega$ is therefore a zero of the aggregate excess demand function $z(., \omega)$: $S \to \mathbb{R}^\ell$ for that economy $\omega \in \Omega$. Equilibrium theory consists in the study of the equation $z(p, \omega) = 0$ when the parameter or economy ω is varied in the parameter or endowment space Ω.

Let $W(\omega)$ be the set of equilibrium price vectors associated with the economy $\omega \in \Omega$. At the moment, there is not much that can be said about the set $W(\omega)$ except that it is a subset of the price set S. With so few assumptions regarding consumers' demand functions, it is impossible to determine when the set $W(\omega)$ is non-empty and, when non-empty, whether it contains one or several elements.

The equilibrium correspondence $W : \Omega \rightrightarrows S$ associates the subset $W(\omega)$ with the economy $\omega \in \Omega$. The domain of this correspondence is the endowment set Ω and the range is the price set S. (A function or map or mapping is a special case of a correspondence because it associates one and only one element of its range with every element of its domain.) At the current level of generality, the equilibrium correspondence is not even a function.

The equilibrium correspondence is also known in the literature as the Walras correspondence. To a large extent, equilibrium theory amounts to the study of the equilibrium correspondence $W : \Omega \rightrightarrows S$.

1.5. The Equilibrium Manifold

Definition 1.6. The equilibrium manifold E is the subset of $S \times \Omega$ defined by the equilibrium equation $z(p, \omega) = 0$.

Despite the term of "manifold", the equilibrium manifold E is at this stage and at this level of generality nothing more than a subset of the Cartesian product $S \times \Omega$. It will be shown in later chapters that the equilibrium manifold E is indeed a smooth manifold and, even better, a smooth submanifold of the Cartesian product $S \times \Omega$ under quite mild additional assumptions regarding the collection of consumers' demand functions (f_i).

1.6. The Natural Projection

The properties of the equilibrium manifold E play an important role in the study of the equilibrium equation $z(p, \omega) = 0$. Some of these properties deal with the way the equilibrium manifold E is embedded or, in other words, is a subset of the Cartesian product $S \times \Omega$. This leads to the following:

Definition 1.7. The natural projection is the map $\pi : E \to \Omega$ that is the restriction to the equilibrium manifold E viewed as a subset of $S \times \Omega$ of the projection map $(p, \omega) \to \omega$ from $S \times \Omega$ onto Ω.

In practice, this means that $\pi(p, \omega) = \omega$. In this formula, (p, ω) is an equilibrium, not an arbitrary element of $S \times \Omega$. The natural projection map $\pi : E \to \Omega$ is a mathematical object that is different from the projection map $S \times \Omega \to \Omega$ even if these two maps have the same "formula". The domain of the projection $S \times \Omega \to \Omega$ is the Cartesian product $S \times \Omega$ while the domain of the "natural projection" $\pi : E \to \Omega$ is the equilibrium manifold E, a subset of $S \times \Omega$.

1.7. Conclusion

The equilibrium correspondence W and the natural projection are related through the equality,

$$\pi^{-1}(\omega) = W(\omega) \times \{\omega\}. \tag{3}$$

The study of the natural projection $\pi : E \to \Omega$ is therefore equivalent to the study of the equilibrium correspondence. The definite advantage of the natural projection over the equilibrium correspondence is that a map carries more structure than a correspondence. A map is a special case of a correspondence. A function is characterized by the fact that it associates one and only one value with every element of its domain. In the case of the natural projection, these properties are obvious: the image of the equilibrium $(p, \omega) \in E$ by the natural projection $\pi : E \to \Omega$ is the (unique) element $\omega \in \Omega$.

The property that the natural projection $\pi : E \to \Omega$ is a map, a map that will be shown to be differentiable under suitable assumptions, will open up the way for the application of some of the most powerful tools of elementary Differential Topology.

1.8. Notes and Comments

The observation that market prices equate aggregate supply and demand is made for the first time by Adam Smith in 1776 [34]. The identification of market prices to solutions of the equilibrium equation starts the analytical phase of economic theory. Walras's [41] definition of consumers' demand functions as maximizing utility functions subject to budget constraints follows Adam Smith's definition of an equilibrium by almost a 100 years. This formulation of consumer's demand enables Walras to be the first economist to write down the equilibrium equation of an exchange economy at the level of generality considered in the current book. Walras is also the first economist to start doing equilibrium analysis in a modern sense. Walras' approach is interesting and full of insights even if it does not satisfy the modern standards of rigor.

For example, Walras deals with the existence and structure of equilibria by merely counting equations and unknowns, checking that their numbers are the same. Walras also describes an out-of-equilibrium process where the price of a commodity in short supply is revised upwardly, and downwardly in case of excess supply. Walras's approach is very interesting from the modern perspective of differential topology and the theory of dynamical systems. With differential topology, the counting equation argument becomes an important step in proving the generic determinateness of the equilibrium solutions.

The first rigorous proof of the existence and uniqueness of an equilibrium solution is given by Wald in 1936 under the additional assumption of gross substitutability at all prices [39] (English translation in [40]). The first existence proofs without gross substitutability and differentiability are published in 1954 by Arrow and Debreu in [4] and McKenzie in [26].

Walras misses the economic importance of the uniqueness vs. multiplicity issue because he wrongly believes that equilibrium is unique whenever the number of goods is greater than or equal to three [41]. For Walras, the multiplicity of equilibrium solutions he acknowledges in the case of two goods is at best a mathematical curiosity. Auspitz and Lieben are the first to fully understand the economic importance of the multiplicity issue. In their 1889 treatise [5], they circumvent this problem by assuming that equilibrium is unique. But, it follows from their correspondence with Walras [23] and an article published in 1909 [6] that they make this assumption only for simplicity's sake, not because they think that equilibrium is always unique. But, at the time, there are no theory of singularities of smooth maps in general and no catastrophe theory in particular around. Auspitz and Lieben address bare-handed the difficult multiplicity problem and, unsurprisingly, are rewarded with little success. Nevertheless, Schumpeter's view that [33, p. 969] "...from the standpoint of *any* exact science, the existence of a 'uniquely determined equilibrium (set of values)' is ...of the utmost importance, even if proof has to be purchased at the price of very restrictive assumptions" is the guiding principle that underlies the uniqueness results of Wald, Arrow and Hurwicz, and Arrow, Block and Hurwicz under the gross substitution assumption or variations of this assumption.

When uniqueness cannot be established, the least Schumpeter expects is what in modern terms amounts to the local determinateness of the equilibrium solutions. In an article that marks the introduction of the techniques of differential topology in economic theory [13], Debreu shows in 1970 that equilibrium solutions are locally determined for a category of economies he calls regular, the set of these regular economies being an open and dense (in fact with full Lebesgue measure) subset of the endowment set.

The history of the uniqueness problem and of the more general determinateness problem illustrates the belief that was widely dominant among economists up to the 1970s that real-world economies are so well behaved that any relevant model is to have unique or at least locally determined solutions. This view not only explains the search for sufficient conditions for uniqueness that are reasonably general, but also denies economic reality to the phenomena that can be predicted in the presence of multiple or undetermined equilibria. These phenomena involve discontinuities, jumps and even chaos. Debreu's 1970 result comforts the dominant view by excluding such discontinuities at regular economies.

The real-world importance of discontinuities in a variety of fields ranging from biology to sociology is underlined by Thom and Zeeman in the early 1970s in what they call catastrophe theory [36, 37]. The mathematical setup of catastrophe theory is formally identical to the one of the natural projection, namely a map $\pi : E \rightarrow \Omega$. In the original version of catastrophe theory, the issue is the determination of the map π (for example, the determination of a local set of coordinates) from the qualitative picture of some local singularity of the map. Catastrophe theory has gradually evolved from a modeling tool into a theory of discontinuous phenomena within differentiable models [2]. The formulation of the general equilibrium model within the setup of the natural projection $\pi : E \rightarrow \Omega$ and, therefore, its identification with the mathematical model underlying catastrophe theory is due to Balasko in 1975 [7]. The economic importance of the discontinuities that occur at critical equilibria is highlighted in [9]. The question remains of a rigorous identification of the discontinuities predicted by the general equilibrium model with those observed in the real world.

1.9. Exercises

1.1. Let $a = (a_i^1, \ldots, a_i^\ell)$ where $\sum_j a_i^j = 1$ and $a_i^j > 0$ for $1 \le j \le \ell$.
Define $f_i(p, w_i)$ for $p = (p_1, p_2, \ldots, p_\ell) \in S$ and $w_i > 0$ by

$$f_i(p, w_i) = \left(\frac{a_i^1}{p_1}, \ldots, \frac{a_i^\ell}{p_\ell} \right) w_i.$$

(i) Show that the function $f_i : S \times \mathbb{R}_{++} \to X$ satisfies (S) and (W).

(ii) Show that the function f_i is a diffeomorphism (i.e., is differentiable up to any order, is a bijection, and its inverse map is also differentiable up to any order.)

1.2. (i) Show that the identity $p \cdot z(p, \omega) = 0$ is satisfied for every $(p, \omega) \in S \times \Omega$.

(ii) Give an example of an exchange model with m demand functions f_i, some of which do not satisfy (W), such that $p \cdot z(p, \omega) \ne 0$ for every $(p, \omega) \in S \times \Omega$. Prove that the equilibrium manifold E is then the empty set $\emptyset$.

1.3. Assume that each demand function $f_i : S \times \mathbb{R} \to X$ satisfies (S) and (W). Let $B = S \times \mathbb{R}^m$. Let $f : B \to S \times \Omega$ be the map defined by $f(p, w_1, \ldots, w_m) = (p, f_1(p, w_1), \ldots, f_m(p, w_m))$. Let $T = f(B)$ be the subset of $S \times \Omega$ that is the image of B.

(i) Prove that T is a subset of the equilibrium manifold E.

(ii) Derive from (i) that T is non-empty.

(iii) Prove that T is a closed subset of $S \times \Omega$ that is homeomorphic to B.

(iv) Prove that T is a smooth submanifold of $S \times \Omega$. (Apply for example the regular value theorem to the equations defining T as a subset of $S \times \Omega$.)

(v) Prove that T is a diffeomorphic to B. (Show that the map f viewed as a map from B to T has a smooth inverse.)

1.4. Assume that each demand function $f_i : S \times \mathbb{R} \to X$ satisfies (S) and (W). Give an example where the natural projection $\pi : E \to \Omega$ is not onto.

Chapter 2

A Simple Linear Version
of the Exchange Model

2.1. Introduction

The theory of general equilibrium can be quite simple under suitable
assumptions regarding demand functions or, more accurately, on the
utility functions that generate these demand functions. It suffices
to have preferences represented by log-linear (or Cobb–Douglas)
utility functions. Every coordinate of the equilibrium equation can
be turned into a linear equation through multiplication by the
commodity price. Then, all that is needed for the study of the general
equilibrium model is basically some general linear algebra. Most
properties are simpler to establish than in the general case because
of the many linearities. For example, existence and uniqueness of
equilibrium is a direct consequence of the Perron–Frobenius theorem
of linear algebra. No differential topology is necessary.

2.2. Log-Linear Utility Functions and their
Associated Demand Functions

As an exception to the general case treated in the previous and
introductory chapters, the consumption set X is the strictly positive
orthant in the current chapter, i.e., $X = \mathbb{R}^{\ell}_{++}$. To preserve the
symmetry that exists between the various goods, it is also more

elegant not to normalize the price system $p = (p_1, \ldots, p_{\ell-1}, p_\ell) \in \mathbb{R}^{\ell}_{++}$ for a while.

2.2.1. Log-linear utilities

The utility of consumer i is defined by the log-linear utility function,

$$u_i(x_i) = \sum_{j=1}^{\ell} a_i^j \log x_i^j,$$

where the coefficients a_i^j are all strictly positive and normalized to sum up to 1, i.e., $\sum_j a_i^j = 1$.

2.2.2. Individual demand functions

Let $p \in X$ be some non-normalized price vector and w_i a strictly positive real number: $w_i > 0$. The following proposition gives an analytic expression of consumer i's demand function.

Proposition 2.1. *The demand function* $f_i : \mathbb{R}^{\ell}_{++} \times \mathbb{R}_{++} \to \mathbb{R}^{\ell}_{++}$ *associated with the utility function* $u_i(x_i) = \sum_{j=1}^{\ell} a_i^j \log x_i^j$ *is equal to*

$$f_i(p, w_i) = \begin{bmatrix} a_i^1/p_1 \\ \vdots \\ a_i^j/p_j \\ \vdots \\ a_i^\ell/p_\ell \end{bmatrix} w_i. \tag{1}$$

Proof. Consumer i's demand $f_i(p, w_i)$ solves the problem:

$$\text{Maximize} \quad u_i(x_i)$$

subject to the budget constraint

$$p \cdot x_i = w_i. \tag{2}$$

The first-order conditions for this maximization problem take the form,

$$\frac{\partial u_i}{\partial x_i^j} = \lambda p_j \tag{3}$$

for $j = 1, 2, \ldots, \ell-1, \ell$ in addition to the budget constraint (2). These conditions are equivalent to

$$\frac{a_i^j}{x_i^j} = \lambda p_j,$$

equivalent to

$$a_i^j = \lambda p_j x_i^j$$

for $j = 1, 2, \ldots, \ell$.

The value of the Lagrange multiplier λ is determined by adding up all these equalities, which yields the equality,

$$1 = \sum_j a_i^j = \lambda \left(\sum_j p_j x_i^j \right) = \lambda w_i,$$

from which follows

$$\lambda = \frac{1}{w_i}.$$

It then comes

$$x_i^j = \frac{a_i^j w_i}{p_j}$$

for $1 \leq j \leq \ell$. $\qquad\qquad\qquad\qquad\qquad\qquad\qquad\square$

This expression of consumer i's demand is independent of the normalization used for the price vector $p = (p_1, \ldots, p_\ell) \in \mathbb{R}_{++}^\ell$. Recall that the numeraire normalization means $p_\ell = 1$ and is often used, including in the case of log-linear utility functions considered in this chapter.

To save space, equality (1) is often written as

$$f_i(p, w_i)^T = \left[a_i^1/p_1, \ldots, a_i^j/p_j, \ldots, a_i^\ell/p_\ell \right] w_i, \tag{4}$$

where $f_i(p, w_i)^T$ is the transposed of the column matrix that represents $f_i(p, w_i)$.

Corollary 2.2. *The demand function $f_i : X \times \mathbb{R}_{++} \to X$ associated with a log-linear utility function $u_i : X \to \mathbb{R}$ is differentiable up to any order.*

Proof. Follows readily for the formula giving the demand terms $f_i^j(p, w_i)$ as a function of w_i and p_j, noting that p_j is different from 0 since it is strictly positive for any j. $\square$

2.3. The Equilibrium Equation Defined by the Equality of Supply and Demand

An exchange economy consists of m consumers, where consumer i is equipped with a log-linear utility function $u_i : X \to \mathbb{R}$ and endowed with goods represented by the commodity bundle $w_i \in X = \mathbb{R}_{++}^\ell$. The parameter space Ω is the set of all possible m-tuples $\omega = (\omega_1, \ldots, \omega_i, \ldots, \omega_m)$ and is equal to the Cartesian product X^m.

Let $r = \sum_i \omega_i \in \mathbb{R}_{++}^\ell$ denote the total resources in the economy associated with $\omega = (\omega_1, \ldots, \omega_m)$. The total resources in good j with $1 \le j \le \ell$ in the economy $\omega = (\omega_1, \ldots, \omega_m)$ is denoted by $r^j = \sum_i \omega_i^j$.

By definition, the non-normalized price vector $p \in X$ is an equilibrium price vector of the economy defined by the m-tuple $\omega = (\omega_1, \ldots, \omega_m) \in \Omega$ if there is equality of aggregate supply and demand:

$$\sum_i f_i(p, p \cdot \omega_i) = \sum_i \omega_i = r. \tag{5}$$

Substituting in (5) the expression of the demand term $f_i(p, p \cdot \omega_i)$ in (1) yields the following equation system of ℓ equations with real coefficients and unknowns:

$$\frac{1}{p_j}\left(\sum_i a_i^j (p \cdot \omega_i)\right) = \sum_i \omega_i^j = r^j, \quad 1 \le j \le \ell. \tag{6}$$

The unknowns are the prices of the ℓ goods: $p_1, \ldots, p_{\ell-1}$ and p_ℓ. Recall that the numeraire normalization is equivalent to setting

$p_\ell = 1$, but we do not need it here. The equation system (6) is not linear because the price p_j, with j varying from 1 to ℓ, appears in the numerator and denominator of the left-hand side terms. Nevertheless, this equation system can easily be reduced to a well-known problem of linear algebra.

2.4. Equivalence between the Equilibrium Equation and a Linear Equation System

To transform the non-linear equation system (6) into an equivalent linear one, it suffices to multiply by the price p_j the equation defined by the equality of total supply and demand for commodity j, with j varying from 1 to ℓ. This yields the equation system,

$$\sum_i a_i^j (p \cdot \omega_i) = p_j r^j \qquad 1 \le j \le \ell. \tag{7}$$

Any solution $p = (p_1, \ldots, p_\ell) \in X$ is then a solution of the equation system (6) and, conversely, any solution $p \in X$ of (6) is a solution of (7). Note the importance for all coordinates of $p = (p_j) \in X$ of being strictly positive and, therefore, different from 0. Equation system (7) is linear with respect to the unknowns $p_1, p_2, \ldots, p_\ell$.

2.5. The Equilibrium Price Vector as an Eigenvector

Proposition 2.3. *There exists an $\ell \times \ell$ matrix $A(\omega)$ with the properties: (1) Matrix $A(\omega)$ has an eigenvalue equal to $\lambda = 1$; (2) Every (non-normalized) price vector $p \in X$ of the economy $\omega \in \Omega$ is an eigenvector of matrix $A(\omega)$ associated with the eigenvalue $\lambda = 1$; (3) Every vector $p \in X$ (i.e., all coordinates are strictly positive) that is also an eigenvector associated with the eigenvalue $\lambda = 1$ of $A(\omega)$ is a non-normalized equilibrium price vector of the economy $\omega \in \Omega$.*

Proof. The $\ell \times \ell$ matrix $A(\omega) = (\alpha_{kj})$ is defined by its coefficient of row k and column j:

$$\alpha_{kj} = \frac{\sum_i a_i^j \omega_i^k}{r^j}.$$

For k varying from 1 to ℓ, multiply the kth row of $A(\omega)$ by r^j. This yields a matrix $\tilde{A}(\omega)$ whose coefficient of row k and column j is equal to

$$\tilde{\alpha}_{kj}(\omega) = \sum_i a_i^j \omega_i^k.$$

Let the $\ell \times \ell$ matrix I be the identity matrix. The matrix $\tilde{I}$ is then defined as the $\ell \times \ell$ diagonal matrix whose coefficient of row and column k is equal to r^k.

Step 1: Matrix $A(\omega)$ has an eigenvalue equal to $\lambda = 1$

A: $\sum_j \tilde{\alpha}_{kj}(\omega) = r^k$. It comes

$$\sum_j \tilde{\alpha}_{kj}(\omega) = \sum_j \left(\sum_i a_i^j \omega_i^k \right)$$

$$= \sum_i \left(\sum_j a_i^j \omega_i^k \right)$$

$$= \sum_i \left(\sum_j a_i^j \right) \omega_i^k,$$

where $\sum_j a_i^j = 1$ and, therefore,

$$\sum_j \tilde{\alpha}_{kj}(\omega) = \sum_i \omega_i^k = r^k.$$

B: **Matrix $\tilde{A}(\omega) - \tilde{I}$ is not invertible.** It follows from (A) that adding up the rows of $\tilde{A}(\omega) - \tilde{I}$ yields the row $(0, 0, \ldots, 0)$ and therefore defines a relation of linear dependence between the rows of $\tilde{A}(\omega) - \tilde{I}$.

C: **$\lambda = 1$ is an eigenvalue of $A(\omega)$.** The eigenvalues λ of the matrix $A(\omega)$ are the solutions of the polynomial equation,

$$\det(A(\omega) - \lambda I) = 0.$$

Therefore, $\lambda = 1$ is an eigenvalue of the matrix $A(\omega)$ if and only if $\det(A(\omega) - I)$ is equal to 0. The relation of linear dependence between the rows of the matrix $\tilde{A}(\omega) - \tilde{I}$ of (B) implies a relation of linear dependence between the rows of matrix $A - I$, which implies that the determinant $\det(A(\omega) - I)$ is equal to 0. The real number $\lambda = 1$ is therefore an eigenvalue of the matrix $A(\omega)$.

Step 2: Every price vector $p \in \mathbb{R}^\ell_{++}$ of the economy $\omega \in \Omega$ is an eigenvector of matrix $A(\omega)$ associated with the eigenvalue $\lambda = 1$. We have seen that the equilibrium price vectors associated with the economy $\omega \in \Omega$ are the solutions $p \in \mathbb{R}^\ell_{++}$ of

$$\sum_i a_i^j (p \cdot \omega_i) = p_j r^j,$$

an equation that has been shown to be equivalent to the equilibrium equation system (6). That equation system can be rewritten under the form,

$$\sum_i a_i^j \left(\sum_k p_k \omega_i^k \right) = p_j r^j.$$

Regrouping the terms in the left-hand side of the equation yields

$$\sum_k p_k \left(\sum_i a_i^j \omega_i^k \right) = p_j r^j.$$

Division by r^j that is strictly positive and, therefore, different from 0, yields the equivalent equation system,

$$\sum_k \frac{\sum_i a_i^j \omega_i^k}{r^j} p_k = p_j \tag{8}$$

with j varying from 1 to ℓ. That equation system can be rewritten in matrix form as

$$A(\omega)p = p, \tag{9}$$

where the price vector p is identified to a column or $\ell \times 1$ matrix. (In matrix notation, the transpose p^T is the row matrix equal to $(p_1, p_2, \ldots, p_{\ell-1}, p_\ell)$). The vector $p \in \mathbb{R}^\ell_{++}$ being different from 0 is therefore an eigenvector of $A(\omega)$ associated with the eigenvalue $\lambda = 1$.

Step 3: *Any eigenvector* $p \in \mathbb{R}^{\ell}_{++}$ *associated with* $\lambda = 1$ *is an equilibrium price vector of the economy* $\omega \in \Omega$. It suffices to go backwards in the calculations of Step 2 to see that $p \in \mathbb{R}^{\ell}_{++}$ satisfying equation (9) also satisfies the equilibrium equation (6) or its equivalent version (7). $\qquad\qquad\qquad\qquad\qquad\qquad\qquad\qquad$ □

It follows from $\lambda = 1$ being a real eigenvalue (real means here that it is a real and not a complex number) that one can associate with it a real eigenvector $p \in \mathbb{R}^{\ell}$, i.e., a vector whose coordinates are all real numbers. But, this does not prove that the coordinates of such an eigenvector are strictly positive. We are still short of proving the existence of an equilibrium price vector for any economy $\omega \in \Omega$. Nevertheless, the properties of matrix $A(\omega)$ will yield a proof of the existence of an equilibrium.

2.6. Existence and Uniqueness of Equilibrium

All the coefficients of matrix $A(\omega)$ being strictly positive, matrix $A(\omega)$ is known as a strictly positive matrix. Those matrices satisfy several remarkable properties that are regrouped in the Perron–Frobenius theorem [21, 8.2.11]. The first property is the existence of a strictly positive eigenvalue $\lambda(A(\omega))$ that is known as the Perron–Frobenius root, an eigenvalue that is strictly larger than the modulus of any other eigenvalue $\lambda \in \mathbb{C}$, i.e., $|\lambda| < \lambda(A(\omega))$ and that has an order of multiplicity equal to one. There is therefore only one ray of eigenvectors associated with the Perron–Frobenius root or eigenvalue. It also follows from the Perron–Frobenius theorem that the ray of associated eigenvectors contains vectors with strictly positive coordinates.

Proposition 2.4. *There exists a unique (numeraire) normalized equilibrium price vector* $p \in S$ *associated with every log-linear exchange economy* $\omega \in \Omega$.

Proof. It suffices to prove that the Perron–Frobenius eigenvalue $\lambda(A(\omega))$ is equal to $\lambda = 1$ for every economy $\omega \in \Omega$.

Step 1: $A(\omega)^T r = r$. This equality follows readily from direct computations. This equality shows us that $\lambda = 1$ is an eigenvalue of the transposed matrix $A(\omega)^T$ and, therefore, of matrix $A(\omega)$. (For an alternative proof, see part (C) in Step 1 of the proof of Proposition 2.3.)

Step 2: $\lambda = 1$ *is the Perron–Frobenius root* $\lambda(A(\omega))$. From the Perron–Frobenius theorem, the Perron–Frobenius root $\lambda(A(\omega))$ is a real eigenvalue that is strictly greater than the modulus of all other eigenvalues of A. By Step 1, that eigenvalue is greater than or equal to 1. If $\lambda = 1$ is not the Perron–Frobenius root $\lambda(A(\omega))$, the strict inequality $1 < \lambda(A(\omega))$ is then satisfied. The proof now proceeds by contradiction by showing that there exists no real number $\mu > 1$ that is an eigenvalue of $A(\omega)$. This is equivalent to showing that the matrix $\mu I - A(\omega)$ is invertible for any $\mu > 1$. We are therefore going to show that $\det(\mu I - A(\omega))$ is different from 0 for $\mu > 1$.

Multiply the first row of $\mu I - A(\omega)$ by r^1, the second row by r^2, ..., up to the ℓth row by r^ℓ. Using matrices $\tilde{I}$ and $\tilde{A}$ used in the proof of Proposition 2.3, we get

$$r^1 \ldots r^\ell \det(\mu I - A(\omega)) = \det(\mu \tilde{I} - \tilde{A}(\omega)).$$

The diagonal coefficient of row and column k of $\tilde{I} - \tilde{A}(\omega)$ is equal to $r^k - \tilde{\alpha}_{kk}(\omega)$. From equality,

$$\sum_{j \neq k} \tilde{\alpha}_{kj}(\omega) = r^k - \tilde{\alpha}_{kk}(\omega)$$

that follows from part (A) of Step 1 in the proof of Proposition 2.3, we see that the diagonal coefficient $r^k - \tilde{\alpha}_{kk}(\omega)$ is strictly positive as equal to a sum of strictly positive real numbers. The off-diagonal coefficients of $\tilde{I} - \tilde{A}(\omega)$ are strictly negative. By writing

$$\mu \tilde{I} - \tilde{A}(\omega) = (\mu - 1)\tilde{I} + (\tilde{I} - \tilde{A}(\omega)),$$

we see that the diagonal coefficients of matrix $\mu \tilde{I} - \tilde{A}(\omega)$ are strictly larger than the absolute value of the sum of the non-diagonal coefficients that belong to the same column. This diagonal column dominant matrix is invertible by the Levy–Desplanques theorem [21, Corollary 5.6.17].

The eigenvalue $\lambda = 1$ is therefore the Perron–Frobenius root $\lambda(A(\omega))$ of the positive matrix $A(\omega)$. The (numeraire normalized) eigenvector $p \in S$ associated with the Perron–Frobenius eigenvalue of matrix $A(\omega)$ is therefore a (numeraire normalized) equilibrium price vector associated with the log-linear exchange economy ω and that (numeraire normalized) equilibrium price vector is unique. $\square$

2.7. Continuity and Differentiability with Respect to Fundamentals

The following theorem will be a direct consequence of the characterization of the equilibrium price vector of a log-linear economy as an eigenvector associated with the Perron–Frobenius root of a strictly positive matrix.

Proposition 2.5. *The unique (numeraire normalized) equilibrium price vector $p(\omega) \in S$ of the log-linear economy $\omega \in \Omega$ is a differentiable function of ω.*

Proof. Step 1: Equilibrium price vector $p(\omega) \in S$ as the solution of a suitable linear equation system. The (numeraire normalized) price vector $p = (\bar{p}, 1) \in S$ where $\bar{p} = (p_1, p_2, \ldots, p_{\ell-1}) \in \mathbb{R}_{++}^{\ell-1}$ is the equilibrium price vector associated the log-linear economy $\omega \in \Omega$ if it solves the linear equation,

$$(A(\omega) - I)p = 0.$$

The $\ell - 1$ unknowns are the coordinates of $\bar{p} = (p_1, \ldots, p_{\ell-1})$. (Recall that $p_\ell = 1$.) Let $A_{\ell\ell}(\omega)$ and $I_{\ell\ell}$ denote the $(\ell - 1) \times (\ell - 1)$ square matrices obtained from $A(\omega)$ and I by deleting their last row and column. Also, let $A_\ell(\omega)$ be the column matrix defined by the ℓth column of $A(\omega)$. Then, $\bar{p} = (p_1, \ldots, p_{\ell-1})$ solves the linear equation system that is equal in matrix form to

$$(A_{\ell\ell}(\omega) - I_{\ell\ell})\bar{p} = -A_\ell(\omega).$$

Step 2: Matrix $A_{\ell\ell}(\omega) - I_{\ell\ell}$ is invertible. Let $\tilde{A}_{\ell\ell}(\omega) - \tilde{I}_{\ell\ell}$ be the matrix derived from $A_{\ell\ell}(\omega) - I_{\ell\ell}$ by multiplying row 1 by r^1, row 2 by r^2, etc., up to row $\ell - 1$ by $r^{\ell-1}$. Obviously, we have

$$\det(\tilde{A}_{\ell\ell}(\omega) - \tilde{I}_{\ell\ell}) = r^1 \dots r^{\ell-1} \det(A_{\ell\ell}(\omega) - I_{\ell\ell}).$$

Equality

$$\sum_{j \neq k} \tilde{\alpha}_{kj}(\omega) = r^k - \tilde{\alpha}_{kk}(\omega)$$

that follows from part (A) of Step 1 in the proof of Proposition 2.3 implies the strict inequality,

$$\tilde{\alpha}_{kk}(\omega) - r^k = - \sum_{j \neq k, \ell} \tilde{\alpha}_{kj}(\omega) - \tilde{\alpha}_{k\ell}(\omega)$$

$$> - \sum_{j \neq k, \ell} \tilde{\alpha}_{kj}(\omega)$$

because $\tilde{\alpha}_{k\ell}(\omega)$ is strictly positive. Matrix $\tilde{A}_{\ell\ell}(\omega) - \tilde{I}_{\ell\ell}$ is another instance of diagonal column dominant matrix and its invertibility follows again from the Levy–Desplanques theorem [21, Corollary 5.6.17].

Step 3: Differentiability of $\bar{p}(\omega) = -(A_{\ell\ell}(\omega) - I_{\ell\ell})^{-1} A_\ell(\omega)$. Cramer's formula expresses the coefficients of the inverse of a square matrix in terms of its cofactors and (non-zero) determinant. Each one of these terms is here a polynomial function and therefore differentiable function of ω and, in addition, the determinant (that appears in the denominators of Cramer's formula) is different from 0. The inverse matrix is then differentiable with respect to $\omega \in \Omega$ because all its coefficients are differentiable with respect to ω. The same applies to the coefficients of $A_\ell(\omega)$ and therefore to $A_\ell(\omega)$. The differentiability of $\bar{p}(\omega)$ as a function of $\omega \in \Omega$ follows readily from the differentiability of the matrix product of two differentiable matrix functions. This evidently implies the differentiability of the numeraire normalized equilibrium price vector $p(\omega) = (\bar{p}(\omega), 1)$. □

Corollary 2.6. *The unique equilibrium allocation* $x(\omega) = (x_i(\omega)) \in \Omega$ *of the log-linear economy* $\omega \in \Omega$ *is a differentiable function of* ω.

2.8. The Equilibrium Manifold

The equilibrium manifold E of the log-linear model consisting of m log-linear consumers is the subset of $S \times \Omega$ defined by the equilibrium equation,

$$\sum_i f_i(p, p \cdot \omega_i) = \sum_i \omega_i,$$

where consumer i's utility function is the log-linear function,

$$u_i(x_i) = \sum_j a_i^j \log x_i^j.$$

The equilibrium manifold E is the set of price-endowment pairs $(p, \omega) \in S \times \Omega$ that satisfy the equation system,

$$(A_{\ell\ell}(\omega) - I_{\ell\ell})\bar{p} + A_{\ell}(\omega) = 0.$$

From Proposition 2.5, we know that $p(\omega) = (\bar{p}(\omega), 1)$ is a differentiable function of $\omega \in \Omega$.

Proposition 2.7. *The equilibrium manifold E is the graph of the function $\omega \to p(\omega)$ from Ω into S.*

Proof. Obvious from the definition of the graph of a mapping.   □

Proposition 2.7 reduces the study of the equilibrium manifold to the study of the smooth mapping $\Omega \to S$ defined by $\omega \to p(\omega)$. The following properties are then obvious consequences of this observation.

Proposition 2.8. *The equilibrium manifold E is a smooth submanifold of $S \times \Omega$ and is diffeomorphic to Ω.*

Proof. The smooth submanifold property follows readily from the property that the graph $\{(f(x), x) \mid x \in X\}$ of a smooth mapping $f : X \to Y$ where X and Y are open sets of Euclidean spaces is a smooth submanifold of $Y \times X$. The diffeomorphism of the equilibrium manifold E with Ω is defined by the map $\omega \to (p(\omega), \omega)$ from $\Omega \to E$ whose inverse map $E \to \Omega$ is the projection map $(p(\omega), \omega) \to \omega$.   □

Corollary 2.9. *The equilibrium manifold E is diffeomorphic to a Euclidean space of dimension ℓm.*

Proof. Follows from $\Omega = X^m$ where $X = \mathbb{R}_{++}^\ell$. ☐

2.9. Conclusion

We have seen in this chapter that the study of the exchange model consisting of an arbitrary number of goods and an arbitrary number of log-linear consumers boils down to an algebra problem. These economies are interesting from two perspectives at least. First, their equilibrium equation system is sufficiently simple for their study to be accessible with just the tools of linear algebra and, in particular, the very nice Perron–Frobenius theory of positive and strictly positive matrices. Second, equilibrium not only always exists but is also unique. The properties that emerge from this approach are relatively easy to prove and confirm the intuition of the early theoreticians who more or less believed that these properties were satisfied by much more general exchange economies. We now know that this is not true and that the study of exchange models with consumers having utility functions that are more general than the log-linear ones is going to be far more difficult.

2.10. Exercises

2.1. For $r \in X = \mathbb{R}_{++}^\ell$ given, define the parameter space $\Omega(r) = \{\omega = (\omega_i) \in \Omega = X^m \mid \sum_i \omega_i = r\}$. Justify the economic interest of that parameter space. Show that the equilibrium manifold associated with this parameter space is a smooth submanifold of $S \times \Omega(r)$ that is diffeomorphic to $\Omega(r)$.

2.2. Let $x(\omega) = (x_i(\omega)) \in \Omega = X^m$ denote the equilibrium allocation associated with the endowment vector $\omega = (\omega_i) \in \Omega$. Give an explicit formula for the utility $u_i(x_i(\omega))$. Show that an increase in the endowment ω_i, the endowments of the other consumers being kept constant, yields a new equilibrium allocation that gives a higher utility level to consumer i. Are the utility levels of all the other consumers also increased at the new equilibrium allocation?

2.3. Assume $\ell = 2$ and identify S with $\mathbb{R}_{++}$ through the normalization $p_2 = 1$. The equilibrium manifold E is a subset of $\mathbb{R}_{++} \times \Omega$ defined by a single real equation and is known as a hypersurface. Show that E can be defined by a quadratic polynomial in p_1 and the coordinates w_i^j of $w \in \Omega$. (Such hypersurfaces are known as quadrics.) In the special case where $m = 2$ and total resources $r \in X = \mathbb{R}_{++}^2$ are fixed (i.e., $w_1 + w_2 = r$), draw a picture of the equilibrium manifold in $\mathbb{R}_{++}^3$. Show that the equilibrium manifold is a subset of a quadric that is a hyperboloid of one sheet. Hyperboloids of one sheet are known to be doubly ruled surfaces. Show that a set of straight lines for the equilibrium manifold E are horizontal (i.e., parallel to the parameter space $\Omega(r)$).

2.4. For $w = (w_i) \in \Omega$ given, let $r = \sum_i w_i$ and $A(w)$ defined in Proposition 2.3. Define the dynamical system $p(t+1) = A(w)p(t)$ for $t \geq 0$ with $p(0) \in \mathbb{R}_{++}^\ell$, a non-normalized price vector. Show that $p(t) \cdot r$ is equal to a constant $w > 0$. Give an economic interpretation of the dynamical system. Show that the sequence $p(t)$ tends to a limit $p^* \in \mathbb{R}_{++}^\ell$ that is the non-normalized equilibrium price vector of the economy $w \in \Omega$ such that $p^* \cdot r = w$.

2.5. Let w_i be given. Let $u_i(x_i) = \sum_i a_i^j \log x_i^j$ a log-linear utility functions ($a_i^j > 0$, and $\sum_j a_i^j = 1$). Consider the map $p \to f_i(p, p \cdot w_i)$ from $\mathbb{R}_{++}^\ell$ into itself. Prove the following expression for the (j, k) coefficient of the Jacobian matrix L of the above map:

$$\frac{df_i^j(p, p \cdot w_i)}{dp_k} = \begin{cases} -\dfrac{1}{p_j^2} a_i^j (p \cdot w_i) + \dfrac{1}{p_j} a_i^j w_i^j & j = k \\[2ex] \dfrac{1}{p_j} a_i^j w_i^k & j \neq k \end{cases}.$$

(1) Show that, for $w_i = f_i(p, w_i)$, the Jacobian matrix L of the map $p \to f_i(p, p \cdot w_i)$ from $\mathbb{R}_{++}^\ell$ into itself is symmetric.

(2) Show that the determinant of the Jacobian matrix L is equal to 0.

(3) Prove that the $\ell - 1$ remaining eigenvalues (counted with their order of multiplicity) of the Jacobian matrix L are strictly negative.

2.6. Using the above exercise, show that the Jacobian matrix J of the map $p \rightarrow \sum_i f_i(p, p \cdot \omega_i)$ from $\mathbb{R}^{\ell}_{++}$ into itself is symmetric, with determinant equal to 0, and such that the $\ell - 1$ remaining eigenvalues are strictly negative.

Chapter 3

The Exchange Model with Two Goods and Two Consumers

3.1. Introduction

The global approach to the study of the exchange model in the general case of an arbitrary number of goods and consumers that is to be developed in the next chapters will exploit properties of exchange economies that can be proved through the equilibrium manifold and natural projection approach. In addition to point-set topology, this approach requires some knowledge of differential topology. But that knowledge does not go very far beyond the most elementary properties of smooth manifolds and submanifolds combined with those of smooth mappings and their singularities. The goal of this chapter is therefore to facilitate the introduction to these tools and concepts by considering the special case of two consumers, two goods and fixed total resources. The study of that case requires little else than some point-set topology, some elementary properties of real analysis and some familiarity with plane and solid geometry. A major outcome of this undertaking is now known as the "Edgeworth–Bowley box" representation of a pure exchange economy with two goods, two consumers and fixed total resources. Equilibrium allocations are then identified with the intersection points of individual demand curves. Even then, a rigorous mathematical analysis is not that simple. There is in particular a difference between our presentation and the traditional one found in almost every textbook. Instead of focusing on individual endowment vectors given once and for all, and looking at the intersection points of the associated individual demand curves, we adopt the global point of view that consists in simultaneously considering the full collection of individual endowments, demand curves and their intersection points. This global approach based on the equilibrium manifold and the natural projection approach is typical of modern general equilibrium theory. It enables one to deal with questions of comparative statics that are beyond the scope of the traditional approach. A good illustration is the characterization of economies with a unique equilibrium that is missed in the more traditional treatments. To sum up, the Edgeworth–Bowley box gives us a visual and highly intuitive content to properties of a model that, otherwise, are rather abstract. With this chapter, readers should be able to develop a geometric intuition that will prove very helpful in the later chapters.

3.2. Utility Functions for Two Goods

In this chapter, the commodity space is $\mathbb{R}^2$. The set of numeraire normalized price vectors $p = (p_1, p_2)$ is the set $S = \mathbb{R}_{++} \times \{1\}$. That set is often identified to $\mathbb{R}_{++}$. The consumption set of every consumer is the strictly positive quadrant $X = \mathbb{R}_{++}^2$.

3.2.1. Utility functions

Consumer i's preferences are defined by a real-valued function u_i whose domain is the consumption set X. The commodity bundle $y_i \in X$ is said to be preferred to the commodity bundle $x_i \in X$ if and only if the inequality $u_i(x_i) \leq u_i(y_i)$ is satisfied. This defines a binary relation on the consumption set X that is denoted by $\preceq_i$ and that represent consumer i's preferences $\preceq_i$. The preference relation $\preceq_i$ may be represented by an infinity of functions. For example, it suffices to compose the function u_i with a strictly increasing function $\theta : \mathbb{R} \to \mathbb{R}$ to obtain a utility function $\theta \circ u_i$. In this chapter, we use one and only one utility function u_i for consumer i and the properties of the preference relation $\preceq_i$ are expressed in terms of the utility function u_i.

3.2.2. First- and second-order derivatives

We assume from now on that the utility function u_i is indefinitely differentiable. The first-order derivative of u_i at the point $x_i \in X$ is represented by the gradient vector or, in matrix form, the $\ell \times 1$ column vector $Du_i(x_i)$ whose coordinates are the first-order derivatives of u_i computed at x_i. In the two-good case considered in this chapter, we have $\ell = 2$, which gives for the derivative of the utility function u_i:

$$Du_i(x_i) = \begin{bmatrix} \dfrac{\partial u_i}{\partial x^1}(x_i) \\[2mm] \dfrac{\partial u_i}{\partial x^2}(x_i) \end{bmatrix}.$$

The Hessian matrix of u_i at $x_i \in X$ is the $\ell \times \ell = 2 \times 2$ matrix defined by the second-order partial derivatives. This gives us here:

$$D^2 u_i(x_i) = \begin{bmatrix} \dfrac{\partial^2 u_i}{(\partial x^1)^2} & \dfrac{\partial^2 u_i}{\partial x^1 \partial x^2} \\[3mm] \dfrac{\partial^2 u_i}{\partial x^1 \partial x^2} & \dfrac{\partial^2 u_i}{(\partial x^2)^2} \end{bmatrix}.$$

The bordered Hessian matrix of u_i at x_i is the $(\ell+1) \times (\ell+1) = 3 \times 3$ square matrix equal to

$$Hu_i(x_i) = \begin{bmatrix} D^2 u_i(x_i) & Du_i(x_i) \\[2mm] Du_i(x_i)^T & 0 \end{bmatrix}.$$

Lemma 3.1. *For $\ell = 2$,*

$$\det Hu_i(x_i) = v^T D^2 u_i(x_i) v,$$

where $v^T = \left(-\dfrac{\partial u_i}{\partial x^2}(x_i) \quad \dfrac{\partial u_i}{\partial x^1}(x_i) \right).$

Proof. Obvious. □

3.2.3. Properties of utility functions

The fact that the domain of the utility function u_i is the strictly positive quadrant $X = \mathbb{R}^2_{++}$ implies that every good is necessary. We will also assume that the utility tends to $+\infty$ when the resources in already one of the two goods tend to infinity. The other standard properties of utility functions in the two-good case are as follows:

Assumption 3.2.

(i) *The function u_i is smooth, i.e., has partial derivatives of any order.*

(ii) *The first-order derivatives $\dfrac{\partial u_i}{\partial x^1}(x_i)$ and $\dfrac{\partial u_i}{\partial x^2}(x_i)$ are strictly positive (i.e., $Du_i(x_i) \in X$) for any $x_i \in X$.*

(iii) *The only column matrix $z \in \mathbb{R}^2$ that satisfies $z^T D^2 u_i(x_i) z \geq 0$ and $z^T Du_i(x_i) = 0$ is $z = 0$.*

Property (i) expresses differentiability. Property (ii) is known as the smooth monotonicity and (iii) as the smooth quasi-concavity of the utility function u_i. The economic interpretations of (ii) and (iii) are obvious.

One sees readily that every indifference curve has two asymptotes, the vertical and the horizontal coordinate axes. This property is equivalent to (loosely speaking) the indifference curves not "intersecting" the coordinate axes at finite distance. The two goods are necessary because the consumption set is the strictly positive quadrant instead of the (slightly) larger non-negative quadrant. It follows from these assumptions that it is always possible to maintain a given utility level by compensating any quantity (of a given commodity) by sufficiently large quantities of the other commodity as it appears from the picture on the right side of Figure 3.1.

Equivalent formulations of Assumption 3.2

Proposition 3.3. *The following inequalities are equivalent to Property (iii) in Assumption 3.2 at $x_i \in X$. (All partial derivatives are taken at that point.)*

(i)
$$v^T D^2 u_i(x_i)\, v < 0 \quad \text{for } v^T = \left(-\frac{\partial u_i}{\partial x^2} \quad \frac{\partial u_i}{\partial x^1}\right). \tag{1}$$

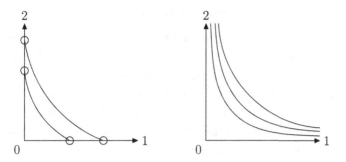

Figure 3.1: Indifference curves in $\mathbb{R}^2_{++}$

(ii) $$\left(-\frac{\partial u_i}{\partial x^2} \quad \frac{\partial u_i}{\partial x^1}\right) D^2 u_i(x_i) \begin{pmatrix} -\dfrac{\partial u_i}{\partial x^2} \\[2mm] \dfrac{\partial u_i}{\partial x^1} \end{pmatrix} < 0. \qquad (2)$$

(iii) $$\left(\frac{\partial u_i}{\partial x^2}\right)^2 \frac{\partial^2 u_i}{(\partial x^1)^2} - 2 \left(\frac{\partial u_i}{\partial x^1}\right)\left(\frac{\partial u_i}{\partial x^2}\right) \frac{\partial^2 u_i}{\partial x^1 \partial x^2}$$

$$+ \left(\frac{\partial u_i}{\partial x^1}\right)^2 \frac{\partial^2 u_i}{(\partial x^2)^2} < 0. \qquad (3)$$

(iv) $$\det H u_i(x_i) > 0. \qquad (4)$$

Proof.

(i) Let $z \neq 0 \in \mathbb{R}^2$. Condition $z^T D u_i(x_i) = 0$ means that the vector z is perpendicular to the vector $D u_i(x_i)$. In the plane $\mathbb{R}^2$, this is equivalent to the vector z being collinear to the vector v where

$$v^T = \left(-\frac{\partial u_i}{\partial x^2}(x_i) \quad \frac{\partial u_i}{\partial x^1}(x_i)\right).$$

Then, there exists a real number $\lambda \neq 0$ such that $z = \lambda v$ and Property (iii) becomes equivalent to the strict inequality (1).

(ii) Inequality (2) is nothing more than inequality (1) with the explicit formulation of v^T.

(iii) Inequality (3) is simply inequality (2) spelt out.

(iv) Inequality (4) follows from Lemma 3.1 combined with inequality (3). □

3.3. Consumer i's Demand Function

Let the price vector $p \in S$ and wealth $w_i \in \mathbb{R}_{++}$ be given. Consumer i maximizes the utility $u_i(x_i)$ subject to the budget constraint $p \cdot x_i \leq w_i$. See Figure 3.2. Four propositions of which three of them are of increasing levels of generality express the main properties of demand functions. We will see in Chapter 4 that deals with any number of goods and consumers that these properties generalize quite well to the more general cases.

Proposition 3.4. *Consumer i's utility maximization problem subject to the budget constraint $p \cdot x_i \leq w_i$ for $(p, w_i) \in S \times \mathbb{R}_{++}$ has a unique solution $x_i \in X$. The budget constraint is then binding.*

Proof.

Step 1: Existence of a solution. Pick some $y_i \in X$ that satisfies the budget constraint $p \cdot y_i \leq w_i$. The budget set $B = \{z_i \in \mathbb{R}_+^2 \mid p \cdot z_i \leq w_i\}$ is defined by the inequalities $z_i^1 \geq 0$, $z_i^2 \geq 0$, and $pz_i^1 + z_i^2 \leq w_i$. This set is closed. In addition, the inequalities $0 \leq z_i^1 \leq w_i/p$ and $0 \leq z_i^2 \leq w_i$ imply that the set B is bounded and, therefore, compact in $\mathbb{R}^2$. The continuous function u_i reaches a maximum value at some point(s) x_i of the compact set B. That maximum value $u_i^* = u_i(x_i)$ is uniquely defined and does not depend on the point x_i where that maximum is reached.

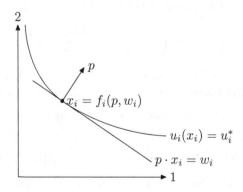

Figure 3.2:   Demand $f_i(p, w_i)$

Step 2: The budget constraint is binding. Assume the contrary. Let $x_i \in X$ be a solution of the maximization problem that satisfies the strict inequality $p \cdot x_i < w_i$. For ϵ that satisfies $0 < \epsilon < w_i - p \cdot x_i$, let $y_i = x_i + (0, \epsilon) \in X$. It comes $p \cdot y_i = p \cdot x_i + \epsilon < w_i$ while the strict inequality $u_i(x_i) < u_i(y_i)$ follows from the monotonicity of u_i, hence a contradiction.

Step 3: The first-order necessary condition for optimality. Let $x_i \in X$ be one of the solutions whose existence follows from Step 1. The budget constraint $p \cdot x_i = w_i$ is satisfied by Step 2. The first-order necessary conditions then take the form,

$$Du_i(x_i) = \lambda p, \quad p \cdot x_i = w_i$$

for the pair $(x_i, \lambda) \in X \times \mathbb{R}_{++}$.

Step 4: Uniqueness. It now follows from Assumption 3.2(iii) that all the points from the tangent line to the indifference curve through x_i, but different from x_i, yield a utility level strictly less than x_i. □

Proposition 3.5. *Consumer i's demand function $f_i : S \times \mathbb{R}_{++} \to X$ satisfies Walras law: $p \cdot f_i(p, w_i) = w_i$ for every $(p, w_i) \in S \times \mathbb{R}_{++}$.*

Proof. Walras law says that the budget constraint $p \cdot x_i \leq w_i$ is binding, which follows from Proposition 3.4. □

The solution to the consumer's maximization problem whose existence and uniqueness is proved in Proposition 3.4 is therefore a function $f_i(p, w_i)$ of the price vector $p = (p_1, 1)$ and wealth w_i. That function $f_i : S \times \mathbb{R}_{++} \to X$ is known as consumer i's demand function. What properties of this function f_i can be derived from those of the utility function u_i that represents consumers' preferences? Is f_i differentiable? Are its first-order partial derivatives continuous? Is f_i differentiable up to any order, i.e., smooth?

Proposition 3.6. *Consumer i's demand function $f_i : S \times \mathbb{R}_{++} \to X$ is smooth.*

Proof. The proof is going to be proved by a direct application of the implicit function theorem to the "implicit equation" that results from the first-order necessary condition that expresses that x_i^1 maximizes the utility $u_i(x^1, w_i - p_1 x^1)$. The condition is that the derivative of the utility with respect to x^1 is equal to zero at x_i^1:

$$\Phi(x_i^1, p_1, w_i) = \frac{\partial u_i}{\partial x^1}(x_i) - p_1 \frac{\partial u_i}{\partial x^2}(x_i) = 0. \tag{5}$$

(Note that this necessary condition is sufficient here, but we do not need to use this fact.) By the implicit function theorem, the solution x_i^1 of equation (5) is a smooth function $f_i(p_1, 1, w_i)$ of p_1 and w_i in some neighborhood of some p_i^* and w_i^* if the partial derivative $\partial \Phi / \partial x^1$ at (x_i^{*1}, p_1^*, w_i^*) (where $x_i^* = f_i(p_1^*, 1, w_i^*)$) is different from 0. This derivative is equal to

$$\frac{\partial^2 u_i}{\partial (x^1)^2} + \varphi'(x^1) \frac{\partial^2 u_i}{\partial x^1 \partial x^2} - p_1 \frac{\partial^2 u_i}{\partial x^1 \partial x^2} - p_1 \varphi'(x^1) \frac{\partial^2 u_i}{\partial (x^2)^2}. \tag{6}$$

At the point x_i, we have by (5) that $\phi'(x_i^1) = -p_1$. Expression (6) is strictly negative by Proposition 3.3(iii) and, therefore, different from 0. $\qquad\square$

The property that the demand is smooth is reinforced by the following proposition that requires a few more powerful properties that are nevertheless satisfied in the case defined by demand functions derived from preference maximization:

Proposition 3.7. *Consumer i's demand function $f_i : S \times \mathbb{R}_{++} \to X$ is a diffeomorphism.*

Proof. We already know that f_i is smooth. We are going to prove that f_i^{-1} exists and is smooth. Let $g_i : X \to S \times \mathbb{R}_{++}$ be the map that associates with $x_i \in X$ the price vector $p \in S$ that is collinear with the gradient vector $Du_i(x_i)$) and the wealth $w_i = p \cdot x_i$. This map is differentiable and, in fact, easily seen to be smooth. One also checks readily that the composition $g_i \circ f_i$ is the identity map of $S \times \mathbb{R}_{++}$. $\qquad\square$

Remark 1. Inspection of Figure 3.2 is considered in many undergraduate courses and textbooks to be sufficient to prove Propositions 3.5 and 3.6 in particular.

3.4. Exchange of Two Goods between Two Consumers

There are now two consumers so that i can be equal to either 1 or 2. In addition, total resources $\omega_1 + \omega_2 = r$ are fixed and equal to some vector $r \in X$. The parameter space Ω is then the subset of $X^2 = (\mathbb{R}^2_{++}) \times (\mathbb{R}^2_{++})$ of $\mathbb{R}^4$ defined by

$$\Omega = \{\omega = (\omega_1, \omega_2) \in X^2 \mid \omega_1 + \omega_2 = r\}.$$

3.4.1. Two coordinate systems for Ω

The endowment vector for the two consumers $\omega = (\omega_1, \omega_2)$ can be represented by the coordinates (ω_1^1, ω_1^2) of consumer 1's endowment vector ω_1. Then, consumer 2's endowment vector ω_2 is equal to $\omega_2 = r - \omega_1$. It is nevertheless convenient to consider the following two coordinate systems as far as possible:

- A first coordinate system with perpendicular axes in the plane that is arbitrary. The origin of coordinates is a point denoted by O_1. That coordinate system is associated with consumer 1 in the sense that the coordinates (x_1^1, x_1^2) represent quantities of goods 1 and 2 allocated to consumer 1.
- Let O_2 be the point whose coordinates (in the first and so far only coordinate system) are equal to (r^1, r^2). Draw from O_2 two oriented lines parallel to the coordinate axes of the first coordinate system but with opposite directions. These two lines (and their common origin O_2) define the second coordinate system.

The coordinates of a point M in these two coordinate systems are $x_1 = (x_1^1, x_1^2)$ in the first and $x_2 = (x_2^1, x_2^2)$ in the second coordinate system. The vector $x_1 = (x_1^1, x_1^2)$ represents consumer 1's allocation. Similarly, the vector $x_2 = (x_2^1, x_2^2)$ represents consumer 2's allocation. Those coordinates are related by equality $x_1 + x_2 = r$.

3.4.2. One picture for the two consumers

Let $C_1(\omega_1) = \{x_1 \in X \mid u_1(x_1) = u_1(\omega_1)\}$ be consumer 1's indifference curve through the point $\omega_1 \in X$. Let $P_1(\omega_1) = \{x_1 \in X \mid u_1(x_1) \geq u_1(\omega_1)\}$ be the set of consumption bundles preferred to the bundle ω_1 also by the first consumer. Using the first coordinate system, these two sets can be identified to subsets of Ω. Similarly, let $C_2(\omega_2) = \{x_2 \in X \mid u_2(x_2) = u_2(\omega_2)\}$ and $P_2(\omega_2) = \{x_2 \in X \mid u_2(x_2) \geq u_2(\omega_2)\}$ be the indifference curve through $\omega_2 \in X$ and the set of consumption bundles preferred by the second consumer to the bundle ω_2. Using the second coordinate system, these two sets can again be identified to subsets of Ω. We have therefore the possibility of representing what happens to the two consumers with only one picture.

3.5. Equilibrium Allocations

Let $\omega = (\omega_1, \omega_2) \in \Omega$ be given. Let $C_1(\omega)$ and $C_2(\omega)$ represent the demand curves of the two consumers considered in the first and second coordinate systems respectively for the endowment vectors ω_1 and ω_2, respectively. Since ω belongs to $C_1(\omega)$ and $C_2(\omega)$, we have $\{\omega\} \subset C_1(\omega) \cap C_2(\omega)$. The following characterization of the equilibrium allocations associated with the endowment vector $\omega = (\omega_1, \omega_2) \in \Omega$ justifies the interest and importance of this geometric representation of Ω that is now known as the Edgeworth–Bowley representation. Let us state first a lemma that will be immediately useful.

Lemma 3.8. *Let $p \in S$ be some price vector. Let M_1 be the point in Ω whose coordinates in the first coordinate system are equal to $x_1 = f_1(p, p{\cdot}\omega_1)$. Similarly, let M_2 denote the point in Ω whose coordinates in the second coordinate system are equal to $x_2 = f_2(p, p \cdot \omega_2)$. The coordinates of the vector $M_1 M_2 \in \Omega$ in the first coordinate system are then equal to $r - f_1(p, p \cdot \omega_1) - f_2(p, p \cdot \omega_2)$.*

Proof. The coordinates of M_2 in the first coordinate system are equal to $r - x_2 = r - f_2(p, p \cdot \omega_2)$. Therefore, the coordinate of the vector $M_1 M_2$ in Ω where the total resources are fixed and equal to r are equal to $(r - f_2(p, p \cdot \omega_2)) - f_1(p, p \cdot \omega_1)$. ☐

Proposition 3.9. *Assume $M = M_1 = M_2$ in the Edgeworth–Bowley representation. Then, the allocation $x = (x_1, x_2)$ where x_1*

and x_2 are the coordinates of the point M in the first and second coordinate system respectively is an equilibrium allocation for $\omega = (\omega_1, \omega_2)$ and some price vector $p = (p_1, 1) \in S$.

Proof. Assume that $M_1 = M_2$ is different from $\omega = (\omega_1, \omega_2)$. The price vector p that is perpendicular to the line ωM then satisfies the equality $r - f_2(p, p \cdot \omega_2) = f_1(p, p \cdot \omega_1)$ since the points M_1 and M_2 are equal. This proves that $p \in S$ is indeed an equilibrium price vector and $M = (x_1, x_2)$ is the corresponding equilibrium allocation for $\omega = (\omega_1, \omega_2)$.

Assume now that $M_1 = M_2$ is equal to $\omega = (\omega_1, \omega_2)$. The indifference curves of both consumers through $\omega = (\omega_1, \omega_2)$ are exterior to each other except for the point $\omega = (\omega_1, \omega_2)$. The common tangent line to $C_1(\omega_1)$ and to $C_2(\omega_2)$ through $\omega = (\omega_1, \omega_2)$ then defines a unique price vector $p = (p_1, 1) \in S$ that is an equilibrium for $\omega = (\omega_1, \omega_2)$. In addition, we have $\omega_1 = f_1(p, p \cdot \omega_1)$ and $\omega_2 = f_2(p, p \cdot \omega_2)$. $\qquad\square$

In both cases, the price vector $p = (p_1, 1)$ that supports the allocation $M_1 = M_2$ in the Edgeworth–Bowley representation of Ω is an equilibrium price of the economy defined by the resources $\omega = (\omega_1, \omega_2) \in \Omega$.

3.5.1. Existence of an equilibrium

We are now ready to prove or, more precisely, to almost prove that an equibrium exists for any given $\omega = (\omega_1, \omega_2) \in \Omega$.

Proposition 3.10. *For any $N = (\omega_1, \omega_2)$ in the Edgeworth–Bowley representation of an exchange economy, there exists an allocation $M = (x_1, x_2)$ and an equilibrium price system $p = (p_1, 1)$ such that $x_1 = f_1(p, p \cdot \omega_1)$ and $x_2 = f_2(p, p \cdot \omega_2)$ and, of course, $x_1 + x_2 = \omega_1 + \omega_2$.*

Proof. We first consider the case where the indifference curves $C_1(\omega_1)$ and $C_2(\omega_2)$ are tangent to each other. Their intersection is then reduced to the point $\omega = (\omega_1, \omega_2)$ and these two curves have the same tangent line at the point $\omega = (\omega_1, \omega_2)$. The curves $C_1(\omega_1)$ and

$C_2(\omega_2)$ therefore belong each one to one side of this common tangent line. The price vector $p = (p_1, 1) \in S$ that is perpendicular to that tangent line is an equilibrium price vector for $\omega = (\omega_1, \omega_2)$ and the corresponding equilibrium allocation is equal to $\omega = (\omega_1, \omega_2)$.

We now consider the case where the indifference curves $C_1(\omega_1)$ and $C_2(\omega_2)$ are not tangent to each other at $\omega = (\omega_1, \omega_2)$. Let us define the curve $F_i(\omega_i) = \{x_i \in X \mid x_i = f_i(p, p \cdot \omega_i)$ for $0 < p_1 < +\infty\}$ for i equal to 1 and 2. The point $\omega = (\omega_1, \omega_2)$ then belongs to the intersection $F_1(\omega_1) \cap F_2(\omega_2)$ but is not an equilibrium point because there is no $p = (p_1, 1) \in S$ such that $\omega_1 = f_1(p, p \cdot \omega_1)$ and $\omega_2 = f_2(p, p \cdot \omega_2)$.

However, the news is not that bad because the two curves $F_1(\omega_1)$ and $F_2(\omega_2)$ that have already an intersection point (the point $\omega = (\omega_1, \omega_2)$) have at least another intersection point and that point is different from $\omega = (\omega_1, \omega_2)$. Let $M = (x_1, x_2)$ denote one of these points. The line ωM is then well defined and perpendicular to a price vector $p = (p_1, 1)$. It is then straightforward to check that this price vector $p = (p_1, 1)$ is an equilibrium price system. □

Remark 2. We already mentioned above that this was almost a proof, but not a fully rigorous proof. The main reason is because we conclude from the intersection $F_1(\omega_1) \cap F_2(\omega_2)$ having more than the element $\omega = (\omega_1, \omega_2)$ in common that any other element is indeed an equilibrium allocation associated with $\omega = (\omega_1, \omega_2)$. The reader can easily prove this part.

3.6. The Equilibrium Manifold

The ambient space is now three-dimensional. By definition, the Cartesian product $S \times \Omega$ can be identified to the coordinate system $(p_1, \omega_1^1, \omega_1^2)$ with $(\omega_1^1, \omega_1^2) \in \Omega$ and $p_1 > 0$. The equilibrium manifold E is the subset of $S \times \Omega$ that consists of the pairs $(p, \omega) \in S \times \Omega$ that are equilibria. It comes as follows:

Proposition 3.11. *The equilibrium manifold E is the subset of $S \times \Omega$ defined by equation,*

$$F^1(p, \omega) = f_1^1(p, p \cdot \omega_1) + f_2^1(p, p \cdot \omega_2) - r^1 = 0. \tag{7}$$

Proof. Let $(F^1(p, \omega), F^2(p, \omega)) = f_1(p, p \cdot \omega_1) + f_2(p, p \cdot \omega_2) - r$. It comes from the identities $p \cdot (f_1(p, p \cdot \omega_1) - \omega_1) = 0$ and $p \cdot (f_2(p, p \cdot \omega_2) - \omega_2) = 0$ that F^1 and F^2 are related by $p_1 F^1 + F^2 = 0$. The equilibrium manifold E is defined by the two equations:

$$F^1(p, \omega) = 0, \quad F^2(p, \omega) = 0, \tag{8}$$

but only one is necessary, for example the first one. $\qquad\square$

Proposition 3.12. *The equilibrium manifold E is a smooth surface in $S \times \Omega$.*

Proof. The set E is a smooth surface of the subset $S \times \Omega$ of $\mathbb{R}^3_{++}$ if there is a tangent plane at every point $(p, \omega_1^1, \omega_1^2)$ of E. To have such a plane, it suffices that the vector defined by the first-order partial derivatives,

$$\left(\frac{\partial F_1}{\partial p_1}, \frac{\partial F_1}{\partial \omega_1^1}, \frac{\partial F_1}{\partial \omega_1^2} \right)$$

is different from 0. This means that at least one of these coordinates is different from 0. That vector is then normal to the surface E by being perpendicular to the tangent plane to E at $(p, \omega_1^1, \omega_1^2)$. Explicit computations yield for that normal vector:

$$\left(\frac{\partial f_1^1}{\partial p_1} + \frac{\partial f_2^1}{\partial p_1} + \frac{\partial f_1^1}{\partial w_1} \omega_1^1 + \frac{\partial f_2^1}{\partial w_2} (r^1 - \omega_1^1), \left(\frac{\partial f_1^1}{\partial w_1} - \frac{\partial f_2^1}{\partial w_2} \right) p_1, \frac{\partial f_1^1}{\partial w_1} - \frac{\partial f_2^1}{\partial w_2} \right).$$

If $(\partial f_1^1 / \partial w_1) \neq (\partial f_2^1 / \partial w_2)$, the normal vector is different from 0 and there is nothing more to prove. If $(\partial f_1^1 / \partial w_1) = (\partial f_2^1 / \partial w_2)$, the second and third coordinates of the normal vector are equal to 0 and the first coordinate is equal to

$$\frac{\partial f_1^1}{\partial p_1} + \frac{\partial f_2^1}{\partial p_1} + \frac{\partial f_2^1}{\partial w_2} r^1 = \left(\frac{\partial f_1^1}{\partial p_1} + \frac{\partial f_1^1}{\partial w_1} f_1^1 \right) + \left(\frac{\partial f_2^1}{\partial p_1} + \frac{\partial f_2^1}{\partial w_2} f_2^1 \right).$$

That term is the sum of two strictly negative terms. See, for example, Exercise 3.3. It is therefore strictly negative, i.e., different from 0. $\qquad\square$

3.7. Conclusion

It would be interesting to know more about the surface E itself and also about the surface E as a subset of $S \times \Omega$. However, the picture is far more complicated than in the previous chapter and this study will require indeed several chapters. The interesting fact is that the mathematical techniques will then work for arbitrary numbers of consumers and goods. We will then return to the special case of two goods, two agents and fixed total resources to add somewhat more to this subject.

3.8. Notes and Comments

The first presentation in print of the theory of general equilibrium except that it was limited to the case of two goods is due to Jevons [24]. That, incidentally, led Walras to increase the speed of the publication of his own work conceived independently of Jevons and that contained an arbitrary number of goods and agents [41]. Walras' book was first published in 1874.

3.9. Exercises

3.1. Identifying the price–income set $S \times \mathbb{R}_{++}$ to a subset of $\mathbb{R}^2$ using the coordinates (p_1, w_i), what is the geometric nature of the set $D = \{(p_1, w_i) \in \mathbb{R}^2 \mid w_i = p_1 w_i^1 + w_i^2, p_1 > 0\}$? Prove the equality $f_i(D) = \Gamma_i(w_i)$ where $\Gamma_i(w_i)$ is the demand curve associated with $w_i \in X$.

3.2. Let (p^t, w_i^t) be a sequence in $S \times \mathbb{R}_{++}$ that tends to (p^*, w_i^*) where $p^* = (p_1^*, 1)$ is such that either $p_1^* = 0$ or $p_1^* = +\infty$ and $w_i^* > 0$. Show that the sequence $\|f_i(p^t, w_i^t)\|$ then tends to $+\infty$.

3.3. Let $(p, w_i) \in S \times \mathbb{R}_{++}$. With the assumptions on consumer's behavior made for the case of two goods, prove the inequality,

$$\frac{\partial f_i^1}{\partial p_1}(p, w_i) + \frac{\partial f_i^1}{\partial w_i}(p, w_i)\, f_i^1(p, w_i) < 0.$$

Chapter 4

Consumer Theory

4.1. Introduction

This chapter develops the theoretical analysis of the consumer. The main theme is that consumers have preferences for commodity bundles and that these preferences translate into buying and selling decisions. The goal of this chapter is to derive a set of useful properties regarding these buying and selling activities from standard assumptions about consumers' preferences. The content of this chapter can be found in the chapters on consumer theory that are in all graduate textbooks.

4.2. Preference Relations

Preference relations are traditionally defined after the definition of the consumption set or sets. One definition of the consumption set is that it consists of the commodity bundles that can be effectively consumed by one consumer at least. Some economists consider that consumers can consume only non-negative quantities of goods. This is certainly true if one has a very restrictive idea of consumption and, more generally, of the reasons that lead economic agents to buy and sell goods in markets. Nevertheless, there are markets where it is perfectly conceivable that, when they close, some consumers (or, may be better, agents) end up with being allotted some "negative" quantities of some goods. In practice, this means that, when these markets reopen at some future date, these agents will have to deliver to the market those quantities of goods. In that sense, it is perfectly conceivable to allocate negative quantities of some of the goods traded in a market to some of the consumers. A well-established tradition in consumer theory is therefore to define a subset X of the commodity space $\mathbb{R}^\ell$ as the set of "feasible" consumption bundles. In most parts of this book, the consumption set X is the full commodity space $\mathbb{R}^\ell$. The only exceptions are those in Chapter 2 for log-linear utility functions and in Chapter 3 for two agents, two goods and fixed total resources. In this chapter, for example, we assume $X = \mathbb{R}^\ell$.

From now on, consumers have preference relations over commodity bundles that belong to the consumption space $X = \mathbb{R}^\ell$. In practice, this means that there exist commodity bundles x_i and y_i in the consumption space $X = \mathbb{R}^\ell$ such that consumer i "prefers in a weak sense" or "weakly prefers" the commodity bundle y_i to the commodity bundle x_i. The notation $x_i \preccurlyeq_i y_i$ represents that preference relation.

One says that the preference relation $\preccurlyeq_i$ on X is as follows:

- *Complete* if, for any pair $(x_i, y_i) \in X \times X$, either $x_i \preccurlyeq_i y_i$ or $y_i \preccurlyeq_i x_i$ is satisfied;
- *Monotone* (resp. *strictly monotone*) if $x_i \preccurlyeq_i x_i + y$ for $y \in \mathbb{R}^\ell_+$ (resp. $x_i \prec_i x_i + y$ for $y \in \mathbb{R}^\ell_{++}$);
- *Convex* (resp. *strictly convex*) if the preferred set $\{x \in X \mid x_i \preccurlyeq_i x\}$ is convex (resp. strictly convex);
- *Continuous* if, for every $x_i \in X$, the sets $\{x \in X \mid x_i \preccurlyeq_i x\}$ and $\{x \in X \mid x \preccurlyeq_i x_i\}$ are closed in X;
- *Bounded from below* if the preferred set $\{x \in X \mid x_i \preccurlyeq_i x\}$ is bounded from below for all $x_i \in X$.

The above definitions are here to enrich the concept of preference relations with economically interesting properties. Nevertheless, we will switch very quickly to utility functions that are even easier to deal with.

4.3. Utility Functions

By definition, the function $u_i : X \to \mathbb{R}$ represents the preference relation $\preccurlyeq_i$ if and only if $x_i \preccurlyeq_i y_i$ is equivalent to $u_i(x_i) \leq u_i(y_i)$. Utility functions are a convenient mathematical way of representing preference relations. Not all preference relations $\preccurlyeq_i$ on the set X can be represented by continuous functions not to mention smooth functions, a possibility that depends on the preference relation $\preccurlyeq_i$ having suitable properties. More specifically, the following conditions provide necessary and sufficient conditions for the existence of continuous utility functions.

Proposition 4.1. *A necessary condition for the preference relation $\preccurlyeq_i$ on X to be represented by a continuous utility function $u_i : X \to \mathbb{R}$ is that $\preccurlyeq_i$ is a continuous complete preorder.*

Proof. (i) $\preccurlyeq_i$ *is a preorder*: two properties of the binary relation $\preccurlyeq_i$ have to be checked for it to be a preorder: reflexivity and transitivity. Reflexivity follows from $u_i(x_i) = u_i(x_i)$ that is equivalent to $x_i \preccurlyeq_i x_i$ for every $x_i \in X$. To prove transitivity, assume $x_i \preccurlyeq_i y_i$ and $y_i \preccurlyeq_i z_i$. This implies the inequalities $u_i(x_i) \leq u_i(y_i)$ and $u_i(y_i) \leq u_i(z_i)$ and, therefore, the inequality $u_i(x_i) \leq u_i(z_i)$, an inequality that implies $x_i \preccurlyeq_i z_i$.

(ii) $\preccurlyeq_i$ *is complete*: let x_i and y_i arbitrary in X. There is no loss of generality in assuming that the inequality $u_i(x_i) \leq u_i(y_i)$ is satisfied. This inequality implies $x_i \preccurlyeq_i y_i$ and the preference relation is necessarily complete.

(iii) $\preccurlyeq_i$ *is continuous*: the sets $\{x \in X \mid u_i(x_i) \leq u_i(x)\}$ and $\{x \in X \mid u_i(x_i) \geq u_i(x)\}$ are closed in X as the preimages by the continuous utility function $u_i : X \to \mathbb{R}$ of the closed interval $[u_i(x_i), +\infty)$ and $(-\infty, u_i(x_i)]$. $\square$

Here is a partial converse to the above proposition.

Proposition 4.2. *A sufficient condition for the preference relation $\preccurlyeq_i$ on X to be representable by a continuous utility function $u_i : X \to \mathbb{R}$ is that the preference relation $\preccurlyeq_i$ is a continuous, complete and monotone preorder.*

Proof. Let $e = (1, \ldots, 1)$ be the vector in X with every coordinate equal to one. Let now $x \in X$ be some commodity bundle. Define $u_i(x)$ be a real number such that the bundle $u_i(x)e = (u_i(x), u_i(x), \ldots, u_i(x)) \in X$ is equivalent to the bundle $x \in X$. One first needs to show that this real number $u_i(x)$ exists and is uniquely defined for every $x \in X$.

Define the following subsets of the set of real numbers: $A_+ = \{t \in \mathbb{R} \mid x \preccurlyeq_i te\}$ and $A_- = \{t \in \mathbb{R} \mid te \preccurlyeq_i x\}$. The union $A_+ \cup A_-$ is obviously equal to $\mathbb{R}$. It follows from the continuity of the preorder $\preccurlyeq_i$ that the sets A_+ and A_- are closed in X. Let us show that they are non-empty. Indeed, let $x = (x^1, x^2, \ldots, x^\ell)$; it follows from the monotonicity of $\preccurlyeq_i$ that for $t \geq \sup\{x^1, \ldots, x^\ell)$, it comes $x \preccurlyeq_i te$. Then, t belongs to the set A_+. Similarly, for $t \leq \inf\{x^1, x^2, \ldots, x^\ell\}$, the real number t belongs to the set A_-. It then follows from the connectedness of $\mathbb{R}$ combined with the non-emptiness of the sets A_+ and A_- that their intersection is necessarily non-empty. Therefore, the set of real numbers $t \in \mathbb{R}$ such that te is indifferent with x is non-empty. The monotonicity of $\preccurlyeq_i$ now implies that this set contains at most one element. This establishes the existence and uniqueness of $u_i(x)$ for any $x \in X = \mathbb{R}^\ell$.

In order to prove that the function u_i represents the preference relation $\preccurlyeq_i$, let x and y satisfy $x \preccurlyeq_i y$. Since x and y are indifferent with $u_i(x)e$ and $u_i(y)e$, respectively, this yields the preference relation $u_i(x)e \preccurlyeq_i u_i(y)e$. Monotonicity then implies the inequality $u_i(x) \leq u_i(y)$. Conversely, let x and y satisfy the inequality $u_i(x) \leq u_i(y)$. The preference relation $u_i(x)e \preccurlyeq_i u_i(y)e$ follows from the monotonicity of $\preccurlyeq_i$, which implies the preference relation $x \preccurlyeq_i y$. This proves the equivalence of the relation $x \preccurlyeq_i y$ and the inequality $u_i(x) \leq u_i(y)$.

One readily sees that the function u_i is onto because the equality $u_i(te) = t$ is satisfied for every $t \in \mathbb{R}$. To prove the continuity of the utility function u_i, it suffices that we show that the preimage by u_i of any open subset of the set of real numbers $\mathbb{R}$ is open. It is a well-known property of the usual topology of the set of real numbers $\mathbb{R}$ that any open subset of $\mathbb{R}$ is the disjoint union of a (countable) collection of open intervals. In addition, it is well known in set theory that the preimage by a function of a union of sets is the union of the preimages of those sets. It therefore suffices that we show that the preimage by u_i of any open real interval (a, b) in $\mathbb{R}$ is open.

Let x_α and x_β be two bundles in X that satisfy $u_i(x_\alpha) = a$ and $u_i(x_\beta) = b$, respectively. We have seen above that these bundles exist. Furthermore, it comes

$$u_i^{-1}(a, b) = \{x \in X \mid x_\alpha \prec_i x \prec_i x_\beta\}.$$

This set is open as the intersection of the sets $\{x \in X \mid x_\alpha \prec_i x\}$ and $\{x \in X \mid x \prec_i x_\beta\}$, sets that are both open by the continuity of the preference relation $\precsim_i$. $\qquad\qquad\square$

4.3.1. Complements on utility functions

Indifference classes

Given an equivalence relation, the equivalence class of an elements is by definition the set of all the elements that are equivalent to that element. In the case of the indifference relation $\sim_i$, the equivalence class $\{x \in X \mid x \sim_i x_i\}$ is the indifference set (for consumer i) that contains the commodity bundle $x_i \in X$. For $\ell = 2$ and 3, indifference sets are known as indifference curves and indifference surfaces, respectively.

Ordinal utility functions

Let u_i be a continuous utility function that represents the preference relation $\precsim_i$ on $X = \mathbb{R}^\ell$. Let $\phi : \mathbb{R} \to \mathbb{R}$ be a continuous function that is strictly increasing. Then, the composition $\phi \circ u_i$ is continuous and also represents $\precsim_i$. It is therefore another utility function for consumer i. The continuous utility functions associated with a given preorder $\precsim_i$ are therefore defined up to some continuous strictly increasing real valued function ϕ. That property is encapsulated in the term of *ordinal utility functions* used to represent preorders defined on the consumption space $X = \mathbb{R}^\ell$. To sum up, one often says that the properties of the utility function u_i that are invariant by composition with any strictly increasing and continuous real valued function of the real numbers ϕ are in fact properties of the underlying preference preorder $\preccurlyeq_i$.

4.4. Differentiable Utility Functions

Our definition of a utility function is very convenient for describing general preferences. A couple of economic concepts that involve the gradient and the second derivative of that utility function are also useful. We begin by defining these concepts.

4.4.1. The gradient vector of the utility function

The gradient vector $Du_i(x_i)$ of the utility function $u_i : X : \mathbb{R}^\ell \to \mathbb{R}$ at $x_i \in X$ is written as a column matrix. Using the transpose of $Du_i(x_i)$ as a line matrix, we write

$$(Du_i(x_i))^T = \left[\frac{\partial u_i}{\partial x^1}, \frac{\partial u_i}{\partial x^2}, \ldots, \frac{\partial u_i}{\partial x^\ell} \right]. \tag{1}$$

4.4.2. The normalized gradient vector of the utility function

The normalized gradient $D_n u_i(x_i)$ of the utility function u_i at x_i is then the column matrix,

$$D_n u_i(x_i) = \frac{1}{\frac{\partial u_i}{\partial x^\ell}} Du_i(x_i). \tag{2}$$

The ℓth coordinate of the normalized gradient vector $D_n u_i(x_i)$ is therefore equal to 1. This implies that the gradient and normalized gradient vectors are collinear. For $x_i \in X$, there exists a real number $\lambda(x_i)$ such that $Du_i(x_i) = \lambda(x_i) D_n u_i(x_i)$.

4.4.3. The Hessian matrix of the utility function

The Hessian matrix of the utility function $u_i : X \to \mathbb{R}$ is the $\ell \times \ell$ matrix $D^2 u_i(x_i)$ of second-order partial derivatives of the utility function u_i at x_i:

$$D^2 u_i(x_i) = \begin{bmatrix} \dfrac{\partial^2 u_i}{(\partial x^1)^2} & \cdots & \dfrac{\partial^2 u_i}{\partial x^1 \partial x^k} & \cdots & \dfrac{\partial^2 u_i}{\partial x^1 \partial x^\ell} \\ \vdots & \cdots & \vdots & \cdots & \vdots \\ \dfrac{\partial^2 u_i}{\partial x^h \partial x^1} & \cdots & \dfrac{\partial^2 u_i}{\partial x^h \partial x^k} & \cdots & \dfrac{\partial^2 u_i}{\partial x^h \partial x^\ell} \\ \vdots & \cdots & \vdots & \cdots & \vdots \\ \dfrac{\partial^2 u_i}{\partial x^\ell \partial x^1} & \cdots & \dfrac{\partial^2 u_i}{\partial x^\ell \partial x^k} & \cdots & \dfrac{\partial^2 u_i}{(\partial x^\ell)^2} \end{bmatrix}.$$

Note that the Hessian matrix $D^2 u_i(x_i)$ is symmetric as soon as the utility function u_i shows enough regularity by being two-times continuously differentiable.

4.4.4. First- and second-order derivatives at the same time

We also introduce for any $x_i \in \mathbb{R}^\ell$ the following $(\ell + 1) \times (\ell + 1)$ matrix,

$$\begin{bmatrix} D^2 u_i(x_i) & D u_i(x_i) \\ D u_i^T(x_i) & 0 \end{bmatrix}.$$

4.5. Basic Assumptions about Utility Functions

We now give some flesh to the concept of utility functions by issuing a few properties of the functions and of their first and second derivatives. First, we assume that every utility function has partial derivatives of any order and that these partial derivatives are differentiable. It therefore follows from differentiability that the partial derivatives are also continuous.

4.5.1. Condition on the utility function and its first and second derivatives

From now on, we assume that consumer i has a utility function $u_i : \mathbb{R}^{\ell} \to \mathbb{R}$ that satisfies the following assumptions:

Assumption 4.3. *The set $u_i^{-1}([c, +\infty))$ is strictly convex in $X = \mathbb{R}^{\ell}$ for every $c \in \mathbb{R}$.*

Assumption 4.4. *The set $u_i^{-1}([c, +\infty))$ is bounded from below in $X = \mathbb{R}^{\ell}$ for every $c \in \mathbb{R}$.*

Assumption 4.5. *The gradient vector $Du_i(x_i)$ is strictly positive for any $x_i \in X = \mathbb{R}^{\ell}$.*

This assumption implies in particular that u_i is strictly increasing, i.e., that $u_i(x_i) < u_i(y_i)$ whenever $x_i \leq y_i$ and $x_i \neq y_i$.

Assumption 4.6. *Let Z denote some column vector in $\mathbb{R}^{\ell}$. The only solution to the inequalities,*

$$Z^T D^2 u_i(x_i) Z \geq 0, \quad Du_i(x_i)^T Z = 0$$

is $Z = 0$ for any $x_i \in X = \mathbb{R}^{\ell}$.

We then have the following:

Proposition 4.7. *The point x_i is the unique intersection point of the set $u_i^{-1}([c, +\infty))$ and of the tangent hyperplane to that same set at $x_i \in u_i^{-1}(c)$ for every $c \in \mathbb{R}$.*

Proof. Obvious. □

The matrix,

$$\begin{bmatrix} D^2 u_i(x_i) & Du_i(x_i) \\ Du_i^T(x_i) & 0 \end{bmatrix}$$

that is defined for any $x_i \in X = \mathbb{R}^{\ell}$ is then invertible. See, e.g., Math 6.5.

4.6. The Consumer's Demand Function

Let the price vector $p \in S$ and consumer i's wealth $w_i \in \mathbb{R}$ be given. Wealth is a real number that defines consumer i's budget set. That set is the set of commodity bundles $x_i \in X$ that satisfy the budget inequality $p \cdot x_i \leq w_i$. In other words, that set consists of the commodity bundles that can be bought by consumer i.

Proposition 4.8. *Consumer i's budget constrained utility maximization problem has a unique solution for every $(p, w_i) \in S \times \mathbb{R}$.*

Proof. The map $\mathbb{R}^\ell \to \mathbb{R}$ defined by $x_i \to p \cdot x_i$ is onto. Let therefore y_i be an element of $\mathbb{R}^\ell$ such that the inner product $p \cdot y_i$ is less than or equal to w_i. If x_i is a solution of the utility maximization problem subject to a budget constraint, then $u_i(x_i)$ must be larger than or equal to $u_i(y_i)$. This implies that one does not change the solution set of this maximization problem by adding the constraint $u_i(x_i) \geq u_i(y_i)$.

Let us now show that the subset K of $\mathbb{R}^\ell$ defined by the two constraints $p \cdot x_i \leq w_i$ and $u_i(x_i) \geq u_i(y_i)$ is compact. This is equivalent to showing that the set K is closed and bounded in $\mathbb{R}^\ell$.

The subset of $\mathbb{R}^\ell$ defined by the inequality $\{x_i \in \mathbb{R}^\ell \mid u_i(x_i) \geq u_i(y_i)\}$ is closed in $\mathbb{R}^\ell$. The set K is therefore closed in $\mathbb{R}^\ell$ as the intersection of the two closed sets $\{x_i \in \mathbb{R}^\ell \mid u_i(x_i) \geq u_i(y_i)\}$ and the half-space bounded by the hyperplane $\{x_i \in \mathbb{R}^\ell \mid p \cdot x_i \leq w_i\}$.

The continuous utility function u_i reaches its maximum on the compact set K. Let us now prove that this solution whose existence has been established is unique. Suppose the contrary, i.e., that two distinct solutions x_i and x_i' exist. The fact that they are solutions to the same maximization problem implies the equality $u_i(x_i) = u_i(x_i')$. Then, it comes $u_i((x_i + x_i')/2) > u_i(x_i) = u_i(x_i')$, a contradiction. $\square$

4.6.1. Walras law

Proposition 4.9. *The demand function $f_i : S \times \mathbb{R} \to \mathbb{R}^\ell$ satisfies the identity $p \cdot f_i(p, w_i) = w_i$ for $p \in S$ and $w_i \in \mathbb{R}$.*

Proof. This proposition simply tells us that if x_i is the solution to consumer i's utility maximization problem, then the equality $p \cdot x_i = w_i$ is satisfied.

Let us assume the contrary, i.e., that we have $p \cdot x_i < w_i$. The difference $\varepsilon = w_i - p \cdot x_i$ is > 0. Define the commodity bundle $x = (x^1, x^2, \ldots, x^\ell)$ by the conditions,

$$x^1 = x_i^1, \ x^2 = x_i^2, \ldots, \ x^{\ell-1} = x_i^{\ell-1}, \ x^\ell = x_i^\ell + \varepsilon.$$

It follows from the definition of ε (combined with the numeraire assumption, i.e., the equality $p^\ell = 1$) that we have $p \cdot x \leq w_i$ (actually, there is equality) while the inequality $u_i(x) > u_i(x_i)$ follows from Assumption 4.5. This contradicts the definition of x_i. $\square$

4.6.2. Smoothness of the individual demand functions

Another important property of individual demand functions is their smoothness.

Proposition 4.10. *The demand function* $f_i : S \times \mathbb{R} \rightarrow \mathbb{R}^\ell$ *is smooth.*

Proof. This proposition follows from a straightforward application of the implicit function theorem. The point $x_i = f_i(p, w_i)$ is such that there exists some $\lambda > 0$ such that the pair (x_i, λ) is a solution (in fact the solution!) of the equation system defined by the first-order conditions:

$$Du_i(x_i) - \lambda p = 0,$$
$$p \cdot x_i - w_i = 0.$$

Therefore, all we have to prove is that (x_i, λ) is a smooth function of p and w_i. This is a direct consequence of the implicit function theorem if it can be proved that the Jacobian matrix obtained by taking the derivatives of the equation system defined by the first-order conditions with respect to the coordinates of x_i and λ at the point (x_i, λ, p, w_i) is invertible.

This Jacobian matrix is equal to the matrix,

$$J = \begin{bmatrix} D^2 u_i(x_i) & -p \\ p & 0 \end{bmatrix}.$$

The determinant $\det J$ is different from zero if and only if the determinant of the matrix obtained by multiplying the last column by -1, a matrix equal to

$$\begin{bmatrix} D^2 u_i(x_i) & p \\ p & 0 \end{bmatrix},$$

is different from 0. Again, the determinant of this matrix is different from 0 if and only if the matrix obtained by multiplying the last row and column by λ is different from 0. This new matrix is equal to

$$\begin{bmatrix} D^2 u_i(x_i) & Du_i(x_i) \\ Du_i(x_i)^T & 0 \end{bmatrix},$$

a matrix that has a non-zero determinant by Maths 6.5. $\qquad \square$

The smoothness property of individual demand functions is strengthened by the following more powerful theorem:

Proposition 4.11. *The demand function* $f_i : S \times \mathbb{R} \to \mathbb{R}^\ell$ *is a diffeomorphism.*

This statement simply means that the individual demand function f_i is smooth, is a bijection, and that its inverse $g_i = f_i^{-1}$ (whose existence is ensured by the property that the function f_i is a bijection) is also smooth.

Proof. The mapping $g_i : \mathbb{R}^\ell \to S \times \mathbb{R}$ is defined by the formula,

$$g_i(x_i) = \big(D_n u_i(x_i), D_n u_i(x_i) \cdot x_i \big).$$

The mapping $x_i \to D_n u_i(x_i)$ is smooth. The inner product $(x, y) \to x \cdot y$ is bilinear, hence smooth. Therefore, the mapping $x_i \to x_i \cdot D_n u_i(x_i)$ is also smooth. This implies that the mapping g_i is smooth.

Let us establish that the maps f_i and g_i are inverse to each other. In other words, let us show that the relations $f_i \circ g_i = \mathrm{id}_{\mathbb{R}^\ell}$ and $g_i \circ f_i = \mathrm{id}_{S \times \mathbb{R}}$ are satisfied.

Computation of $f_i \circ g_i$.

By definition, we have $g_i(x_i) = (p, w_i)$ where $p = D_n(u_i(x_i))$ and $w_i = x_i \cdot D_n u_i(x_i)$. Then, it comes $f_i \circ g_i(x_i) = f_i(p, w_i) = f_i(D_n(u_i(x_i)), x_i \cdot D_n u_i(x_i))$, a term that is equal to x_i. This is equivalent to $f_i \circ g_i = \mathrm{id}_{R^\ell}$.

Computation of $g_i \circ f_i$.

By definition of g_i, we have

$$g_i\big(f_i(p, w_i)\big) = \big(D_n u_i\big(f_i(p, w_i)\big), f_i(p, w_i) \cdot D_n u_i\big(f_i(p, w_i)\big)\big),$$

which is equal to (p, w_i). This proves the equality $g_i \circ f_i = \mathrm{id}_{S \times \mathbb{R}}$.

We have therefore established that the maps f_i and g_i are bijections which are inverse to each other, and that the map g_i is smooth. Finally, it also follows from Proposition 4.10 that the map f_i is smooth. □

Corollary 4.12. *The Jacobian matrix of the map $f_i : S \times \mathbb{R} \to \mathbb{R}^\ell$ is invertible.*

Proof. Take the derivatives of the following maps:

$$f_i \circ g_i = \mathrm{id}_{\mathbb{R}^\ell}, \quad g_i \circ f_i = \mathrm{id}_{S \times \mathbb{R}}.$$

One gets the equalities,

$$D(f_i \circ g_i) = D(\mathrm{id}_{\mathbb{R}^\ell}) = \mathrm{id}_{\mathbb{R}^\ell}, \quad D(g_i \circ f_i) = D(\mathrm{id}_{S \times \mathbb{R}}) = \mathrm{id}_{S \times \mathbb{R}}.$$

One then concludes from the equalities,

$$D(f_i \circ g_i) = D(f_i) \circ D(g_i), \quad D(g_i \circ f_i) = D(g_i) \circ D(f_i)$$

(relationships that follow readily from the chain rule) that the linear maps Df_i and Dg_i are inverse to each other from which follows that the Jacobian matrix of the map f_i, i.e., the matrix of the linear map Df_i, is therefore invertible. □

The Jacobian matrix $Df_i(p, w_i)$ of the individual demand function f_i at (p, w_i) is equal to

$$
Df_i(p, w_i) = \begin{bmatrix}
\dfrac{\partial f_i^1}{\partial p_1} & \dfrac{\partial f_i^1}{\partial p_2} & \cdots & \dfrac{\partial f_i^1}{\partial p_{\ell-1}} & \dfrac{\partial f_i^1}{\partial w_i} \\[2mm]
\dfrac{\partial f_i^2}{\partial p_1} & \dfrac{\partial f_i^2}{\partial p_2} & \cdots & \dfrac{\partial f_i^2}{\partial p_{\ell-1}} & \dfrac{\partial f_i^2}{\partial w_i} \\[2mm]
\vdots & \vdots & \ddots & \vdots & \vdots \\[2mm]
\dfrac{\partial f_i^\ell}{\partial p_1} & \dfrac{\partial f_i^\ell}{\partial p_2} & \cdots & \dfrac{\partial f_i^\ell}{\partial p_{\ell-1}} & \dfrac{\partial f_i^\ell}{\partial w_i}
\end{bmatrix}.
$$

We then have the following:

Corollary 4.13.

$$\det Df_i(p, w_i) \neq 0.$$

Proof. Follows from Corollary 4.12 since the matrix $Df_i(p, w_i)$ is the Jacobian matrix of the demand function $f_i : S \times \mathbb{R} \to \mathbb{R}^\ell$. $\square$

4.7. Some Properties of the Consumer's Demand Function

4.7.1. Alternative expressions of the first-order derivative of the individual demand function

Proposition 4.14. *We have $D_n u_i\big(f_i(p, w_i)\big) = p$ for every $p \in S$ and $w_i \in \mathbb{R}$.*

Proof. From $Du_i(x_i) = \lambda(x_i)p$, with $\lambda(x_i) \neq 0$, the normalized gradient vector $D_n u_i(x_i)$ and the price vector p are collinear. Since the ℓ coordinates of these two collinear vectors are equal to 1 and, therefore, equal, these two vectors are equal. $\square$

Proposition 4.15. *Let $x_i \in \mathbb{R}^\ell$. We then have*

$$x_i = f_i\big(D_n u_i(x_i), D_n u_i(x_i) \cdot x_i\big).$$

Proof. Pick some point $x_i \in \mathbb{R}^\ell$. Let p and λ be defined by

$$p = D_n u_i(x_i), \quad \lambda = \frac{\partial u_i}{\partial x^\ell}(x_i).$$

We then have $\lambda p = D u_i(x_i)$. It suffices to define w_i by the inner product $w_i = p \cdot x_i$ to conclude that we have $x_i = f_i(p, w_i)$. $\square$

4.7.2. Important identities between the first-order derivatives

Proposition 4.16. *The following relationships are satisfied by the first-order derivatives of the individual demand function* $f_i : S \times \mathbb{R} \to \mathbb{R}^\ell$.

$$p \cdot \frac{\partial f_i}{\partial w_i} = 1, \tag{3}$$

$$p \cdot \frac{\partial f_i}{\partial p_j} = -f_i^j(p, w_i) \qquad j = 1, 2, \dots, \ell - 1. \tag{4}$$

Proof. Equality (3) is obtained by taking the derivative of Walras law $p \cdot f_i(p, w_i) = w_i$ with respect to w_i. By taking the derivative with respect to p_j, one gets $f_i^j(p, w_i) + p \cdot (\partial f_i / \partial p_j)(p, w_i) = 0$, hence equality (4). $\square$

4.8. The Slutsky Matrix

Let us associate with the demand function $f_i : S \times \mathbb{R} \to \mathbb{R}^\ell$ the following matrix:

Definition 4.17. The Slutsky matrix $M_i(p, w_i)$ defined for $(p, w_i) \in S \times \mathbb{R}$ is the square matrix of order $\ell - 1$ with (j, k) coefficient (for row j and column k) equal to

$$m_i^{jk}(p, w_i) = \frac{\partial f_i^j}{\partial p_k} + \frac{\partial f_i^j}{\partial w_i} f_i^k(p, w_i).$$

Proposition 4.18. *We have*

$$\frac{df_i^j}{dp_k} = \left(\frac{\partial f_i^j}{\partial p_k} + f_i^k \frac{\partial f_i^j}{\partial w_i}\right) + (\omega_i^k - f_i^k)\frac{\partial f_i^j}{\partial w_i}.$$

Proof. It suffices to apply the chain rule to the (derivative of the) function $p \to f_i(p, p \cdot \omega_i)$ after having observed that the price vector is both a direct and an indirect argument of the demand function f_i. $\square$

Proposition 4.18 alone would suffice to justify the interest in the Slutsky matrix. The following subsection gives us other reasons.

4.8.1. The substitution and the income effects

Definition 4.19. The income effect is equal to

$$\left(\omega_i^k - f_i^k(p, w_i)\right)\frac{\partial f_i^j}{\partial w_i}(p, w_i). \tag{5}$$

The substitution effect is equal to

$$\frac{\partial f_i^j}{\partial p_k}(p, w_i) + f_i^k(p, w_i)\frac{\partial f_i^j}{\partial w_i}(p, w_i). \tag{6}$$

The term of income effect is rather easy to justify. The justification of the term of substitution effect is less immediate and requires an alternative expression of this coefficient. Since this expression is not directly useful for our purpose, these calculations are left to the reader.

Proposition 4.20. *The coefficient $m_i^{jk}(p, w_i)$ of the Slutsky matrix at (p, w_i) is equal to the corresponding substitution effect.*

Proof. Follows readily from the definition of the substitution effects. $\square$

4.8.2. Invertibility of the Slutsky matrix

Proposition 4.21. *The Slutsky matrix has a non-zero determinant:*

$$\det M_i(p, w_i) \neq 0.$$

Proof. The Jacobian matrix of the individual demand function f_i : $(p, w_i) \rightarrow f_i(p, w_i)$ is invertible by Corollary 4.13. This Jacobian matrix is equal to

$$\begin{bmatrix} \dfrac{\partial f_i^1}{\partial p_1} & \dfrac{\partial f_i^1}{\partial p_2} & \cdots & \dfrac{\partial f_i^1}{\partial p_{\ell-1}} & \dfrac{\partial f_i^1}{\partial w_i} \\[2ex] \dfrac{\partial f_i^2}{\partial p_1} & \dfrac{\partial f_i^2}{\partial p_2} & \cdots & \dfrac{\partial f_i^2}{\partial p_{\ell-1}} & \dfrac{\partial f_i^2}{\partial w_i} \\[1ex] \vdots & \vdots & \ddots & \vdots & \vdots \\[1ex] \dfrac{\partial f_i^\ell}{\partial p_1} & \dfrac{\partial f_i^\ell}{\partial p_2} & \cdots & \dfrac{\partial f_i^\ell}{\partial p_{\ell-1}} & \dfrac{\partial f_i^\ell}{\partial w_i} \end{bmatrix}.$$

It follows from Linear Algebra that we do not change the value of the determinant of this (Jacobian) matrix if we add to the last row some linear combination of the other rows of the matrix. Therefore, let us add to the last row the first row multiplied by p_1, the second row multiplied by $p_2, \ldots$, up to the $\ell - 1$th row multiplied by $p_{\ell-1}$. It follows from Proposition 4.16 that this yields a last row equal to

$$\begin{pmatrix} -f_i^1 & -f_i^2 & \cdots & -f_i^{\ell-1} & 1 \end{pmatrix}.$$

Again, we do not change the value of the determinant if we add to the first column the last column multiplied by f_i^1, if we add to the second column the last column multiplied by f_i^2, etc., up to the $\ell - 1$th column to which we add the last column multiplied by $f_i^{\ell-1}$. This operation yields the matrix,

$$\begin{pmatrix} M_i & \vdots \\ 0 \ldots 0 & 1 \end{pmatrix},$$

whose determinant is equal to the determinant of the Slutsky matrix. $\square$

4.8.3. Negative semi-definiteness and symmetry

Let (p^*, w_i^*) be a given price–income pair. Let $\omega_i^* = f_i(p^*, w_i^*)$. Let us consider the map $h_i : S \to \mathbb{R}$ defined by the formula,

$$h_i(p) = u_i\big(f_i(p, p \cdot \omega_i^*)\big).$$

Lemma 4.22. *The function $p \to h_i(p)$ reaches an absolute minimum at $p = p^*$.*

Proof. Let $x_i = f_i(p, p \cdot \omega_i^*)$. This is the solution of the problem of maximizing $u_i(x)$ subject to the budget constraint $p \cdot x \leq p \cdot \omega_i^*$. Note that $x = \omega_i^*$ satisfies the budget constraint. This implies the inequality $u_i(\omega_i^*) \leq u_i(x_i)$, which is equivalent to $h_i(p^*) \leq h_i(p)$ for any $p \in S$. $\square$

Lemma 4.23. *The first-order derivative of the function h_i with respect to the price p_j is equal to*

$$\frac{\partial h_i}{\partial p_j} = -\lambda(x_i)\,\big(f_i^j(p, p \cdot \omega_i^*) - \omega_i^{*j}\big).$$

Proof. The computation of the first-order derivative exploits the chain rule:

$$\frac{\partial h_i}{\partial p_j} = Du_i \cdot \frac{df_i}{dp_j},$$

$$\frac{\partial h_i}{\partial p_j} = \lambda(x_i)\, p \cdot \left(\frac{\partial f_i}{\partial p_j} + \frac{\partial f_i}{\partial w_i}\omega_i^{j*}\right),$$

$$\frac{\partial h_i}{\partial p_j} = \lambda(x_i)\left(p \cdot \frac{\partial f_i}{\partial p_j}\right) + \omega_i^{j*}\left(p \cdot \frac{\partial f_i}{\partial w_i}\right)$$

From $p \cdot \dfrac{\partial f_i}{\partial p_j} = -f_i^j(p, p \cdot \omega_i^*)$ and $p \cdot \dfrac{\partial f_i}{\partial w_i} = 1$, it comes

$$\frac{\partial h_i}{\partial p_j} = -\lambda(x_i)\,\big(f_i^j(p, p \cdot \omega_i^*) - \omega_i^{*j}\big).$$

$\square$

One can use Lemma 4.23 to check that the first-order derivatives of the function h_i at p^* are equal to 0. This can also be viewed as a consequence that the function h_i has an absolute minimum at $p = p^*$.

Proposition 4.24. *The second-order derivative $\left(\frac{\partial^2 h_i}{\partial p_j \partial p_k}\right)$ at $p = p^*$ for $1 \leq j, k \leq \ell - 1$ is equal to*

$$\frac{\partial^2 h_i}{\partial p_j \partial p_k}\bigg|_{p=p^*} = -\lambda(\omega_i^*) m_i^{jk}.$$

Proof. Using Lemma 4.23, the second-order derivative at the price vector p is equal to

$$\frac{\partial^2 h_i}{\partial p_j \partial p_k} = -\frac{d\lambda}{dp_k}(x_i)\left(f_i^j(p, p \cdot \omega_i^*) - \omega_i^{*j}\right) - \lambda(x_i)\frac{df_i^j}{dp_k}(p, p \cdot \omega_i^*).$$

For $p = p^*$, we have $f_i^j(p^*, p^* \cdot \omega_i^*) = \omega_i^{*j}$, which implies the equality,

$$\frac{\partial^2 h_i}{\partial p_j \partial p_k}\bigg|_{p=p^*} = -\lambda(\omega_i^*)\left(\frac{\partial f_i^j}{\partial p_k}(p^*, p^* \cdot \omega_i^*) + \frac{\partial f_i^j}{\partial w_i}(p^*, p^* \cdot \omega_i^*)\omega_i^{*k}\right),$$

$$\frac{\partial^2 h_i}{\partial p_j \partial p_k}\bigg|_{p=p^*} = -\lambda(\omega_i^*) m_i^{jk}.$$

$\square$

Proposition 4.25. *The numeraire normalized Slutsky matrix $M_i(p^*, w_i^*)$ is equal to the Hessian matrix of the function $p \to h_i(p)$ at p^* multiplied by $-\lambda(\omega_i^*)$.*

Proof. Obvious. $\square$

The following statement is remarkable in the sense that it states relatively strong properties of the individual demand functions. Its importance will appear very quickly in the following chapters.

Proposition 4.26 (Slutsky). *The numeraire normalized Slutsky matrix is symmetric negative definite.*

Proof. The function $p \to h_i(p)$ is smooth. Therefore, its Hessian matrix is symmetric. In addition, this function reaches an absolute minimum at $p = p^*$. Corollary 4.25 implies that the Slutsky matrix is symmetric and negative semi-definite. It now follows from Linear Algebra that a negative semi-definite quadratic form is definite if and only if the determinant of the associated matrix is different from 0. This follows from Proposition 4.21. $\square$

4.9. Revealed Preferences

The next property is global because it involves two different pairs (p, w_i) and (p', w_i') that are not necessarily close to each other.

Proposition 4.27. *Let (p, w_i) and (p', w_i') be two distinct price–income pairs. If the inequality $p \cdot f_i(p', w_i') \leq w_i$ is true, then the strict inequality $p' \cdot f_i(p, w_i) > w_i'$ is also satisfied.*

Proof. The mapping f_i being a diffeomorphism and the pairs (p, w_i) and (p', w_i') being different, $f_i(p, w_i)$ and $f_i(p', w_i')$ are different. The inequality $p \cdot f_i(p', w_i') \leq w_i$ means that $f_i(p', w_i')$ satisfies the budget constraint $p \cdot x_i \leq w_i$. Since $f_i(p, w_i)$ maximizes the utility $u_i(x_i)$ subject to the budget constraint $p \cdot x_i \leq w_i$, the inequality,

$$u_i(f_i(p', w_i')) \leq u_i(f_i(p, w_i))$$

is therefore satisfied. Furthermore, this inequality is strict since the solution $f_i(p, w_i)$ that maximizes $u_i(x_i)$ subject to the constraint $p \cdot x_i \leq w_i$ is unique.

In order to prove the inequality $p' \cdot f_i(p, w_i) > w_i'$, let us assume that the opposite inequality is satisfied, i.e., that we have $p' \cdot f_i(p, w_i) \leq w_i'$. It follows from the same line of reasoning as above that this inequality implies the strict inequality $u_i(f_i(p, w_i)) < u_i(f_i(p', w_i'))$, hence a contradiction. $\square$

4.10. The Properties of the Demand Function

The main properties of consumer i's demand function $f_i : S \times \mathbb{R} \to \mathbb{R}^\ell$ that will be used over and over in the following pages in order to reflect assumptions made on preferences are the following ones in particular:

- (Walras law) $p \cdot f_i(p, w_i) = w_i$;
- (Differentiability) $f_i : S \times \mathbb{R} \to \mathbb{R}^\ell$ is differentiable;
- (Diffeomorphism) $f_i : S \times \mathbb{R} \to \mathbb{R}^\ell$ is a diffeomorphism.

The properties associated with the Slutsky matrix and with the revealed preference property are also important and are also used at various places. There are a few other properties like the fact that the demand is going to be bounded from below for endowments that belong to a compact subset of the commodity space that are also satisfied. They are either proved in the exercises or put in later chapters when they become necessary.

4.11. Conclusion

The content of this chapter is known in all textbooks as Consumer Theory. In this book, we focus on preferences that are defined on the full commodity space and represented by smooth utility functions. Extension to preferences that are bounded from below is almost straightforward. We are now ready to study the general equilibrium model with an arbitrary number of goods and agents.

4.12. Notes and Comments

A natural question to ask at this stage is whether the revealed preference property and Slutsky's theorem are not different facets of the property that individuals maximize their preferences subject to a budget constraint defined by prices and income. This is true, but only up to a certain extent. Furthermore, proving that equivalence requires a lot more of mathematics.

Given a smooth mapping $f_i : S \times \mathbb{R} \to \mathbb{R}^\ell$ that satisfies Walras relation and the conditions of the Slutsky's theorem, it is possible to construct a utility function u_i for which the corresponding demand function is precisely the function f_i. We do not develop this topic here for the reason that the appropriate mathematical setup involves Frobenius theorem and related topics, a rather specialized area of Pure Mathematics (see, for example, [16, (10.9.4)] and [25]). Slutsky's theorem can then be viewed as the expression of a necessary and sufficient condition for the vector field defined by associating with every $x_i \in \mathbb{R}^\ell$ the price vector p that supports x_i to be identical to a normalized gradient field. For a thorough analysis of this question, we refer the reader to [14].

For the revealed preference property, Samuelson has shown that in the case of two commodities, it is possible to associate with any smooth function satisfying the revealed preference property (and Walras relation) a utility function. But, when there are more than two commodities, the property of strong revealed preference is necessary by opposition to the weak revealed preference property considered in this book. For details about this approach to consumer theory, see more particularly the original papers on the subject with, in particular, [22] and [38].

4.13. Exercises

4.1. Let $x_i^* = \lim_{n \to \infty} x_i^n$ with $u_i(x_i^n) \geq u_i^*$. Define $y_i^n = \lambda_n x_i^n$ with $u_i(y_i^n) = u_i^*$ and $0 < \lambda_n \leq 1$. (1) Show that the sequence y_i^n has a subsequence that converges to some y_i^*. (2) Prove the inequality $y_i^* \leq x_n^*$. (3) Deduce that the set $\{x_i \in \mathbb{R}^\ell \mid u_i(x_i) \geq u_i^*\}$ is closed.

4.2. Define $\lambda_i(p, w_i)$ by the formula $Du_i(f_i(p, w_i)) = \lambda_i(p, w_i)\, p$. (1) Show that the map $(p, w_i) \to \lambda_i(p, w_i)$ is differentiable. (2) Extend this property by showing that the same map is indefinitely differentiable.

Chapter 5

The Equilibrium Manifold

We assume in the next two chapters that total resources are variable in addition to the numbers of goods ℓ and consumers m being only finite. We therefore have $\Omega = \mathbb{R}^{\ell m}$.

5.1. Closedness of the Equilibrium Manifold

We endow the equilibrium manifold which is a subset E of $S \times \Omega$ with the topology induced by that of $S \times \Omega$. This simply means that once a distance (for example, the Euclidean distance) has been chosen on $S \times \Omega$, one defines a distance on the subset E simply by taking the restriction to the subset E of the distance defined on $S \times \Omega$. This enables one to define in a meaningful way neighborhoods and limits of sequences in E and, therefore, a topology on E. The set E then becomes a topological subspace of $S \times \Omega$. Note that we do not know yet that the topological space E is a differentiable manifold.

Proposition 5.1. *The equilibrium manifold E is a closed subset of $S \times \Omega$.*

Proof. The equilibrium manifold E consists of the pairs $(p, \omega) \in S \times \Omega$ which satisfy the equality $z(p, \omega) = \sum_i f_i(p, p \cdot \omega_i) - \sum_i \omega_i = 0$. This set is closed in $S \times \Omega$ as the preimage of the closed set reduced to the point (or vector) $0 \in \mathbb{R}^\ell$ by the continuous map $(p, \omega) \to z(p, \omega)$. $\quad\square$

Note that this closedness property requires only the continuity of individual demand functions. This property is obviously satisfied by smooth pure exchange models.

5.2. Smooth Manifolds and Submanifolds

5.2.1. Smooth parameterizations

One of the most convenient ways of describing a set consists in parameterizing its elements by continuous or, even much better, differentiable functions. For example, a curve in the three-dimensional space $\mathbb{R}^3$ is parameterized by some map $t \in \mathbb{R} \to \big(f(t), g(t), h(t)\big) \in \mathbb{R}^3$. A parameterized set can therefore be identified with the graph of one or several real-valued functions of one or several real variables. Note that "most" subsets of $\mathbb{R}^n$ cannot have smooth parameterizations. Therefore, the existence of a smooth parametrization appears to be a rather strong property of the set.

We address the structure problem of the equilibrium manifold E as the one of finding suitable smooth parameterizations. There are essentially two versions of that structure problem: the local one consists in showing that "small" open sets can be smoothly parameterized; the global one corresponds to the existence of some smooth parametrization of the full set E. If it is evidently more interesting to have a solution of the global problem, the local version is easier to deal with, and not without its own interest. We therefore start with the study of the local problem, a step towards getting an understanding of the global structure.

5.2.2. Smooth manifolds

The local structure problem leads us readily to the mathematical concepts of differentiable or smooth manifolds, and of diffeomorphisms. A reader unfamiliar with the concept of a smooth manifold should consult the mathematical appendix and the references cited there. The aim of the following heuristic presentation is simply to give some intuition of the smooth manifold concept and of its relationship with the smooth local parametrization problem.

Roughly speaking, a smooth manifold is a topological space that can be locally identified with a Euclidean space, i.e., to $\mathbb{R}^n$ for some finite n. More precisely, at every point of the manifold, it is possible to find at least one open neighborhood U that is homeomorphic to $\mathbb{R}^n$. The set U is called a chart of the manifold. The inverse map $\phi : U \to \mathbb{R}^n$ is continuous and constitutes a parametrization of the chart U by n real numbers. This parametrization is said to define a local coordinate system of the smooth manifold.

It may happen that two distinct charts U and V have a non-empty intersection. Then, there exist at least two ways of parametrizing the points that belong to the intersection $U \cap V$: one through the map $\phi : U \to \mathbb{R}^n$, another through the map $\psi : V \to \mathbb{R}^p$. The sets $\phi^{-1}(U \cap V)$ and $\psi^{-1}(U \cap V)$ are then open subsets of $\mathbb{R}^n$ and $\mathbb{R}^p$, respectively. These sets are related by two bijections:

$$\psi^{-1} \circ \phi : \phi^{-1}(U \cap V) \to \psi^{-1}(U \cap V),$$
$$\phi^{-1} \circ \psi : \psi^{-1}(U \cap V) \to \phi^{-1}(U \cap V).$$

These maps can be interpreted as changes of local coordinates; they are often called transition morphisms.

By definition, a set is a smooth manifold if, in addition to being the countable union of a collection of charts, all these transition morphisms, i.e., the $\psi^{-1} \circ \phi$ and $\phi^{-1} \circ \psi$, are smooth. The smooth manifold structure therefore consists of a (countable) collection of local coordinate systems covering up the whole space and such that coordinate substitutions are all smooth.

5.2.3. Dimension of a smooth manifold

The dimension of a smooth manifold at a point is the number of local coordinates of an arbitrary chart containing that point. One checks easily that this number does not depend on the choice of the chart. If the dimension is the same for all the points of the manifold — this happens in particular for connected manifolds — then this number is known as the dimension of the manifold.

5.2.4. Smooth submanifolds

The concept of smooth manifold extends to the one of smooth submanifold. Roughly speaking, a submanifold of a given smooth manifold X is a subspace Y of X that is not only a smooth manifold on its own but also whose manifold structure is derived from the one of X very simply. This takes the following form. First, we know that for every open subset V of Y, there exists an open subset U of X such that $V = U \cap Y$. Second, for V small enough, we can take V to be diffeomorphic to $\mathbb{R}^m$ and U to $\mathbb{R}^n$ for every $y \in V$, with $m \leq n$.

5.3. The Equilibrium Manifold as a Smooth Manifold

Proposition 5.2. *The equilibrium manifold E is a smooth submanifold of the set $S \times \Omega$ having dimension ℓm.*

The regular value theorem is a very simple method of proving that a subset of some Euclidean space $\mathbb{R}^n$ is a smooth submanifold of that set.

The regular value theorem goes as follows. Let $f : X \to Y$ be a smooth map from the manifold X into the manifold Y. The point $x \in X$ is a critical point of the map f if the tangent map $(df)_x : T_x(X) \to T_{f(x)}Y$ is not onto. Then, the image $f(x)$ of the critical point $x \in X$ is by definition a singular value of the map f. The element $y \in Y$ is a regular value of the map f if it is not a singular value, i.e., the image of some critical point of f. The regular value theorem then states that the preimage $f^{-1}(y)$ of the regular value $y \in Y$ is a smooth manifold whose dimension is equal to the dimension of X minus the dimension of Y. In addition, the manifold $f^{-1}(y)$ is a smooth submanifold of X.

We already know from $E = z^{-1}(0)$ that E is the preimage of $0 \in \mathbb{R}^\ell$. Therefore, it would suffice for $0 \in \mathbb{R}^\ell$ to be a regular value of the map $z : S \times \Omega \to \mathbb{R}^\ell$. Unfortunately, $0 \in \mathbb{R}^\ell$ cannot be a regular value of the map z because of Walras law. The solution is then to consider the map $\bar{z} : (p, \omega) \to \mathbb{R}^{\ell-1}$ that is the composition of the map $z : S \times \Omega \to \mathbb{R}^\ell$ with the projection map $x \to \bar{x}$ from $\mathbb{R}^\ell$ to $\mathbb{R}^{\ell-1}$ that associates with $x = (x^1, x^2, \ldots, x^{\ell-1}, x^\ell)$ the element $\bar{x}$ defined by the first $\ell - 1$ coordinates $\bar{x} = (x^1, x^2, \ldots, x^{\ell-1})$. We then have the following:

Lemma 5.3. *The equilibrium manifold E is equal to $\bar{z}^{-1}(0)$.*

Proof. The inclusion $E = z^{-1}(0) \subset \bar{z}^{-1}(0)$ is obvious. Conversely, let $(p, \omega) \in \bar{z}^{-1}(0)$. From $p \cdot z(p, \omega) = 0$, we get the equality $p_1 z^1(p, \omega) + \cdots + p_{\ell-1} z^{\ell-1}(p, \omega) + p_\ell z^\ell(p, \omega) = 0$, which implies $z^\ell(p, \omega) = 0$ given that $p_\ell = 1$. This proves (p, ω) belongs to $z^{-1}(0)$, from which follows the inclusion $\bar{z}^{-1}(0) \subset z^{-1}(0)$. $\qquad\square$

5.3.1. Proof of the smooth manifold structure

Proof. [Proof of Proposition 5.2] We know by Lemma 5.3 that the "equilibrium manifold" E is the preimage of $0 \in \mathbb{R}^{\ell-1}$ by the map $\bar{z} : S \times \Omega \to \mathbb{R}^{\ell-1}$. It therefore suffices that we show that $0 \in \mathbb{R}^{\ell-1}$ is a regular value of the map $\bar{z}$. This is equivalent to showing that $0 \in \mathbb{R}^{\ell-1}$ is not the value of the function $\bar{z}$ at some critical point. This follows from the property that we now prove that the map $\bar{z}$ has no critical point whatsoever.

The latter property is equivalent to the Jacobian matrix of the map $\bar{z}$ having everywhere full rank. This rank must be equal to $\ell - 1$, the number of rows of the Jacobian matrix since this matrix has $\ell - 1 + m\ell$ columns, a number strictly larger than the number $\ell - 1$ of rows.

Let us extract from the Jacobian matrix of $\bar{z}$ at $(p, \omega) \in S \times \Omega$ the $(\ell - 1) \times \ell$ submatrix whose elements are the partial derivatives of the (coordinates of the) function $\bar{z}$ with respect to the variables $\omega_i^1, \omega_i^2, \ldots, \omega_i^\ell$ for some arbitrarily chosen agent or consumer i. Let us show that this $\ell - 1 \times \ell$ matrix has rank $\ell - 1$. This matrix is equal to

$$
\begin{bmatrix}
\dfrac{\partial f_i^1}{\partial w_i} p_1 - 1 & \dfrac{\partial f_i^1}{\partial w_i} p_2 & \cdots & \dfrac{\partial f_i^1}{\partial w_i} p_{\ell-1} & \dfrac{\partial f_i^1}{\partial w_i} \\[2ex]
\dfrac{\partial f_i^2}{\partial w_i} p_1 & \dfrac{\partial f_i^2}{\partial w_i} p_2 - 1 & \cdots & \dfrac{\partial f_i^2}{\partial w_i} p_{\ell-1} & \dfrac{\partial f_i^2}{\partial w_i} \\[2ex]
\vdots & \vdots & \ddots & \vdots & \vdots \\[2ex]
\dfrac{\partial f_i^{\ell-1}}{\partial w_i} p_1 & \dfrac{\partial f_i^{\ell-1}}{\partial w_i} p_2 & \cdots & \dfrac{\partial f_i^{\ell-1}}{\partial w_i} p_{\ell-1} - 1 & \dfrac{\partial f_i^{\ell-1}}{\partial w_i}
\end{bmatrix}.
$$

Let us subtract from the first column the last column multiplied by p_1, an operation that we repeat from the second to the $(\ell - 1)$th column with $p_2, \ldots, p_{\ell-1}$. We end up with the matrix,

$$
\begin{bmatrix}
-1 & & 0 & \frac{\partial f_i^1}{\partial w_i} \\
& \ddots & & \vdots \\
0 & & -1 & \frac{\partial f_i^{\ell-1}}{\partial w_i}
\end{bmatrix},
$$

which, by construction, has the same rank as the original matrix. The first $\ell - 1$ columns of this new matrix define a square matrix that is invertible, and therefore has rank $\ell - 1$.

The dimension of the equilibrium manifold E is then, again by the regular value theorem, equal to $\dim E = \dim S \times \mathbb{R}^{\ell m} - \dim \mathbb{R}^{\ell-1} = \ell - 1 + \ell m - (\ell - 1) = \ell m$. □

Proposition 5.2 implies that it is possible to parametrize sufficiently small open subsets of the equilibrium manifold E by ℓm "local coordinates."

5.4. The No-trade Equilibria

The existence of local smooth structure for E is already interesting for its own sake; but an explicit system of local coordinates or, even better, a global parametrization of the equilibrium manifold E would be much more useful, from both theoretical and practical perspectives. This will lead us to the study of the global properties of the equilibrium manifold E. But, before, our goal is to get a better understanding of the equilibrium manifold E, of how it is embedded in $S \times \Omega$ and, more surprisingly, of how the equilibrium manifold E can be viewed as a fibered space on the price–income set B. Before that, we therefore study the set of no-trade equilibria.

Definition 5.4. The pair $(p, \omega) \in S \times \Omega$ is a no-trade equilibrium if the equality $f_i(p, p \cdot \omega_i) = \omega_i$ is satisfied for every consumer i. The set of no-trade equilibria is denoted by T.

Equality $f_i(p, p \cdot \omega_i) = \omega_i$ in the above definition being equivalent to the condition $f_i(p, p \cdot \omega_i) - \omega_i = 0$, a no-trade equilibrium $(p, \omega) \in S \times \Omega$ is characterized by the condition that all individual excess demands $f_i(p, p \cdot \omega_i) - \omega_i$ are equal to 0. We still have to prove (even if this is more or less obvious) that a "no-trade equilibrium" is an "equilibrium."

Proposition 5.5. *Every no-trade equilibrium is an equilibrium, i.e., $T \subset E$.*

Proof. Let $(p, \omega) \in T$ be a no-trade equilibrium. The individual excess demand $f_i(p, p \cdot \omega_i) - \omega_i$ is equal to 0 for i varying from 1 to m. Summing up yields the aggregate excess demand $z(p, \omega) = \sum_{i=1}^{m} (f_i(p, p \cdot \omega_i) - \omega_i) = 0$. □

The definition of the no-trade equilibrium concept may appear to be paradoxical. This concept conflicts with the very idea that the role of markets is to facilitate exchange activities. In fact, markets where exchange activities are very small are quickly closed. Therefore, one can expect that no-trade equilibria are never or almost never observed in real markets. Despite this observation, the no-trade equilibrium concept, however, turns out to be a very important tool in understanding the properties of competitive equilibria.

In fact, the concept of no-trade equilibrium highlights the importance of the intensity of net trades as an explanatory factor of the properties of economic equilibria. The net trades are represented by the excess demand vector $(f_i(p, p \cdot \omega_i) - \omega_i)_{i=1,2,\ldots,m}$. The intensity of net trade then provides a measure of how far an equilibrium is from a no-trade equilibrium.

Concepts with no real-world realization exist in many areas of Science. The perfect vacuum and the absolute zero of temperature are good examples of that. These concepts extrapolate real-world situations to extremes that are never achieved. Nevertheless, their theoretical and practical usefulness is tremendous. The no-trade equilibrium concept belongs to the same category.

5.4.1. A useful lemma

The following mathematical lemma is very convenient in a number of questions in the theory of general equilibrium. We will apply this lemma here to establish the global structure of the set of no-trade equilibria. We will see shortly after that another application of the same lemma to the global structure of the equilibrium manifold.

Lemma 5.6. *Let* $\alpha : X \to Y$ *and* $\beta : Y \to X$ *be two smooth mappings between smooth manifolds such that the composition* $\alpha \circ \beta :$ $Y \to Y$ *is the identity map. Then, the set* $Z = \beta(Y)$, *the image of the map* β, *is a smooth submanifold of* X *diffeomorphic to* Y.

Proof. The strategy of proof is to show that the smooth map $\beta : Y \to X$ is an embedding, i.e., by the definition of an embedding, a map that is an immersion and a homeomorphism between the domain Y and the image $Z = \beta(Y)$. It is then a standard property of an embedding that its image is a smooth submanifold diffeomorphic to the domain. Here, this means that the image Z is a smooth submanifold of X diffeomorphic to Y.

To prove the homeomorphism part, we first remark that β, viewed as a map from Y to $Z = \beta(Y)$, is a surjection. From $\alpha \circ \beta = \mathrm{id}_Y$, the identity map of Y, it follows that the map β is also an injection, hence a bijection. Let $\alpha \mid Z$ denote the restriction of α to Z. The relation $\alpha \circ \beta = \mathrm{id}_Y$ implies $(\alpha \mid Z) \circ \beta = \mathrm{id}_Y$. With the map β now being a bijection between Y and Z, the inverse map is therefore equal to $\alpha \mid Z$. The definition of the induced topology of Z implies, the maps $\alpha : X \to Y$ and $\beta : Y \to X$ being continuous (in fact, these maps are smooth), that their counterparts $\alpha \mid Z : Z \to Y$ and $\beta : Y \to Z$ are also continuous. (Note that the fact that Z is simply a subset of X equipped with the induced topology does not make it a "nice" subset of X yet, and prevents us from using the above argument to infer that $\alpha \mid Z : Z \to Y$ and $\psi : Y \to Z$ are smooth mappings.)

To prove the immersion part, take $y \in Y$. The relation $\alpha \circ \beta = \mathrm{id}_Y$ yields for the tangent maps the relation $T_{\beta(y)} \alpha \circ T_y \beta = \mathrm{id}_{T_y(Y)}$ where

$T_y(Y)$ denotes the tangent space to the manifold Y at y. Therefore, the linear map between tangent spaces $T_y\beta : T_y(Y) \to T_{\alpha(y)}(X)$ is an injection. □

5.4.2. The global structure of the set of no-trade equilibria

In the following developments, the price–income vector $(p, w_1, \ldots, w_m) \in B = S \times \mathbb{R}^m$ plays an important role. We also consider the following two maps:

The map $f : B \to S \times \Omega$ is defined by the expression,

$$f(p, w_1, \ldots, w_m) = \big(p, f_1(p, w_1), f_2(p, w_2), \ldots, f_m(p, w_m)\big).$$

This map is smooth since its coordinates are smooth.

The map $\varphi : S \times \Omega \to B$ is defined by the expression,

$$\varphi(p, \omega_1, \ldots, \omega_m) = (p, p \cdot \omega_1, \ldots, p \cdot \omega_m).$$

This map is polynomial and, therefore, smooth.

Proposition 5.7. *The map f obviously takes its values in E. Similarly, we will consider only the restriction of the map φ to E. The set of no-trade equilibria T is a smooth submanifold of $S \times \Omega$ diffeomorphic to B.*

Proof. Let us show that the maps $f : B \to E$ and $\varphi : E \to B$ just defined satisfy the assumptions of Lemma 5.6.

We have $\varphi \circ f(p, w_1, \ldots, w_m) = (p, p \cdot f_1(p, w_1), \ldots, p \cdot f_m(p, w_m))$ which is equal, by Walras law, to $(p, w_1, \ldots, w_m)$. This proves the equality $\varphi \circ f = \mathrm{id}_B$.

Let us now prove the equality $T = f(B)$. Let

$$(p, \omega_1, \ldots, \omega_m) = f(p, w_1, \ldots, w_m) \in f(B).$$

By the definition of the map f, we have

$$\omega_i = f_i(p, w_i) \qquad \text{for } i = 1, \ldots, m.$$

Walras law implies $w_i = p \cdot \omega_i$, from which follows

$$w_i = f_i(p, p \cdot \omega_i) \qquad \text{for } i = 1, 2, \ldots, m$$

and, therefore, $(p, \omega_1, \ldots, \omega_m) \in T$, hence the inclusion $T \subset f(B)$.

Let now $(p, \omega_1, \ldots, \omega_m) \in T$. Define $w_i = p \cdot \omega_i$ for $i = 1, \ldots, m$. It follows from the definition of a no-trade equilibrium that we have $w_i = f_i(p, p \cdot \omega_i) = f_i(p, w_i)$ for every i and, therefore, $(p, \omega_1, \ldots, \omega_m) = f(p, w_1, \ldots, w_m)$ by the definition of the map f, which proves that $(p, \omega_1, \ldots, \omega_m)$ belongs to T, hence the inclusion $f(B) \subset T$. □

5.5. The Fibers of the Equilibrium Manifold

The aim of this section is to show that the equilibrium manifold E is a collection of remarkable subsets called its fibers. One notices that if the price vector p and the income $p \cdot \omega_i$ for i varying from 1 to m are kept constant, then aggregate demand $\sum_i f_i(p, p \cdot \omega_i)$ remains constant when $\omega = (\omega_i)$ is varied. Therefore, (p, ω) remains an equilibrium if the total resources $\sum_i \omega_i$ are kept constant in addition to having the price vector p and the incomes $p \cdot \omega_i$ constant. This leads us to the following definition:

Definition 5.8. The fiber $V(b)$ associated with $b = (p, w_1, \ldots, w_m) \in B$ is the set of pairs $(p, \omega) \in S \times \Omega$ that satisfy the following equations:

$$p \cdot \omega_i = w_i \qquad \text{for } i = 1, 2, \ldots, m, \tag{1}$$

$$\sum_i \omega_i = \sum_i f_i(p, w_i). \tag{2}$$

Equality (2) combined with (1) implies that $(p, \omega) \in V(b)$ satisfies the equilibrium equation. Therefore, every fiber $V(b)$ is a subset of the equilibrium manifold E.

5.5.1. The fiber $V(b)$

The structure of the fiber $V(b)$ associated with $b \in B$ is described in the following proposition:

Proposition 5.9. *The fiber $V(b)$ associated with $b \in B$ is a linear manifold of dimension $(\ell - 1)(m - 1)$.*

Proof. The equations defining the fiber $V(b)$ for $b = (p, w_1, \ldots, w_m) \in B$ are linear with a constant term. This proves that the fiber $V(b)$ is a linear manifold. To obtain the dimensionality property, it then suffices to find a system of $(\ell - 1)(m - 1)$ coordinates for this linear set.

Let $r = f_1(p, w_1) + \cdots + f_m(p, w_m)$. The equality $\sum_i \omega_i = r$ implies $\omega_m = r - \sum_{i=1}^{m-1} \omega_i$. It therefore suffices to know ω_1, ω_2, $\ldots$, up to ω_{m-1} to determine ω_m.

It then follows from $p \cdot \omega_i = w_i$ that we have

$$\omega_i^\ell = w_i - (p_1 \omega_i^1 + \cdots + p_{\ell-1} \omega_i^{\ell-1}).$$

The first $(\ell - 1)$ coordinates $\bar{\omega}_i = (\omega_i^1, \omega_i^2, \ldots, \omega_i^{\ell-1})$ therefore suffice to determine the quantity ω_i^ℓ of the ℓth commodity, with i varying from 1 to $m - 1$.

This proves that $(\bar{\omega}_i^1, \bar{\omega}_i^2, \ldots, \bar{\omega}_{m-1}) \in \mathbb{R}^{(\ell-1)(m-1)}$ does define a linear parametrization of the fiber $V(b)$ associated with $b = (p, w_1, w_2, \ldots, w_m) \in B$. $\square$

It is evidently possible to use other coordinate systems to parametrize the fiber $V(b)$. For example, one could use coordinates that would be more symmetrical with respect to consumers and goods. This does not seem, however, to have much importance in the forthcoming developments.

Proposition 5.9 implies that every fiber is non-empty. We shall see in a moment that each fiber $V(b)$ contains one and only one no-trade equilibrium in addition to being diffeomorphic to $\mathbb{R}^{(\ell-1)(m-1)}$.

Proposition 5.10. *The set of fibers $V(b)$, with $b \in B$, constitute a partition of the equilibrium manifold E.*

Proof. Let $(p, \omega) \in E$. Then, a necessary condition for the equilibrium (p, ω) to belong to the fiber $V(b)$ is that we have $b = \phi(p, \omega)$, i.e.,

$$b = (p, w_1 = p \cdot \omega_1, \ldots, w_m = p \cdot \omega_m).$$

This proves that if (p, ω) belongs to some fiber $V(b)$, then $b \in B$ is uniquely determined by (p, ω). From the equilibrium equation,

$$\sum_i f_i(p, p \cdot \omega_i) = \sum_i \omega_i$$

that is satisfied by definition by the equilibrium (p, ω), the sum $\sum_i f_i(p, w_i) = r$ is equal to the sum $\sum_i \omega_i$. This proves that the equilibrium (p, ω) does belong to the fiber $V(b)$ with $b = (p, w_1, \ldots, w_m) = \phi(p, \omega)$.   □

5.5.2. The no-trade equilibrium belonging to a fiber

Proposition 5.11. *For any $b \in B$, we have $V(b) \cap T = \{f(b)\}$.*

Proof. Let $b = (p, w_1, \ldots, w_m) \in B$. By definition, we have

$$f(b) = (p, f_1(p, w_1), \ldots, f_m(p, w_m)).$$

That $f(b)$ is a no-trade equilibrium follows from Walras law $w_i = p \cdot f_i(p, w_i)$ with i varying from 1 to m because it implies $f_i(p, w_i) = f_i(p, p \cdot f_i(p, w_i))$ for every i. That $f(b)$ belongs to the fiber $V(b)$ follows readily from $w_i = p \cdot f_i(p, p \cdot \omega_i)$, a direct consequence of Walras law.

To prove that the intersection $V(b) \cap T$ is reduced to the unique element $f(b)$ follows from the property that the map $f : B \to T$ defined by $f(b) = (p, f_1(p, w_1), \ldots, f_m(p, w_m))$ is a bijection whose inverse map is the map ϕ restricted to T by Proposition 5.7.   □

It is by now possible to provide a better geometric picture of the equilibrium manifold E. It is the union of disjoint sets, the fibers. The fibers are themselves parametrized by the no-trade equilibria $f(b)$, where b is varied in B. The fibers are linear manifolds. Furthermore, they have a remarkably simple structure. The non-linearities depend on how the fibers $V(b)$ get "glued" together to make up the equilibrium manifold E.

5.6. Pathconnectedness of the Equilibrium Manifold

A topological space is pathconnected if it is always possible to link two arbitrarily chosen points of this space by a continuous path. For example, every convex set is pathconnected because any two points of the convex set are linked by the continuous path that is the line segment defined by these two points. Other sets than the convex sets are also pathconnected. This is in particular true for the equilibrium manifold E:

Proposition 5.12. *The equilibrium manifold E is pathconnected.*

Proof. Let (p, ω) and (p', ω') be two equilibria. The idea of the proof is to construct a continuous path contained in the equilibrium manifold E and linking these two equilibria. Let $b = \phi(p, \omega)$ and $b' = \phi(p', \omega')$ and consider the no-trade equilibria $f(b)$ and $f(b')$. The equilibria (p, ω) and $f(b)$ belong to the same fiber $V(b)$. It follows from the linear structure of the fiber $V(b)$ that the segment $[(p, \omega), f(b)]$ is contained in the fiber $V(b)$. Similarly, the segment $[(p', \omega'), f(b')]$ is contained in the fiber $V(b')$. To construct a continuous path linking the no-trade equilibria $f(b)$ and $f(b')$, it suffices to consider the segment $[b, b']$ linking b and b' in $B = S \times \mathbb{R}^m$. The image $f([b, b'])$ of this segment by the continuous map f then defines a continuous path linking $f(b)$ and $f(b')$. By piecing together the three continuous paths $[(p, \omega), f(b)]$, $f([b, b'])$, and $[f(b'), (p', \omega')]$, one defines a continuous path contained in the equilibrium manifold E and linking the equilibria (p, ω) and (p', ω'). □

The mathematical implications of pathconnectedness regarding the properties of the natural projection $\pi : E \to \Omega$ are considerable. The direct economic interpretation of the idea of pathconnectedness as the possibility of some continuous transition from the equilibrium (p, ω) to the equilibrium (p', ω') is straightforward and interesting.

An unexpected consequence of the pathconnectedness property of the equilibrium manifold E is an additional argument in favor of economic reformism in the old debate of the late 19th and early

20th century between reformism and revolution. One often used argument in favor of revolution is that the end point, i.e., the equilibrium (p', ω'), could not be attained continuously from all initial points, here from all equilibrium (p, ω). In mathematical terms, this can be rephrased as the initial and end points belonging to two different pathconnected components of the equilibrium manifold. That argument is vitiated by the proof that the equilibrium manifold is pathconnected.

5.7. Simple Connectedness of the Equilibrium Manifold

It follows from pathconnectedness that there exists at least one continuous path linking the equilibrium (p, ω) to the equilibrium (p', ω'). But generally there will exist more than one path. It is then natural to try to compare these paths. In particular, given two such paths, is it possible to deform continuously one path into the other? When this mathematical property is true of all continuous paths of a topological space linking two arbitrarily given points, this space is said to be simply connected. The property of simple connectedness has a nice geometric illustration. A connected manifold is simply connected if and only if it has no "holes". For example, the sphere is simply connected while the torus is not.

The two properties of pathconnectedness and simple connectedness are found in an important class of topological spaces, namely the *contractible spaces*. A topological space is contractible if it can be continuously deformed to being one point. Let a and b be two points. In the deformation process that collapses the topological space to a point, the points a and b follow two continuous paths that end up at the same point. Therefore, combining these two paths yields a continuous path linking a to b, which implies pathconnectedness. It is intuitively obvious that a contractible space cannot have any "hole," hence is simply connected. An important class of contractible spaces consists of the starshaped subsets of $\mathbb{R}^n$, i.e., subsets that contain all the line segments linking some well-defined point of that set, the "center," to the other points of the set. This class obviously includes the convex sets and, in particular, the Euclidean space $\mathbb{R}^n$.

Proposition 5.13. *The equilibrium manifold E is simply connected.*

Proof. This will follow from Proposition 5.16, every contractible space being simply connected. □

If we identify paths on the equilibrium manifolds with the economic policies that generate these paths, the continuous deformation property can be viewed as a sequence of tiny policy changes. Then, simple connectedness means that it is always possible to move from one policy to another one through tiny incremental steps.

5.8. Contractibility of the Equilibrium Manifold

We now turn to the issue of contractibility, which implies simple connectedness. Our goal is to show that the contractibility of the equilibrium manifold is a direct consequence of its structure of linear fibers parametrized by the no-trade equilibria. We get the following:

Lemma 5.14. *The set of no-trade equilibria T is contractible.*

Proof. It follows from Proposition 5.7 that the set of no-trade equilibria T is homeomorphic to $B = S \times \mathbb{R}^m$. Since the set of (normalized) prices S can be identified to $\mathbb{R}^{\ell-1}_{++} \times \{1\}$, the set B is homeomorphic to $\mathbb{R}^{\ell-1}_{++} \times \mathbb{R}^m$ and, hence, to $\mathbb{R}^{\ell+m-1}$. One concludes by observing that $\mathbb{R}^{\ell+m-1}$ is contractible. □

The second property shows that the equilibrium manifold E can be continuously collapsed into the set of no-trade equilibria T. (Mathematicians then say the subset T is a deformation retract of the set E.) We state this property as follows:

Proposition 5.15. *There exists a continuous map $h : E \times [0,1] \to E$ with the following properties:*

(i) *The partial map $h(.,0) : E \to E$ is the identity map;*
(ii) *The partial map $h(.,1) : E \to E$ takes its values in the set T;*

(iii) *The restriction of the map $h(.,t) : E \rightarrow E$ for $t \in [0,1]$ to the subset T is the identity of T.*

Proof. Let $x = (p, \omega_1, \ldots, \omega_m)$ be an equilibrium, i.e., an element of E. Let $\varphi(x) = (p, p \cdot \omega_1, \ldots, p \cdot \omega_m)$. Similarly, let

$$f(p, \omega_1, \ldots, \omega_m) = (p, f_1(p, \omega_1), \ldots, f_m(p, \omega_m)).$$

The maps $\varphi : E \rightarrow B = S \times \mathbb{R}^m$ and $f : B \rightarrow E$ are continuous. In addition, we have $f(B) = T$.

We now define $h(x,t)$ for $x \in E$ and $t \in [0,1]$ by the expression $h(x,t) = (1-t)x + t f \circ \varphi(x)$. Let us check that this map satisfies the properties listed in the Proposition. This map is continuous as a linear combination of continuous maps. We have $h(x,0) = x$ and $h(x,1) = f(\varphi(x)) \in T$. Last, let $x \in T$. Then, there exists some $b = (p, w_1, \ldots, w_m) \in B$ with $x = f(b)$. It then comes

$$h(x,t) = h(f(b),t),$$
$$h(x,t) = (1-t)f(b) + tf(\varphi(f(b))),$$

from which follows $h(x,t) = (1-t)f(b) + tf(b) = f(b) = x$ by $\varphi \circ f = \mathrm{id}_B$. $\qquad\square$

This proposition shows us that the equilibrium manifold E can be continuously deformed into the set of no-trade equilibria T. Note that the "contraction map" $h(.,t)$ for t given contracts every fiber in the direction of the no-trade equilibrium of that fiber. This leads us to the following property:

Proposition 5.16. *The equilibrium manifold E is contractible.*

Proof. It follows from Proposition 5.15 that the equilibrium manifold can be continuously contracted into the set of no-trade equilibria T. It follows from Lemma 5.14 that the set of no-trade equilibria itself is contractible, i.e., can be continuously deformed into a single point. By combining these two operations, one defines a continuous deformation of the equilibrium manifold E into a point. $\qquad\square$

5.9. Diffeomorphism of the Equilibrium Manifold with a Euclidean Space

This section is devoted to proving the strongest possible global property of the equilibrium manifold E, namely its diffeomorphism with the Euclidean space $\mathbb{R}^{\ell m}$. This property improves on all the results obtained so far on the equilibrum manifold E. The proof that we follow here, however, requires a strong and difficult result published by Meigniez in 2002.

Proposition 5.17. *The equilibrium manifold E is diffeomorphic to* $S \times \mathbb{R}^m \times \mathbb{R}^{(\ell-1)(m-1)}$.

Proof. In his Corollary 31, Meigniez [27] states that the surjective submersion $\varphi : E \to B$ with fibers diffeomorphic to a Euclidean space is a fiber map that is locally trivial. This is all we need here because, then, we can easily prove that this fibration is trivial. For this, it suffices to observe that the base space B is contractible because it is diffeomorphic to the Euclidean space $S \times \mathbb{R}^m$. Therefore, the equilibrium manifold E is diffeomorphic to the Cartesian product $B \times \mathbb{R}^{(\ell-1)(m-1)}$, hence to the Euclidean space $S \times \mathbb{R}^m \times \mathbb{R}^{(\ell-1)(m-1)}$. The dimensionality $\ell m = (\ell - 1) + m + (\ell - 1)(m - 1)$ is then straightforward. $\square$

Corollary 5.18. *The equilibrium manifold E is diffeomorphic to $\mathbb{R}^{\ell m}$.*

Proposition 5.17 readily implies that E is pathconnected, simply connected and contractible. This result provides therefore an alternative way of proving these properties.

5.10. Conclusion

We have therefore proved that the equilibrium manifold is a smooth manifold diffeomorphic to a Euclidean space under the standard assumptions of smooth consumer theory. Weaker properties like the connectedness, the pathconnectedness and even the contractibility of the equilibrium manifold can be proved with the help of much weaker theorems.

5.11. Notes and Comments

The proof that the equilibrium manifold with variable total resources considered in this chapter is indeed a smooth manifold is due to Delbaen [15]. All the other results are due to Balasko [7, 8, 10].

5.12. Exercises

5.1. It has been shown that a necessary and sufficient condition for the subset E of the smooth manifold X to be a smooth submanifold of codimension k is that for every point $x \in E$, there exists a chart (φ, U, V) (i.e., U and V are open subsets of X and some $\mathbb{R}^n$ and such that $\varphi : U \to V$ is a diffeomorphism) with $x \in U$ and such that $\varphi(E \cap U) = V \cap \mathbb{R}^k \times \{0\}$).

   (1) Let $f : X \to Y$ be a smooth map (i.e., differentiable up to any order) where $X = \mathbb{R}^p$ and $Y = \mathbb{R}^q$. Consider the maps ψ and θ from $X \times Y$ into itself defined by $\psi(x, y) = (x, y - f(x))$ and $\theta(x, z) = (z, z + f(x))$, respectively. Prove that ψ and θ are both smooth. Show that the composition $\theta \circ \psi$ and $\psi \circ \theta$ are the identity maps of $X \times Y$.

   (2) Using the definition of a smooth submanifold recalled at the beginning of the exercise, show that the graph E of f, i.e., the set $\{(x, y) \in X \times Y \mid y = f(x)\}$ is a smooth submanifold of $X \times Y$.

   (3) Show that E is diffeomorphic to X.

5.2. Let $X = \mathbb{R}^p$ and $Y = \mathbb{R}^q$ and $f : X \to Y$ be a smooth function. Let $E = \{(x, y) \in X \times Y \mid x = y\}$ be the graph of the function f.

   (1) Prove that the map $j_f : X \to X \times Y$ defined by $j_f(x) = (x, f(x))$ is a smooth map.

   (2) Show that the image $j_f(X)$ is the graph E of the function f.

   (3) Let $p : X \times Y \to X$ be the projection map $p(x, y) = x$. Show that the composition $p \circ j_f$ is equal to the identity map of X.

(4) Using the results of the previous questions, show that the smooth map $j_f : X \to X \times Y$ is an embedding.

5.3. Let $X = \mathbb{R}^p$ and $Y = \mathbb{R}^q$ and $f : X \to Y$ be a smooth function. Let $E = \{(x, y) \in X \times Y \mid x = y\}$ be the graph of the function f.

(1) Prove that the map $j_f : X \to X \times Y$ defined by $j_f(x) = (x, f(x))$ is a smooth map.

(2) Show that E is a closed subset of $X \times Y$.

(3) Let $p : X \times Y \to X$ be the projection map $p(x, y) = x$ and $p_E : E \to X$ be the restriction of E of the projection p. Let E be equipped with the topology induced by the topology of $X \times Y$. Show that $p_E : E \to X$ is continuous.

(4) Prove that the compositions $p_E \circ j_f : X \to X$ and $j_f \circ p_E : E \to E$ are the identity maps of X and E, respectively.

(5) Show that Question 4 implies that E and X are homeomophic.

Chapter 6

The Natural Projection

Remember that we have normalized the price system by the convention $p_\ell = 1$ and that the price system is therefore $S = \mathbb{R}_{++}^{\ell-1} \times \{1\}$. From now on, we assume one more thing regarding the demand functions or, in fact, just one demand function.

6.1. Properness of the Natural Projection

We denote by $P(S)$ the (projective) closed set associated with S. An element belongs to $P(S)$ if it can be represented by an element different from 0 that belongs to $\mathbb{R}_+^\ell$. Note the unique $+$, which implies that this element may have some coordinates equal to 0. If p and p' represent the same element in $P(S)$, there is a positive number λ such that $p' = \lambda p$. We can now state the boundary condition that we need to simplify the study of the natural projection:

Assumption 6.1 (Boundary condition when some numeraire normalized prices tend to 0 or to $+\infty$). *For every sequence,* $(p^n, w_i^n) \in S \times \mathbb{R}$ *that tends to a limit* (p^0, w_i^0), *with some homogeneous coordinates of* $p^0 \in P(S)$ *being equal to 0 but wealth* w_i^0 *being* > 0, *then* $\lim_{n \to +\infty} \|f_i(p^n, w_i^n)\| = +\infty$.

Given the identification of the equilibrium manifold E with the Cartesian product $B \times (\mathbb{R}^{\ell-1})^{m-1}$, the natural projection $\pi : E \to \Omega$ can be identified with some map from $B \times (\mathbb{R}^{\ell-1})^{m-1}$ to Ω. Since

$B \times (\mathbb{R}^{\ell-1})^{m-1}$ can itself be identified with the subset $\mathbb{R}^{\ell-1}_{++} \times \{1\} \times \mathbb{R}^m \times \mathbb{R}^{(m-1)(\ell-1)}$ through the coordinate system,

$$\left(p_1, \ldots, p_{\ell-1}, 1, w_1, \ldots, w_m, \omega_1^1, \ldots, \omega_1^{\ell-1}, \right.$$
$$\left. \omega_2^1, \ldots, \omega_2^{\ell-1}, \ldots, \omega_{m-1}^1, \ldots, \omega_{m-1}^{\ell-1} \right).$$

The map $\pi : E \to \Omega$ can therefore be viewed as being simply a map from an open subset of $\mathbb{R}^{\ell m}$ into $\mathbb{R}^{\ell m}$.

We will give very soon an explicit expression of the coordinates of the map $\pi : E \to \Omega$. But, before working out this analytical expression, let us first say a few words about smooth proper maps because the map $\pi : E \to \Omega$ is such a map. More generally, a continuous proper map $\pi : M \to N$ where M and N are two locally compact metric spaces (which includes in particular working with submanifolds of $\mathbb{R}^n$) is such that the preimage $\pi^{-1}(K)$ of any compact subset K of N is compact. The following proposition confirms us that the natural projection is that kind of nice map:

Proposition 6.2. *The natural projection* $\pi : E \to \Omega$ *is proper.*

Proof. Let K be an arbitrary compact subset of Ω. All we need to show is that the preimage $\pi^{-1}(K)$ is compact. Let us pick an arbitrary i between 1 and m and consider the projection map $\omega = (\omega_1, \ldots, \omega_m) \to \omega_i$. Let K_i be the image of K by this projection on the ith coordinate space. This set is compact as the image of a compact set by a continuous map. It follows from Assumption 4.4 that the demand $f_i(p, p \cdot \omega_i)$ is bounded from below by some $x_i' \in \mathbb{R}^\ell$ for $\omega_i \in K_i$ and any $p \in S$. This property holds for all values of i taken between 1 and m.

Let us now prove that $f_i(p, p \cdot \omega_i)$ is also bounded from above for all $(p, \omega) \in \pi^{-1}(K)$. We can write

$$f_i(p, p \cdot \omega_i) = \sum_j \omega_j - \sum_{j \neq i} f_j(p, p \cdot \omega_j) \leq \sum_j \omega_j - \sum_{j \neq i} x_j'$$

for $(p, \omega) \in E$. The image of the compact set K by the linear (and continuous) map $(\omega_1, \omega_2, \ldots, \omega_m) \to \omega_1 + \omega_2 + \cdots + \omega_m$ is also a compact set; therefore, the sum $\sum_j \omega_j$ is uniformly bounded from above for every $\omega \in K$. To sum up, we have established that, for every i, there exist x_i' and x_i'' such that the following inequalities are satisfied for every $(p, \omega) \in \pi^{-1}(K)$:

$$x_i' \leq f_i(p, p \cdot \omega_i) \leq x_i''.$$

Let now i be such that the demand function $f_i : S \times \mathbb{R} \to \mathbb{R}^\ell$ satisfies Assumption 6.1. The set $\{x \in \mathbb{R}^\ell \mid x_i' \leq x_i \leq x_i''\}$ is compact. Its preimage by the map f_i is compact. The projection of this compact set on the price set S, denoted by G, is therefore compact.

It follows that the set $\pi^{-1}(K)$ is a subset of the compact set $G \times K$. It is therefore sufficient to show that $\pi^{-1}(K)$ is closed in $G \times K$. The map $\pi : E \to \Omega$ being continuous, the set $\pi^{-1}(K)$ is closed in E, itself a closed subset of $S \times \Omega$. Consequently, $\pi^{-1}(K)$ is closed in $S \times \Omega$. The intersection $\pi^{-1}(K) \cap G \times K$ is therefore a closed subset of $G \times K$. This ends the proof once one notices that $\pi^{-1}(K) \cap G \times K$ is equal to $\pi^{-1}(K)$. $\qquad\square$

6.2. Smoothness of the Natural Projection

The fact that E possesses the structure of a smooth manifold enables one to use the notion of smooth mappings from the set E into the set Ω. A mapping is smooth if one can compute partial derivatives of any order for a system of local coordinates of E (and of Ω).

The first problem which arises is whether the natural projection π is smooth. As a matter of fact, a proof of non-smoothness would lead one to expect serious difficulties of a mathematical nature, while smoothness would put at one's disposal the powerful tools of differential topology. Besides, smoothness is the mathematical property that justifies those linearization techniques used, for example, in econometric modeling.

Proposition 6.3. *The natural projection $\pi : E \to \Omega$ is smooth.*

Proof. We have shown in Proposition 5.2 that the equilibrium set E is not only a smooth manifold but in fact a smooth submanifold of $S \times \Omega$. It follows from the definition of a smooth submanifold that the natural embedding $E \to S \times \Omega$ is smooth. The projection mapping

$S \times \Omega \to \Omega$ being smooth itself, the composition of these two maps, i.e., the natural projection π, is therefore smooth.   □

The property of differentiability amounts to the existence of a linear tangent map, i.e., of some satisfactory linear approximation. In other words, a differentiable map can be linearized for the purpose of local studies. Physicists have used these linearization techniques a lot. Econometricians also have sometimes without any proper justification. Proposition 6.3 provides the theoretical justification for these linearizing practices within the setup of the pure exchange model.

6.3. An Explicit Formula for the Natural Projection

In this section, we identify E with $S \times \mathbb{R}^m \times \mathbb{R}^{(\ell-1)(m-1)}$ while we keep the representation $\Omega = (\mathbb{R}^\ell)^m$ for the set of individual endowments. Recall that $\bar{p} = (p_1, \ldots, p_{\ell-1})$ and $\bar{x}_i = (x_i^1, \ldots, x_i^{\ell-1})$ for $1 \le i \le m$. We then have the following:

Proposition 6.4. *The natural projection* $\pi : E \to \Omega$ *is such that we have* $\omega_i^j = w_i^j$ *for* $1 \le i \le m-1$ *and* $1 \le j \le \ell-1$ *and*

$$\omega_1^\ell = w_1 - \bar{p} \cdot \bar{\omega}_1$$

$$\vdots \qquad \vdots$$

$$\omega_{m-1}^\ell = w_{m-1} - \bar{p} \cdot \bar{\omega}_{m-1},$$

$$\bar{\omega}_m = \sum_{i=1}^{m} \bar{f}_i(p, w_i) - \sum_{i=1}^{m-1} \bar{\omega}_i,$$

$$\omega_m^\ell = w_m - \bar{p} \cdot \left[\sum_{i=1}^{m} \bar{f}_i(p, w_i) - \sum_{i=1}^{m-1} \bar{\omega}_i \right].$$

Proof. We denote by $(p, \omega) = (p_1, \ldots, p_{\ell-1}, 1, w_1, \ldots, w_m, \omega_1^1, \ldots, \omega_{m-1}^{\ell-1})$ the representation in coordinate form of the equilibrium $x = (p, \omega) \in E$. The wealth constraints imply the equalities,

$$\omega_i^\ell = w_i - \bar{p} \cdot \bar{\omega}_i,$$

with $1 \le i \le m - 1$. The total resource constraint then implies the equality,

$$\omega_m^k = \sum_{i=1}^{m} f_i^k(p, w_i) - \sum_{i=1}^{m-1} \omega_i^k,$$

for $1 \le k \le \ell - 1$. The ℓth coordinate is then computed by

$$\omega_m^\ell = w_m - \bar{p} \cdot \bar{\omega}_m,$$

where $\bar{\omega}_m$ has just been computed above. $\qquad\qquad\square$

6.4. Regular and Critical Points of the Natural Projection

6.4.1. Regular and critical points of smooth maps

The study of differentiable maps has led mathematicians to introduce a number of powerful concepts that we are going to apply to the special case of the natural projection. We start with the concept of critical point of a differentiable map.

Let $\pi : M \to N$ be a smooth map between two smooth manifolds. The point $x \in M$ is a critical point for the map π if the tangent map $T_x\pi$ is not onto. The point $y \in N$ is a singular value of the map π if there exists some $x \in M$ that is a critical point of π and such that $\pi(x) = y$. In other words, a singular value of the map π is the image by π of some critical point. A point $x \in M$ is called a regular point of the map $\pi : M \to N$ if it is not a critical point of that map. In other words, the map $T_x\pi$ is then onto.

The point $y \in N$ is a regular value of π if y is not a singular value of the same map π. In other words, the preimage $\pi^{-1}(y)$ contains no critical point. Incidentally, it is worth noting that if the preimage $\pi^{-1}(y)$ is empty, then y is a regular value of the map π. It follows from these definitions that the set of regular values is the complement of the set of singular values. We denote the sets of regular values and singular values of the map $\pi : M \to N$ by $\mathcal{R}$ and by Σ, respectively. By definition, we have $\mathcal{R} = \Omega \backslash \Sigma$ and also $\Sigma = \Omega \backslash \mathcal{R}$. Note also that the set of regular values of the map $\pi : M \to N$ does not coincide in general with the image by the map π of the set of regular points of the map π.

Let us point one apparently paradoxical consequence of the above definitions. If the point $y \in N$ does not belong to the image of the map π, then it is a regular value. Indeed, a point that does not belong to this image cannot be the image of a critical point. It is therefore a regular value. The apparent paradox stems from the rather peculiar use of the expression "regular value" for an element that is not a value of a map.

6.4.2. Economic applications

We now apply those general definitions to the mapping $\pi : E \to \Omega$.

Definition 6.5. The equilibrium $(p, \omega) \in E$ is regular (resp. critical) if it is a regular (resp. critical) point of the natural projection $\pi : E \to \Omega$. The economy $\omega \in \Omega$ is regular (resp. singular) if it is a regular (resp. singular) value of the map $\pi : E \to \Omega$.

The set of regular economies (resp. singular economies) is denoted $\mathcal{R}$ (resp. Σ.).

6.4.3. Sets of critical equilibria and singular economies

The set of critical equilibria is denoted by E_c and we have the following:

Proposition 6.6. *The set of critical equilibria E_c is a closed subset of the equilibrium manifold E.*

Proof. Consider the map that associates with (p, ω) the value of the Jacobian determinant of π at (p, ω). The coefficients of this determinant are continuous (actually smooth) functions of (p, ω). The determinant is also a continuous function of its coefficients. Therefore, the map that we are considering is continuous as a composition of continuous mappings. The set of critical equilibria E_c is the inverse image of 0 by this continuous map and is therefore closed. $\square$

Proposition 6.7. *The set of singular economies* Σ *is a closed subset of measure zero of the endowment set* Ω.

Proof. This set is the image of E_c by the natural projection π. The natural projection is a proper mapping and, as such, the image of a closed set is closed.

Furthermore, it follows from Sard's theorem (Math 1.7) that this set has measure zero. $\quad\square$

6.5. Regular Economies and Equilibria

In this section, we follow the tradition that consists in studying the regular economies and their equilibria. Note that some of these assumptions can easily be made weaker. We have the following:

Proposition 6.8. *The set of regular economies* $\mathcal{R}$ *is an open and dense subset of* Ω.

Proof. The set $\mathcal{R}$ is the complement of Σ in Ω. We now know that it is open as the complement of a closed set. Let us show that $\mathcal{R}$ is dense. Assume the contrary. Then there exists a non-empty open cube U, such that the intersection $\mathcal{R} \cap U$ is empty. This means that U is contained in Σ. Therefore, the measure of Σ must be larger than or at least equal to the measure of U. But the measure of the cube U is the product of the lengths of its sides and, as such, is strictly positive. This yields a contradiction. $\quad\square$

6.5.1. Equilibria over a small set of regular economies

The main result of this section is the description of the preimage $\pi^{-1}(U)$ when the set U is a small enough open subset of the set of regular economies $\mathcal{R}$. We start first by a description of the preimage $\pi^{-1}(\omega)$ for $\omega \in \mathcal{R}$.

Proposition 6.9. *The preimage* $\pi^{-1}(\omega)$ *is a finite set for every regular economy* $\omega \in \mathcal{R}$.

In other words, there is only a finite number of equilibria $(p, \omega) \in E$ associated with the endowment vector $\omega = (\omega_1, \ldots, \omega_m)$ when ω is regular. This is equivalent to saying that the number of equilibrium price vectors $p \in S$ associated with the regular endowment vector $\omega \in \mathcal{R}$ is finite. Note also that, at this stage, we cannot exclude the possibility that this finite number might be equal to 0.

Proof. [Proof of Proposition *6.9*] The topological space $\pi^{-1}(\omega)$ is compact as the preimage of the compact set $\{\omega\}$ by the proper map π. Let us show that the topology of $\pi^{-1}(\omega)$ is discrete, i.e., that each point of $\pi^{-1}(\omega)$ is open and closed. Closedness is almost obvious: every point of $\pi^{-1}(\omega)$ is closed because $\pi^{-1}(\omega)$ is a subspace of the metric space $S \times \Omega$, and therefore, the induced topology on $\pi^{-1}(\omega)$ is metric, and every point of a metric topological space is closed.

For openness, let x be some point of $\pi^{-1}(\omega)$ and let us show that the set $\{x\}$ is open in $\pi^{-1}(\omega)$. The point x cannot be critical for the map π because, otherwise, $\omega = \pi(x)$ would be a singular value of π, which is excluded by the assumption $\omega \in \mathcal{R}$. Therefore, the point x is regular for the map π. This is equivalent to the tangent map $T_x\pi$ being onto. Since the domain and the range have the same dimension, this is equivalent to $T_x\pi$ being a bijection. It then follows from the inverse function theorem (Math 1.2) that the map $\pi : E \to \Omega$ is a local diffeomorphism at the point $x \in E$. This means that there exist open neighborhoods V of x in the equilibrium manifold E and U of ω in the endowment space Ω such that the restriction $\pi \mid V$ is a diffeomorphism. One of the properties of a diffeomorphism is to be a one-to-one map (i.e., a bijection). This is the only property that we need to end the proof.

Let us now show that the intersection $\pi^{-1}(\omega) \cap V$ is reduced to the subset $\{x\}$. Clearly, this intersection contains the element x. Let x' be some element of the intersection $\pi^{-1}(\omega) \cap V$. By the definition of $\pi^{-1}(\omega)$, it comes $\pi(x) = \pi(x') = \omega$. The bijection property (on the set V) then implies the equality $x = x'$, which proves the equality $\{x\} = \pi^{-1}(\omega) \cap V$.

The set $\{x\}$ is therefore the intersection of $\pi^{-1}(\omega)$ with the open subset V of E, hence is open for the topology of $\pi^{-1}(\omega)$ induced by the topology of E.

The preimage $\pi^{-1}(\omega)$ is therefore a discrete and compact topological space. The union of the subsets $\{x\}$ for all $x \in \pi^{-1}(\omega)$ defines an open covering of $\pi^{-1}(\omega)$. By the compactness property, there exists a finite subcovering of the set $\pi^{-1}(\omega)$ made of these sets consisting of a unique element. The set $\pi^{-1}(\omega)$ is therefore the union of a finite number of its elements, hence is finite. $\qquad \square$

Let $\{1, 2, \ldots, k\}$ denote the set of integers between 1 and the natural integer k with $k \geq 1$. We then have the following:

Corollary 6.10. *Let $\omega \in \mathcal{R}$ be a regular economy. There exists an integer $k \geq 1$ such that the preimage $\pi^{-1}(\omega)$ is in bijection with the Cartesian product $\{1, 2, \ldots, k\} \times \{\omega\}$ for $k \geq 1$ and the empty set for $k = 0$.*

Proof. Obvious. $\qquad \square$

A natural question to ask at this stage is whether it is possible to substitute in Proposition 6.9 and in Corollary 6.10 some bigger subset U of the set of regular economies $\mathcal{R}$ than the one-point set $\{\omega\}$. This question has a positive answer provided the subset U is open and sufficiently small. We treat only the case $k \geq 1$ because $k = 0$ is trivial and, in fact, not satisfied under our assumptions as we will see very soon.

Proposition 6.11. *Let $\omega \in \mathcal{R}$ be a regular economy. Let $k \geq 1$ be the finite number of elements of $\pi^{-1}(\omega)$. Then, there exists an open subset U of $\mathcal{R}$ containing ω and k open subsets $V_1, V_2, \ldots, V_k$ of the equilibrium manifolds E such that the following properties are satisfied:*

(i) *The subsets $V_1, V_2, \ldots, V_k$ are two-by-two disjoint;*
(ii) *We have $\pi^{-1}(U) = V_1 \cup V_2 \cup \cdots \cup V_k$;*
(iii) *The restriction $\pi \mid V_j$ of the natural projection to the open subset V_j is a diffeomorphism between V_j and U.*

Proposition 6.11 tells us that the portion $\pi^{-1}(U)$ of the equilibrium manifold E above the open set U is made up of a finite number of layers diffeomorphic to U and stacked over U. This picture excludes the possibility that there are endowments ω' arbitrarily close to ω with a different number of equilibria.

Proof. [Proof of Proposition *6.11*] Let $x_1, \ldots, x_k$ be all the elements of the preimage $\pi^{-1}(\omega)$. Recall that the map π is a local diffeomorphism at each one of these points. Therefore, for every j between 1 and k, there exists an open subset V_j' of the equilibrium manifold such that the restriction of the map π to V_j' is a diffeomorphism with the open subset $U_j = \pi(V_j')$ of Ω.

Let d denote a distance that defines the (metric) topology of the equilibrium manifold E. The points $x_1, x_2, \ldots, x_k$ being distinct, the number $\varepsilon = \inf d(x_j, x_{j'})$, where $j \neq j'$, is then > 0. Let $B(x_j; \varepsilon/2)$ the open ball of center x_j and radius $\varepsilon/2$. The open sets $V_j'' = V_j' \cap B(x_j; \varepsilon/2)$ for $j = 1, 2, \ldots, k$ are by construction two-by-two distinct. In addition, the restriction of the map π to the open set V_j'' is a diffeomorphism between the open set V_j'' and its image $U_j'' = \pi(V_j'')$.

The set $E \backslash (V_1'' \cup \cdots \cup V_k'')$ is closed in E as the complement of an open set. Its image $\pi\big(E \backslash (V_1'' \cup \cdots \cup V_k'')\big)$ by the natural projection π is closed in Ω because the map π is proper. Let W be the open subset of Ω defined by

$$W = \Omega \backslash \pi \big(E \backslash (V_1'' \cup \cdots \cup V_k'') \big).$$

We now define the set $U = (U_1'' \cap U_2'' \cap \cdots \cap U_k'') \cap W$. This set is open in Ω as the finite intersection of the open sets U_j'' (with $j = 1, \ldots, k$) and W.

Let us show that ω belongs to U. This is equivalent to showing that ω belongs to every set U_j'' with $j = 1, \ldots, k$ and to W. It follows from the definition of $U_j'' = \pi(V_j'')$ that $\omega = \pi(x_j)$ belongs to U_j'' for $j = 1, \ldots, k$. To prove that ω belongs to W, let us argue by contradiction. Assume the contrary, i.e., that we have $\omega \in \pi(E \backslash (V_1'' \cup \cdots \cup V_k''))$. Then, there exists $x' \in E \backslash (V_1'' \cup \cdots \cup V_k'')$ such that $\pi(x') = \omega$. This element x' then belongs to $\pi^{-1}(\omega)$ but does not belong to the union $V_1'' \cup \cdots \cup V_k''$. This contradicts the definition of the collection of open sets $V_1'', \ldots, V_k''$.

Let $V_j = V_j'' \cap \pi^{-1}(U)$. The map π restricted to the open set V_j'' being a diffeomorphism (with $\pi(V_j'')$), its restriction $\pi \mid V_j$ is also a diffeomorphism between V_j, and $\pi(V_j) = U$.

The proof ends with the observation that the open sets V_j with $j = 1, \ldots, k$ are two-by-two disjoint by construction. $\square$

Corollary 6.12. *Let* $\omega \in \mathcal{R}$ *be a regular economy. Let* $k \geq 1$ *be the finite number of elements of* $\pi^{-1}(\omega)$. *Then, there exists an open subset* U *of the set of regular economies* $\mathcal{R}$ *containing* ω *such that the preimage* $\pi^{-1}(U)$ *is diffeomorphic to the Cartesian product* $\{1, 2, \ldots, k\} \times U$.

Proof. Obvious. □

Corollary 6.13. *Let* $\omega \in \mathcal{R}$. *There exists an open neighborhood* U *of* ω *and a finite number* $k \geq 0$ *of smooth mappings* $s_i : U \to S$ *such that the set of equilibrium price vectors associated with* $\omega' \in U$ *is the union* $\cup_{1 \leq i \leq k} s_i(\omega')$.

In other words, we have $\pi^{-1}(\omega') = \bigcup_{1 \leq j \leq k} \{(s_j(\omega'), \omega')\}$ for $k \geq 1$ while $\emptyset$ for $k = 0$ and for every $\omega' \in U$.

Proof. If $k = 0$, $\pi^{-1}(\omega')$ is empty for ω' close enough to ω. For $k \geq 1$, let us go back to the proof of Proposition 6.11. It then suffices to compose the inverse map $(\pi \mid V_j)^{-1} : U \to V_j$ of the restriction of the natural projection $\pi \mid V_j$ to U with the projection $S \times \Omega \to S$ to define the map $s_j : U \to S$. □

Proposition 6.11 and its corollaries are important for its numerous applications. For example, it enables one to express the equilibrium prices associated with the regular economy $\omega \in \mathcal{R}$ as a function of the endowment vector ω only.

6.5.2. The number of equilibria of regular economies

Let M be a topological (metric) space. One defines the relation $x \sim y$ between the points x and y of M as meaning that there exists a connected subset N of M that contains the points x and y. One shows readily that the relation $\sim$ is an equivalence relation. By definition, the equivalence class $C(x)$ and $C(y)$ of the point x and y are equal, i.e., $C(x) = C(y)$, if and only if $x \sim y$. It is obvious from the definitions that the equivalence class $C(x)$ is the biggest connected subset of M that contains the point x. The equivalence class for that relation is called a connected component.

Applying this to economies, we partition the set $\mathcal{R}$ into its connected components for the above relation. Note that each connected component of $\mathcal{R}$ is then open.

One says that an integer-valued function $\psi : M \to \mathbb{N}$ is locally constant if, at every point $x \in M$, there exists an open neighborhood U such that the value of the function ψ in that neighborhood is a constant integer. The following property of locally constant integer-valued functions over connected sets is important:

Lemma 6.14. *Every integer-valued locally constant function defined on a connected set is constant.*

Proof. Let $\psi : M \to \mathbb{N}$ be a locally constant function defined on the topological space X. Let us equip the set of natural integers $\mathbb{N}$ with the discrete topology. Then, each set consisting of just the integer n is open. One checks readily that the preimage $\psi^{-1}(V)$ of any open subset V of $\mathbb{N}$ by the function ψ is a neighborhood of every point $x \in \psi^{-1}(V)$ (because the preimage contains an open subset containing the point $x \in \psi^{-1}(V)$). Therefore, the set $\psi^{-1}(V)$ is open as a neighborhood of all of its elements, which proves that the locally constant function $\psi : M \to \mathbb{N}$ is continuous for $\mathbb{N}$ equipped with the discrete topology.

The image of a connected set by a continuous function is connected. Therefore, the image of the connected set M by a locally constant function is a connected subset of the set of natural integers $\mathbb{N}$ endowed with the discrete topology and, therefore, cannot contain more than one element. The function $\psi : M \to \mathbb{N}$ is therefore constant. $\square$

It is possible to use Lemma 6.14 to determine how the number of equilibria varies or, more precisely, does not vary when ω varies a little within the set of regular economies $\mathcal{R}$. More precisely, we have the following:

Proposition 6.15. *The number of equilibria is constant for all the points belonging to the same connected component of $\mathcal{R}$.*

Proof. It follows from Lemma 6.14 that the number of equilibria $N(\omega) = \#\{\pi^{-1}(\omega)\}$ associated with the economy $\omega \in \mathcal{R}$ is an integer-valued locally constant map on the set of regular economies $\mathcal{R}$. It then follows from Lemma 6.14 that this map is constant on every connected component of the set $\mathcal{R}$.   □

6.6. Economic Characterization of Regularity

Our goal now is to get a simpler expression of the fact that the equilibrium $(p, \omega) \in E$ is critical or not. First, we introduce the matrices $M(p, \omega)$ and $N(p, \omega)$ that are both $(\ell + m - 1) \times (\ell + m - 1)$. The matrix $M(p, \omega)$ is equal to

$$
\begin{bmatrix}
\sum_i \dfrac{\partial f_i^1(p, w_i)}{\partial p_1} & \cdots & \sum_i \dfrac{\partial f_i^1(p, w_i)}{\partial p_{\ell-1}} & \dfrac{\partial f_1^1(p, w_1)}{\partial w_1} & \cdots & \dfrac{\partial f_m^1(p, w_m)}{\partial w_m} \\
\vdots & \ddots & \vdots & \vdots & \cdots & \vdots \\
\sum_i \dfrac{\partial f_i^{\ell-1}(p, w_i)}{\partial p_1} & \cdots & \sum_i \dfrac{\partial f_i^{\ell-1}(p, w_i)}{\partial p_{\ell-1}} & \dfrac{\partial f_1^{\ell-1}(p, w_1)}{\partial w_1} & \ddots & \dfrac{\partial f_m^{\ell-1}(p, w_m)}{\partial w_m} \\
-\omega_1^1 & \cdots & -\omega_1^{\ell-1} & 1 & & 0 \\
-\omega_2^1 & \cdots & -\omega_2^{\ell-1} & 0 & & 0 \\
\vdots & \ddots & \vdots & \vdots & \ddots & \vdots \\
-\omega_{m-1}^1 & \cdots & -\omega_{m-1}^{\ell-1} & 0 & & 0 \\
-\omega_m^1 & \cdots & -\omega_m^{\ell-1} & 0 & & 1
\end{bmatrix},
$$

while the matrix $N(p, \omega)$ is equal to matrix $M(p, \omega)$ except for its last line that is

$$
\begin{bmatrix} -r^1 & \cdots & -r^{\ell-1} & 1 & \cdots & 1 & 1 \end{bmatrix}.
$$

We then have the following:

Proposition 6.16. *The equilibrium* $(p, \omega) \in E$ *is such that* $\det T_{(p,\omega)}\pi = \det M(p, \omega)$.

Proof. We use $(p, w_1, \ldots, w_m, \bar{\omega}_1, \ldots, \bar{\omega}_{m-1})$ as coordinates for the equilibrium manifold E and the variables ω_1, ω_2, $\ldots$, ω_{m-1} and r (where $r = \sum_{1 \leq i \leq m} \omega_i$) to parameterize the space of economies Ω. The analytic expression of the mapping π in these coordinates takes the following form:

$$r^1 = \sum_{i=1}^{m} f_i^1(p, w_i),$$

$$\vdots \qquad \vdots$$

$$r^{\ell-1} = \sum_{i=1}^{m} f_i^{\ell-1}(p, w_i),$$

$$w_1^\ell = w_1 - p_1 w_1^1 - \cdots - p_{\ell-1} w_1^{\ell-1},$$

$$\vdots \qquad \vdots$$

$$w_{m-1}^\ell = w_{m-1} - p_1 w_{m-1}^1 - \cdots - p_{\ell-1} w_{m-1}^{\ell-1},$$

$$r^\ell = w_1 + w_2 + \cdots + w_m - p_1 r^1 - p_2 r^2 - \cdots - p_{\ell-1} r^{\ell-1},$$

and $w_i^j = w_i^j$ for $1 \le i \le m - 1$ and $1 \le j \le \ell - 1$.

The Jacobian matrix $T_{(p,w)}\pi$ of π at the equilibrium (p, w) then takes the following form:

$$\begin{bmatrix} N(p, w) & * \\ 0 & I \end{bmatrix},$$

where I is the $(\ell - 1)(m - 1)$ identity matrix. We therefore have $\det T_{(p,w)}\pi = \det N(p, w)$. After subtracting from the last row of $N(p, w)$ the rows ℓ to $\ell + m - 1$ of $N(p, w)$, we obtain the last row of $M(p, w)$, which proves the proposition. □

Let now $J(p, w)$ be the Jacobian matrix of aggregate excess demand $\bar{z}(., w)$ at the equilibrium price vector p that is associated with the equilibrium (p, w). We then have the following:

Proposition 6.17. *The matrices $J(p, w)$ and $M(p, w)$ have the same determinant.*

Proof. We have just seen that the matrix $M(p, w)$ takes the particular form,

$$M(p, w) = \begin{bmatrix} A & B \\ C & I \end{bmatrix},$$

where I denotes the identity matrix. The coefficient $-\omega_i^j$ belonging to row i and column j of matrix C is "killed" by multiplying column $((\ell - 1) + i)$ of $M(p, \omega)$ by ω_i^j and adding the result to the column j of $M(p, \omega)$. We perform this operation for every element of C so that we end up with a matrix which is precisely equal to

$$\begin{bmatrix} J(p, \omega) & B \\ 0 & I \end{bmatrix},$$

where $J(p, \omega)$ is the Jacobian matrix of aggregate demand $\sum_i \bar{f}_i(p, p \cdot \omega_i)$ computed at the equilibrium (p, ω). $\quad\square$

Proposition 6.18. *The equilibrium* $(p, \omega) \in E$ *is regular* (resp. *critical*) *if and only if the determinant of the* $(\ell - 1) \times (\ell - 1)$ *matrix* $J(p, \omega)$ *is different from* 0 (resp. *equal to* 0).

Proof. Obvious. $\quad\square$

Proposition 6.18 enables one to give an alternative description of regular and singular economies which may be useful under certain circumstances.

Corollary 6.19. *The economy* $\omega \in \Omega$ *is regular* (resp. *singular*) *if and only if the vector* $0 \in \mathbb{R}^{\ell-1}$ *is a regular* (resp. *singular*) *value of the aggregate excess demand mapping* $\bar{z}(., \omega) : S \to \mathbb{R}^{\ell-1}$.

Proof. By definition, the vector $0 \in \mathbb{R}^{\ell-1}$ is a regular value of the excess demand mapping $\bar{z}(., \omega) : S \to \mathbb{R}^{\ell-1}$ associated with the economy $\omega \in \Omega$ if and only if, for every equilibrium $(p, \omega) \in E$, $\det J(p, \omega)$ is $\neq 0$. This condition is equivalent to having (p, ω) not a critical point of the mapping π, which also means that ω is a regular value of the natural projection.

For singular values, we can use the same argument. The economy $\omega \in \Omega$ is a singular value of the map $\pi : E \to \Omega$ if and only if there exists $p \in S$ such that the equilibrium $(p, \omega) \in E$ is a critical point of $\pi : E \to \Omega$. Then, the price vector $p \in S$ is a singular or critical value of the map $\bar{z}(., \omega) : S \to \mathbb{R}^{\ell-1}$ and conversely. $\quad\square$

6.7. Economies with a Large Number of Equilibria

Proposition 6.15 does not provide an upper bound for the number of equilibria because it is possible to construct economies with an arbitrarily large number of equilibria. Nevertheless, an upper bound to the size of the set of economies with more than n equilibria does exist. Let us consider a compact subset K of Ω. Let $\Omega_n(K)$ denote the set of economies $\omega \in K$ having at least n equilibria, and let $\mu(\Omega_n(K))$ represent the Lebesgue measure of this set.

Proposition 6.20. *There exists $c(K)$ such that the inequality $\mu(\Omega_n(K)) \leq c(K)/n$ is satisfied for every $n \geq 1$.*

Proof. This argument requires techniques that can be skipped in a first reading because we have not used them yet and shall not use them again. We consider the equilibrium manifold E as a submanifold of $S \times \Omega$, which is itself identified with a Euclidean space. Restricting the scalar product to the tangent spaces to E defines a Riemannian structure on E (see, for example [65] for these rather elementary notions in Riemannian geometry). This implies that there exists a concept of ℓm dimensional area on E. We denote by λ this measure defined on E. It is related to the Lebesgue measure μ of Ω in the following way: The orthogonal projection does not increase the measure of a set. In other words, with the notation $i(U)$ representing the orthogonal projection of U, it comes $\mu(i(U)) \leq \lambda(U)$ for every measurable subset U of E. This property simply extends to arbitrary dimensions and to a non-linear framework the well-known property of solid geometry according to which the area of the orthogonal projection of a triangle is less than or equal to the area of the triangle that is projected.

Since the set K is compact and the natural projection π is proper, the set $\pi^{-1}(K)$ is compact, hence measurable, and $\lambda(\pi^{-1}(K))$ is finite. Let $c(K) = \lambda(\pi^{-1}(K))$.

Consider now the set of regular economies with at least n equilibria in K, i.e., $\Omega_n(K) \cap \mathcal{R}$. Since the set of singular economies E has measure zero, we have

$$\mu(\Omega_n(K)) = \mu(\Omega_n(K) \cap \mathcal{R}).$$

The open subset $\mathcal{R}$ of Ω is equal to a countable union of pairwise disjoint open cubes and of a set of measure zero (for a proof, see, for example, [32, p. 52]). We can neglect the set of measure zero. Each of the cubes is a connected and simply connected set. The connectedness property implies that each cube is contained in one connected component of $\mathcal{R}$, so that each ω in a given cube possesses a constant number of equilibria. Let us consider the sequence of cubes U_j for which each $\omega \in U_j$ has at least n equilibria. Note that $\Omega_n(K)$ is equal, up to a set of measure zero, to the union of the sequence of cubes U_j. The simple connectedness of U_j implies that the covering $\pi^{-1}(U_j)$ of U_j is trivial (see, for example, [17, (16.28.6)]; or (Math 3.3)).

Consequently, $\pi^{-1}(U_j)$ consists of at least n layers, each one having a λ-measure at least equal to $\mu(U_j)$:

$$n\mu(U_j) \leq \lambda(\pi^{-1}(U_j)).$$

Summing up the above inequalities, we get

$$n\mu(\Omega_n(K)) \leq \lambda(\pi^{-1}(\Omega_n(K)) \leq \lambda(\pi^{-1}(K)) = c(K). \qquad \square$$

Remark 4. Let ω be an economy with an infinite number of equilibria. Since every regular economy has a finite number of equilibria, ω cannot be a regular economy. Therefore, the set of economies with an infinite number of equilibria is contained in the set Σ and has measure zero. Proposition 6.20 provides us with an asymptotic version of this property: the size of the set of economies with at least n equilibria tends to zero with at least the same speed as $1/n$.

Remark 5. Proposition 6.20 can also be given the following interpretation: Although the probability of observing economies with multiple equilibria is not equal to zero, it is definitely very small.

6.8. Pareto Optimum

We have already seen that the number of equilibria is constant over every connected component of the set of regular economies $\mathcal{R}$. In order to go further, we consider specific elements of the set Ω.

Definition 6.21. The economy $\omega = (\omega_1, \omega_2, \ldots, \omega_m) \in \Omega$ is a Pareto optimum if no economy $\omega' = (\omega'_1, \omega'_2, \ldots, \omega'_m) \in \Omega$ satisfying the following equalities and inequalities exist:

(i) $\sum_{i=1}^{m} \omega_i = \sum_{i=1}^{m} \omega'_i$,
(ii) $u_i(\omega'_i) \geq u_i(\omega_i)$, at least one inequality being strict,
     $i = 1, 2, \ldots, m$.

The set of Pareto optima is denoted by P.

It follows from this definition that an economy is Pareto optimal if it is impossible to reallocate commodities between the economic agents in order to improve the utility levels of every agent. Note that one excludes the possibility of creating some commodities before the reallocation process takes place, which is reflected by the condition $\sum \omega'_i = \sum \omega_i$.

The notion of Pareto optimality occupies a central place among the concepts developed in economic theory. The first precise formulation of the concept dates back to [80] where it was then described as a property of equilibrium allocations.

6.8.1. Equilibrium allocations and Pareto optima

Proposition 6.22. *Every equilibrium allocation is a Pareto optimum.*

Proof. Let us prove that the allocation $x = (x_i) = (f_i(p, p \cdot \omega_i))$ is a Pareto optimum where (p, ω) is an equilibrium. Assume the contrary, i.e., that there exists a m-tuple $x' = (x'_i) \in \Omega$ for which $\sum_i x_i = \sum_i x'_i$ and $u_i(x_i)$ is less than equal to $u_i(x'_i)$ for every i, with at least one inequality being strict. We readily see that the inequality $u_i(x'_i) \geq u_i(x_i)$ (resp. $u_i(x'_i) > u_i(x_i)$) would contradict the definition of x_i as a Pareto optimum if the inequality $p \cdot x'_i < p \cdot x_i$ (resp. $p \cdot x'_i \leq p \cdot x_i$) is satisfied. This implies the inequality $p \cdot x'_i \geq p \cdot x_i$ (resp. $p \cdot x'_i > p \cdot x_i$).

Let us add all these inequalities for i varying from 1 to m. This yields $\sum p \cdot x_i < \sum p \cdot x_i'$, hence the inequality $p \cdot (\sum x_i) < p \cdot (\sum x_i')$, which obviously contradicts the assumption $\sum x_i = \sum x_i'$. □

Remark 6. The reader may easily check that Proposition 6.22 remains true under much weaker assumptions. This theorem is often described in the literature as the first welfare theorem. The second welfare theorem evidently deals with the converse statement. We will prove this result after the introduction of the notion of supporting prices.

6.8.2. Supporting price system

Definition 6.23. We say that the price vector $p \in S$ supports the allocation $x = (x_1, \ldots, x_m) \in \Omega$ if the relationships $x_i = f_i(p, p \cdot x_i)$ is true for $1 \leq i \leq m$.

This definition simply means that, given the price vector $p \in S$ and the resulting wealth level $w_i = p \cdot x_i$, consumer i's demand for that price vector $p \in S$ and the wealth w_i is just equal to x_i, with i varying from 1 to m.

Proposition 6.24. *Let* $x = (x_1, \ldots, x_m) \in \Omega$ *be the allocation associated with the economy* $\omega = (\omega_1, \ldots, \omega_m) \in \Omega$ *and the equilibrium price vector* $p \in S$. *Then, the price vector* $p \in S$ *supports the allocation* $x = (x_1, \ldots, x_m) \in \Omega$.

Proof. The equality $x_i = f_i(p, p \cdot \omega_i)$ for every i follows from the definition of an equilibrium. The equality $f_i(p, p \cdot \omega_i) = f_i(p, p \cdot x_i)$ follows from $x = (x_i)$ belonging to the fiber associated with $\omega = (\omega_i)$. Hence, the equality $x_i = f_i(p, p \cdot x_i)$ for every i between 1 and m. □

Proposition 6.25. *Let the allocation* $x = (x_1, \ldots, x_m) \in \Omega$ *be an allocation supported by the price vector* $p \in S$. *Then, the allocation* x *is a Pareto optimum.*

Proof. It follows from $x = (x_1, \ldots, x_m) \in \Omega$ being supported by the price vector $p \in S$ that we have $x_i = f_i(p, p \cdot x_i)$ for i between 1 and m.

The price vector $p \in S$ is therefore an equilibrium price vector of the economy x. The allocation x is then a Pareto optimum.   □

Proposition 6.26. *Let* $x = (x_1, \ldots, x_m) \in P$ *be a Pareto optimal allocation. The price vector* $p \in S$ *that supports the allocation* x *is then unique.*

Proof. We consider the following optimisation problem: find $x' = (x'_1, \ldots, x'_m)$ that maximizes $u_m(x'_m)$ subject to the constraints,

$$u_1(x'_1) = u_1(x_1),$$

$$\vdots \qquad \vdots$$

$$u_{m-1}(x'_{m-1}) = u_{m-1}(x_{m-1}),$$

$$\sum x'_i = \sum x_i.$$

One easily checks that $x = (x_1, \ldots, x_m)$ is a solution of this constrained optimization problem. First-order conditions associated with the above optimization problem take the form,

$$Du_m(x_m) = q,$$

$$\mu_1 Du_1(x_1) = q,$$

$$\vdots \qquad \vdots$$

$$\mu_{m-1} Du_{m-1}(x_{m-1}) = q,$$

where μ_i (with $1 \le i \le m - 1$) is the Lagrange multiplier associated with the constraint $u_i(x'_i) - u_i(x_i) = 0$. The first equality implies that the vector q is different from 0 because the vector $Du_m(x_m)$ is always positive. Consequently, no multiplier μ_i can be equal to zero. All vectors $Du_i(x_i)$ are collinear and different from 0. It then suffices to take the normalized price vector p collinear with those vectors. This implies that, for every i, the price vector $p \in S$ satisfies $x_i = f_i(p, p \cdot x_i)$. This proves that the price vector p supports the allocation $x = (x_1, \ldots, x_m) \in \Omega$. Uniqueness is then immediate.   □

Corollary 6.27. *Let an economy* $x \in \Omega$ *be Pareto optimal and let* $p \in S$ *be the price vector that supports* x. *The equilibrium allocation* *associated with the economy* $x \in \Omega$ *and the price vector* $p \in S$ *is identical to* $x \in \Omega$.

Proof. Obvious from the equality $x_i = f_i(p, p \cdot \omega_i)$ for $1 \le i \le m$. □

This corollary does provide a converse to Proposition 6.22. It explicitly defines an economy of which an equilibrium allocation turns out to be the given Pareto optimum.

One should also keep in mind that there exist many other economies $\omega' = (\omega'_1, \ldots, \omega'_m)$ for which the allocation x is an equilibrium allocation. They simply must satisfy the relationships $\sum \omega'_i = \sum x_i$ and $p \cdot \omega'_i = p \cdot x_i$ for $i = 1, 2, \ldots, m$.

Finally, a last but obvious remark: the relationships $x_i = f_i(p, p \cdot x_i)$ for $i = 1, \ldots, m$, show us that (p, x) is a no-trade equilibrium. All this suggests a close link between Pareto optima and no-trade equilibria. This we shall investigate now.

6.9. The Set of Pareto Optima and Regular Economies

6.9.1. Uniqueness of equilibrium associated with a Pareto optimum

Proposition 6.28. *There exists only one equilibrium associated with* $\omega \in P$ *(i.e.,* ω *Pareto optimum).*

Proof. Let $p \in S$ be the price vector that is such that $\omega_i = f_i(p, p \cdot \omega_i)$ for $1 \le i \le m$. Assume now that there exists some $p' \ne p$ in S that is also an equilibrium price vector. The equality,

$$p' \cdot f_i(p, p \cdot \omega_i) = p' \cdot \omega_i$$

is satisfied and implies by the revealed preference property the strict inequality,

$$p \cdot f_i(p', p' \cdot \omega_i) > p \cdot \omega_i.$$

Summing up all these inequalities for i varying between 1 and m yields

$$p \cdot \left(\sum f_i(p', p' \cdot \omega_i) - \sum \omega_i \right) > 0,$$

a contradiction with the definition of p' as an equilibrium price vector associated with $\omega = (\omega_1, \ldots, \omega_m) \in \Omega$. □

Corollary 6.29. *The unique price vector $p \in S$ that is an equilibrium price vector for the Pareto optimum $\omega = (\omega_1, \ldots, \omega_m) \in \Omega$ is such that $\omega_i = f_i(p, p \cdot \omega_i)$ for $1 = 1, 2, \ldots, m$.*

Proof. Obvious. □

Proposition 6.30. *The preimage of the set of Pareto optima P by the natural projection $\pi : E \to \Omega$ is the set of no-trade equilibria: $\pi^{-1}(P) = T$.*

Proof. Obvious. □

6.9.2. Pareto optima and regular economies

Proposition 6.31. *The set of Pareto optima P is contained in one connected component of the set of regular economies $\mathcal{R}$.*

Proof. The first step consists in showing that every Pareto optimum is a regular economy, i.e., in proving the inclusion $P \subset \mathcal{R}$. We have $\pi^{-1}(P) = T$. Therefore, we only need to show that no no-trade equilibrium is critical. This is the same thing as showing that $\det J(p, \omega)$ is $\neq 0$ for any $(p, \omega) \in T$. We know that the matrix $J(p, \omega)$ is negative definite symmetric. Its determinant is therefore $\neq 0$, which ends the first step.

The second step is to show that P belongs to only one connected component of the set of regular economies $\mathcal{R}$. We only have to show that P is connected, which follows from $P = \pi(T)$. □

Proposition 6.32. *There is uniqueness of equilibrium for every economy $\omega = (\omega_1, \ldots, \omega_m) \in \Omega$ that belongs to $\mathcal{R}_1$, the connected* *component of the set of regular economies $\mathcal{R}$ that contains the set of Pareto optima.*

Proof. Obvious. □

6.10. The Number of Equilibria

The result just above establishes the uniqueness of equilibrium for well-specified economies, namely those that belong to the connected component $\mathcal{R}_1$ of $\mathcal{R}$. Combined with the properness of the natural projection, we derive from this uniqueness property general statements about the number of equilibria of an economy by a simple application of degree theory.

6.10.1. A quick entry to degree theory

The smooth proper map $\pi : E \to \Omega$ possesses important topological invariants related to the number of elements of the inverse image $\pi^{-1}(\omega)$ for any regular economy $\omega \in \mathcal{R}$. In fact, there exist two concepts of degree.

The modulo 2 degree of the smooth proper map $\pi : E \to \Omega$ is simply the parity of the number of elements of the set $\pi^{-1}(\omega)$ when ω is a regular economy. A rather deep theorem underlying the definition of the modulo 2 degree of a smooth map states that, even if the number of elements of $\pi^{-1}(\omega)$ may vary with $\omega \in \mathcal{R}$, its parity does not depend on the choice of ω (Math 2.7). The modulo 2 degree is sufficient in most applications.

The Brouwer degree is somewhat more intricate to define. First, one has to choose orientations for both E and Ω. The coordinate system we use for the equilibrium manifold E is defined by the diffeomorphism with $S \times \mathbb{R}^m \times \mathbb{R}^{(\ell-1)(m-1)}$. The coordinate system we use for Ω is simply $(\omega_1, \dots, \omega_m)$. One then associates with every element of $\pi^{-1}(\omega)$, where ω is a regular value of the map $\pi : E \to \Omega$, either $+1$ or -1 depending on the sign of the Jacobian determinant of π. The Brouwer degree is then the sum of $+1$'s and -1's for all elements of $\pi^{-1}(\omega)$. This number is an invariant in the sense that it does not depend on the choice of the regular value ω (Math 2.8).

6.10.2. Oddness and existence of equilibria

Proposition 6.33. *The modulo 2 degree of the natural projection* $\pi : E \to \Omega$ *is equal to* $+1$.

Proof. We know that ω Pareto optimum is a regular economy and that $\pi^{-1}(\omega)$ contains only one element. One just applies the definition of the modulo 2 degree for this ω.   □

Proposition 6.34. *The Brouwer degree of the natural projection* $\pi : E \to \Omega$ *is equal to* $+1$ *for a suitable orientation of the equilibrium manifold* E *and of the endowment space* Ω.

Proof. Let ω be a Pareto optimum and let (p, ω) be the unique element of $\pi^{-1}(\omega)$. We just have to show that, for some orientation of E, the sign of $\det T_{(p,\omega)}\pi$ is positive. Using the proof of 6.16, we have $\det T_{(p,\omega)}\pi = \det M(p, \omega)$ and, similarly, $\det M(p, \omega) = \det J(p, \omega)$. Now, the sign of $\det J(p, \omega)$ is the same as the sign of $(-1)^{\ell-1}$ since the matrix $J(p, \omega)$ is symmetric and negative definite, which ends the proof.   □

Proposition 6.35. *The natural projection* $\pi : E \to \Omega$ *is onto.*

Proof. Follows from the modulo 2 degree of $\pi : E \to \Omega$ being equal to $+1$ for example.   □

This property is important because it proves the existence of equilibria for any economy $\omega = (\omega_1, \omega_2, \ldots, \omega_m) \in \Omega$.

Corollary 6.36. *The number of equilibria associated with every regular economy is odd.*

Note, however, that the above result does not say that the odd number of equilibria is the same over all connected components of the set of regular economies $\mathcal{R}$. In fact, it is the contrary. This number varies with the connected components of $\mathcal{R}$. This number is equal to one at Pareto optima, but it can be much larger at other economies.

6.10.3. The structure of the set of Pareto optima

The results above have shown us the importance of the set of Pareto optima P with respect to the number of equilibria. The next result describes more carefully the structure of that set.

Proposition 6.37. *The set of Pareto optima P is a smooth submanifold of $\Omega = (\mathbb{R}^{\ell m})$ that is diffeomorphic to $\mathbb{R}^{\ell+m-1}$.*

Proof. Let $g(x) = \frac{1}{\frac{Du_1(x_1)}{Dx^\ell}} Du_1(x_1)$. We consider the mapping
$(x_1, \ldots, x_i, \ldots, x_m) \to (g(x_1), g(x_1) \cdot x_1, \ldots, g(x_1) \cdot x_i, \ldots, g(x_1) \cdot x_m)$
from $\mathbb{R}^{\ell m}$ to $S \times \mathbb{R}^m$. We then restrict this mapping to the set of Pareto optima P, a restriction that is a mapping from P into $S \times \mathbb{R}^m$. This map has an inverse map that merely applies $(p, w_1, \ldots, w_m)$ to the Pareto optimum $(f_1(p, w_1), \ldots, f_m(p, w_m))$ so that it suffices to apply Lemma 5.6 to conclude this proof.   □

We have therefore shown that the two maps $\pi \circ f : S \times \mathbb{R}^m \to \Omega$ (where $(p, w_1, \ldots, w_m) \to (f_1(p, w_1), \ldots, f_m(p, w_m))$) and $\rho : P \to S \times \mathbb{R}^m$ (where $\rho(x_1, \ldots, x_m) = (g(x), g(x) \cdot x_1, \ldots, g(x) \cdot x_m)$) are inverse to each other, which yields the following proposition:

Proposition 6.38. *The maps $\pi \circ f : S \times \mathbb{R}^m \to P$ and $\rho : P \to S \times \mathbb{R}^m$ are inverse to each other.*

Proof. Obvious given the above considerations.   □

6.11. Conclusion

This chapter was mainly motivated by the study of the existence and the number of equilibria. This theme is put in this chapter in a wider and more natural perspective, namely, the study of the dependence of equilibria on the parameters defining an economy. As we have already seen in the first chapter, this point of view leads directly to the natural projection. In the general case, we have seen in Chapter 5 that the equilibrium manifold is made of fibers that are parameterized by the no-trade equilibria. This raises the question of the economic significance of these no-trade equilibria and their image by the natural projection. The characterization of the Pareto optima as the image of the set of no-trade equilibria is then equivalent to the two welfare theorems. It is quite remarkable that this approach also enables one to identify the connected component of the set of regular economies that contains the Pareto optima as one where equilibrium is unique. Outside that connected component, the number of equilibria not only varies but, also is generally larger than one. It is still an open question for more than two agents whether the set of regular economies with a unique equilibrium coincides with the set of regular economies that contains the Pareto optima.

6.12. Notes and Comments

There are two main original sources for the content of this chapter. One is Debreu [13] who proved the existence of equilibrium for all economies and the generic finiteness of those equilibria for an open and dense set of economies he called the regular economies. He also proved that, locally, the number of equilibria was constant at regular economies. The second one is Balasko [8] who, in addition to proving that the equilibrium manifold was diffeomorphic to a Euclidean space as seen in the previous chapter, showed that the regular economies where just the regular values of the projection of the equilibrium manifold E onto the space of economies Ω. He also showed that the two welfare theorems that have had such an important role in economic analysis could be simply stated as the equality of the set of equilibrium allocations with the set of Pareto optima or, in other words, the equality $\pi(T) = P$. In fact, Balasko showed that the set of no-trade equilibria T and the set of Pareto optima P are diffeomorphic by the application π. This implies the uniqueness of equilibrium when endowments belong to the connected component of the set of regular economies that contains the set of Pareto optima.

6.13. Exercises

6.1. *The following exercise involves numerical computations. We recommend them to be dealt with only once all qualitative aspects discussed in this exercise have been understood.*

One considers the equilibrium setup $S \times \Omega$ in the case $S = (0, +\infty)$ and $\Omega = (0, +\infty)$. Note also this highly stylized economic setup. One assumes that the equilibrium manifold is the subset,

$$E = \{(p, \omega) \in S \times \Omega \mid 1/\omega = 4.11p^3 - 28p^2 + 50p\}. \quad (1)$$

(1) Draw the picture of the equilibrium manifold E in the $S \times \Omega$ quadrant where the ω-axis is horizontal and the p-axis vertical.

(2) Show that there are two points C' and C'' with coordinates (p', ω') and (p'', ω''), respectively, with $\omega' < \omega''$, such that the tangent lines to the curve E at these points C' and C'' are vertical. Compute the numerical values of (p', ω') and (p'', ω'') up to the second digit for the coordinate ω. How many equilibria are there for ω in the intervals $(0, \omega')$, (ω', ω''), and $(\omega'', +\infty)$?

(3) To fix ideas, assume that $\omega(t) \in (0, +\infty)$ represents the quantity of some agricultural product brought to the market on day t. Let $p(t)$ denote the market price on day t. The value of the resource $\omega(t)$ is then equal to the product $p(t)\omega(t)$. To fix ideas, assume that the production season lasts 100 days, starts at date $t = 0$, and the total resources at date t are represented by the unimodal function,

$$\omega(t) = \frac{a}{2500}t(100 - t),$$

where $a > 0$ is some constant. Show that for $a < \omega'$, the equilibrium is unique for all $t \in [0, 100]$. What is the economic interpretation of $\Phi(a) = \sum_{t=0}^{100} p(t)\omega(t)$? Give an analytic expression of $\Phi(a)$ as a function of $a \in [0, \omega']$. (In this computation, one can approximate this finite sum by the corresponding integral, i.e., work in continuous time.)

(4) Assume now that a belongs to the interval (ω', ω''). Deduce from the continuity principle that all price equilibria $p(t)$ associated with $w(t) \in (\omega', \omega'')$ belong to the upper branch of the curve E. Prove that the properties established in question 3 extend to this case.

(5) Assume now that a is $> \omega''$. Show that the equilibrium prices $p(t)$ for the days t where the resource $w(t)$ is larger than ω'' belong to the lower branch of the curve E. Let t_1 be the last day where $w(t)$ is $\leq \omega''$. Compute the difference $p_{t_1 - 1} - p_{t_1}$. Compare with the difference $p_{t_1} - p_{t_1 + 1}$. Is there an economic interpretation?

(6) One still assumes $a > \omega''$. Let t_2 be the last day where $w(t)$ is $\geq \omega''$ and t_3 the last day where $w(t)$ is $\geq \omega'$. Show by the application of the continuity principle that, for $t \in [t_2 + 1, t_3]$, the price equilibria $p(t)$ belong to the lower branch of the curve E. Compute the expression $\Phi(a) = \sum_{t=0}^{100} p(t)w(t)$ as a function of $a > \omega''$. Compare with the expression of $\Phi(a)$ found in questions 3 and 4. Analyze what happens at $a = \omega''$.

(7) An agency is set to prevent the amount of resources brought to the market to exceed ω''. In practice, one assumes that there is a level $\omega_{\max} \in (\omega', \omega'')$ such that the quantity $w(t) - \omega_{\max}$ is bought by the agency at some price p^*. Let $p_{\max}$ denote the equilibrium price on the upper branch of E associated with $\omega_{\max}$. (Note that we do not assume the equality $p_{\max} = p^*$.) Compute the total intervention cost of the agency as a function of p^*, $p_{\max}$ and a. Express the sum $\sum_{t=0}^{100} p(t)w(t)$ as a function of $a > \omega'$, p^* and $p_{\max}$. Compare the cost of operating the agency with the farmers' income that is saved.

(8) Compare and discuss the results of questions 6 and 7.

Chapter 7

Equilibrium Analysis for Fixed Total Resources

The main goal of this chapter is to extend the results of the previous two chapters on the equilibrium manifold on one hand, and on the natural projection on the other, to the case of fixed total resources.

Imposing fixed total resources is a very natural assumption when doing comparative statics analysis involving only redistributions of endowments. But, restricting the size of the parameter space generally leads to mathematical complications. Therefore, there is no guarantee that the equilibrium analysis of the previous two chapters carries over to the case of fixed total resources. We show, however, that imposing these total resources constraints does not change the nature of the results we have obtained so far. Only a few steps in their proofs have to be adjusted in order to take into account this new assumption. In doing this, we shall find that some diffeomorphism plays a crucial role in solving the problems raised by the fixed resources case. This diffeomorphism property has other by-products that involve aggregate demand functions. Therefore, we study some of these properties in the second part of this chapter.

7.1. The Fixed Total Resources Setting

Let $r \in \mathbb{R}^\ell$ represent the vector of fixed total resources, i.e., $\Sigma \omega_i = r$. We denote by $\Omega(r) = \{\omega = (\omega_1, \ldots, \omega_m) \in (\mathbb{R}^\ell)^m | \Sigma \omega_i = r\}$ the space of economies. Similarly, we define

$$E(r) = \{(p, \omega) \in S \times \Omega(r) | \Sigma f_i(p, p \cdot \omega) = r\}$$

as the set of corresponding equilibria. The restriction of the natural projection $(p, \omega) \to \omega$ to $E(r)$ is still denoted by π, i.e., $\pi : E(r) \to \Omega(r)$. The first problem that naturally arises deals with the structure of the equilibrium set $E(r)$. Formally, this set can be defined as the intersection $E \cap S \times \Omega(r)$. Unless the two submanifolds E and $S \times \Omega(r)$ are transverse, there is little hope for their intersection $E(r)$ to be a submanifold of $S \times \Omega(r)$. This question, however, has to be answered first if one wants to be able to define, in some useful way, the smoothness of the natural projection $\pi : E(r) \to \Omega(r)$. Our strategy is to investigate the submanifold structure of $E(r)$ via the diffeomorphism $\phi : E \to S \times \mathbb{R}^m \times \mathbb{R}^{(\ell-1)(m-1)}$ of (5.17). This leads us to introduce the concept of price–income equilibrium, whose importance will become increasingly more apparent in later developments.

Definition 7.1. The $(m+1)$-tuple $b = (p, w_1, \ldots, w_m) \in S \times \mathbb{R}^m$ is a price–income equilibrium associated with the total resources $r \in \mathbb{R}^\ell$ if the equality $\Sigma f_i(p, w_i) = r$ is satisfied. Let $B(r)$ denote the set of price–income equilibria associated with $r \in \mathbb{R}^\ell$.

The set of price–income equilibria $B(r)$ plays a crucial role in understanding the structure of the equilibrium set $E(r)$ for the following simple reason:

Proposition 7.2. *We have*

$$\phi(E(r)) = B(r) \times \mathbb{R}^{(\ell-1)(m-1)}.$$

Proof. Obvious.   □

7.2. Structure of the Set of Price–Income Equilibria

It has been established in 6.38 that the mapping $\pi \circ f : S \times \mathbb{R}^m \to P$ defined by $(p, w_1, \ldots, w_m) \to (f_1(p, w_1), \ldots, f_m(p, w_m))$ is a diffeomorphism. The set $B(r)$ of price–income equilibria is the inverse image of $P(r) = P \cap \Omega(r)$ by this mapping. Now, $P(r)$ can be defined as being the set of Pareto optima that belong to $\Omega(r)$, i.e., such that the total endowments are equal to $r \in \mathbb{R}^\ell$. Therefore, the structure of $B(r)$ and $P(r)$ are closely related, and this provides us with a way to analyze this structure.

7.2.1. A fundamental lemma

Lemma 7.3. *The mapping $\theta : S \times \mathbb{R}^m \to \mathbb{R}^\ell \times \mathbb{R}^{m-1}$ defined by the formula,*

$$\theta(p, w_1, \ldots, w_m)$$

$$= \left(\sum_i f_i(p, w_i), u_1(f_1(p, w_1)), \ldots, u_{m-1}(f_{m-1}(p, w_{m-1})) \right)$$

is a diffeomorphism.

Note that if $m = 1$, then the mapping θ becomes identical to $f_1 : S \times \mathbb{R} \to \mathbb{R}^\ell$. Therefore, 7.3 can be viewed as an extension of 4.11 to the case of several consumers.

Proof. The strategy is to show that θ is a smooth bijection which is locally invertible. Smoothness is obvious. Let us prove that θ is locally invertible, i.e., that its Jacobian determinant is everywhere non-zero.

Computing this Jacobian determinant involves, besides the partial derivative of the individual demand mappings with respect to prices and incomes, the derivatives of the utility functions $u_1, \ldots, u_{m-1}$. These latter derivatives are proportional to the price vector p; substituting p for them does not alter the vanishing or non-vanishing of the Jacobian determinant; taking into account (4.16) then leads to proving that the matrix,

$$
\begin{bmatrix}
\displaystyle\sum_i \frac{\partial f_i^1}{\partial p_1} & \cdots & \displaystyle\sum_i \frac{\partial f_i^1}{\partial p_{\ell-1}} & \frac{\partial f_1^1}{\partial w_1} & \cdots & \frac{\partial f_{m-1}^1}{\partial w_{m-1}} & \frac{\partial f_m^1}{\partial w_m} \\
\vdots & \vdots & \vdots & \vdots & \vdots & \vdots & \vdots \\
\displaystyle\sum_i \frac{\partial f_i^\ell}{\partial p_1} & \cdots & \displaystyle\sum_i \frac{\partial f_i^\ell}{\partial p_{\ell-1}} & \frac{\partial f_1^\ell}{\partial w_1} & \cdots & \frac{\partial f_{m-1}^\ell}{\partial w_{m-1}} & \frac{\partial f_m^\ell}{\partial w_m} \\
-f_1^1 & \cdots & -f_1^{\ell-1} & 1 & \cdots & 0 & 0 \\
\vdots & \vdots & \vdots & \vdots & \vdots & \vdots & \vdots \\
-f_{m-1}^1 & \cdots & -f_{m-1}^{\ell-1} & 0 & \cdots & 1 & 0
\end{bmatrix},
$$

has non-zero determinant. After multiplying row k by p_k, with k varying from 1 to ℓ, and summing up the results, one gets the following row:

$$
\left(-\sum_i f_i^1, -\sum_i f_i^2, \ldots, -\sum_i f_i^{\ell-1}, 1, \ldots, 1 \right),
$$

which can be substituted for the ℓth row without changing the value of the above determinant. We then subtract from the new ℓth row the last $(m-1)$ rows, which yields as a new row,

$$
\left(-f_m^1, -f_m^2, \ldots, -f_m^{\ell-1}, 0, \ldots, 0, 1 \right).
$$

Moving this expression from the ℓth row to the last row — which, at most, changes only the sign of the determinant — yields the matrix,

$$
\begin{bmatrix}
\displaystyle\sum_i \frac{\partial f_i^1}{\partial p_1} & \cdots & \displaystyle\sum_i \frac{\partial f_i^1}{\partial p_{\ell-1}} & \frac{\partial f_1^1}{\partial w_1} & \cdots & \frac{\partial f_{m-1}^1}{\partial w_{m-1}} & \frac{\partial f_m^1}{\partial w_m} \\
\vdots & \vdots & \vdots & \vdots & \vdots & \vdots & \vdots \\
\displaystyle\sum_i \frac{\partial f_i^{\ell-1}}{\partial p_1} & \cdots & \displaystyle\sum_i \frac{\partial f_i^{\ell-1}}{\partial p_{\ell-1}} & \frac{\partial f_1^{\ell-1}}{\partial w_1} & \cdots & \frac{\partial f_m^{\ell-1}}{\partial w_{m-1}} & \frac{\partial f_m^{\ell-1}}{\partial w_m} \\
-f_1^1 & \cdots & -f_1^{\ell-1} & 1 & \cdots & 0 & 0 \\
\vdots & \vdots & \vdots & \vdots & \vdots & \vdots & \vdots \\
-f_{m-1}^1 & \cdots & -f_{m-1}^{\ell-1} & 0 & \cdots & 1 & 0 \\
-f_m^1 & \cdots & -f_m^{\ell-1} & 0 & \cdots & 0 & 1
\end{bmatrix},
$$

which has the special form $\begin{pmatrix} A & B \\ C & I \end{pmatrix}$, where I is the $m \times m$ identity matrix. Finally, we can cancel the elements of B by suitable combinations of rows: multiply row $(\ell - 1) + j$ by $\partial f_j^k / \partial w_j$; subtract from row k; proceed for all possible combinations of k and j; this eventually yields a matrix that takes the form,

$$\begin{bmatrix} M & 0 \\ * & I \end{bmatrix},$$

and its determinant is obviously equal to det (M), where M is a $(\ell - 1) \times (\ell - 1)$ matrix, which is easily recognized to be the sum of the Slutsky matrices of all consumers, i.e.,

$$M = \sum_i M_i(p, w,).$$

The Slutsky matrix $M_i(p, w_i)$ is symmetric negative definite. Therefore, the matrix M is clearly symmetric. By looking at the quadratic forms associated with each of these symmetric matrices, we see that the form associated with M is the sum of the forms associated with the matrices $M_i(p, w_i)$ where i varies from 1 to m. Therefore, the quadratic form defined by M is negative definite as the sum of negative definite forms. This implies that det (M) is non-zero.

To prove that θ is a bijection, it suffices to define a mapping $\sigma : \mathbb{R}^\ell \times \mathbb{R}^{m-1} \to S \times \mathbb{R}^m$ that is the inverse of θ. This mapping σ can easily be formulated with the help of the classical approach to Pareto optima, which we shall now recall. □

7.2.2. The classical approach to Pareto optima

It is based on the identification of Pareto optima with the solutions of some optimization problem, namely:

Proposition 7.4. *The optimization problem,*

$$Maximize \quad u_m(x_m),$$

$$Subject \ to \quad \begin{cases} \sum_i x_i = r; \\ u_i(x_i) \geq u_i^*, \quad i = 1, 2, \ldots, m - 1, \end{cases}$$

has a unique solution. This solution is a Pareto optimum.

Proof. Let $C = C(r, u_1^*, \ldots, u_{m-1}^*)$ be the set defined by these constraints. It is clearly non-empty. Let $\bar{\bar{x}} = (\bar{\bar{x}}_1, \ldots, \bar{\bar{x}}_m)$ belong to C. Then, maximizing $u_m(\cdot)$ subject to having x belong to C or subject to having the additional constraint $u_m(x_m) \geq u_m(\bar{\bar{x}}_m)$ satisfied are equivalent problems. Let us show that the latter set, defined by C and the additional constraint, is compact. It is clearly closed. Now, with indifference surfaces being bounded from below by Assumption 4.4 of Section 4.5.1, there exists $x_j^* \in \mathbb{R}^\ell$ such that $u_j(x_j) \geq u_j^*$ implies $x_j^* \leq x_j, j = 1, 2, \ldots, m - 1$. Furthermore, we have $u_m(\bar{\bar{x}}_m) \leq u_m(x_m)$. There also exists x_m^* such that $x_m^* \leq x_m$. The equality $\Sigma x_i = r$ combined with these inequalities implies that each x_i is also bounded from above (in fact, $x_i \leq r - \Sigma_{j \neq i} x_j^*$). This proves the compactness assertion, which implies the existence of at least one solution.

Let us show that the solution is unique. Assume the contrary: let x and x' be two solutions, with $x \neq x'$. The set C being convex, one considers $x'' = (x + x')/2$. Clearly, $\Sigma x_i'' = r, u_i(x'') \geq u_i(x_i), i = 1, \ldots, m$.

There exists at least one i for which $x_i \neq x_i'$. If $x_m \neq x_m'$, we immediately get a contradiction because the inequality $u_m(x_m'') > u_m(x_m)$ follows from the strict quasi-concavity of u_m. If $x_i \neq x_i', i \neq m$, then we have $u_i(x_i'') > u_i(x_i) \geq u_i^*$. There exists a vector $h \in \mathbb{R}_{++}^\ell$ such that $u_i(x_i'' - h) \geq u_i^*$. Consider $x''' = (x_1'', \ldots, x_i'' - h, \ldots, x_m'' + h)$. Then, clearly x''' belongs to C, but we have $u_m(x_m'' + h) > u_m(x_m)$. This, once again, implies a contradiction.

This unique solution is denoted by $R(r, u^*, \ldots, u_{m-1}^*)$. It is a Pareto optimum because, otherwise, there would exist $x' \neq x$ such that $u_i(x_i) \leq u_i(x_i')$, $i = 1, 2, \ldots, m$, with at least one inequality being strict, and $\Sigma x_i = \Sigma x_i'$. The same argument as the one used in proving uniqueness would yield a contradiction. $\square$

We have therefore defined a mapping,

$$R : \mathbb{R}^\ell \times \mathbb{R}^{m-1} \to (\mathbb{R}^\ell)^m,$$

which associates with $(r, u_1^*, \ldots, u_m^* - 1)$ the Pareto optimum denoted $R(r, u_1^*, \ldots, u_{m-1}^*)$. The image of R is contained in the set P of Pareto optima. (Note that it follows from the definition of a Pareto optimum that the set P is in fact the image of the mapping R.)

Let now $\rho : P \to S \times \mathbb{R}^m$ be the mapping defined by

$$\rho(x) = (g(x), g(x) \cdot x_1, \ldots, g(x) \cdot x_m),$$

where $g(x)$ is the price vector that supports x. We define $\sigma : \mathbb{R}^\ell \times \mathbb{R}^{m-1} \to S \times \mathbb{R}^m$ as the composition $\rho \circ R$.

Lemma 7.5. *The mapping σ is the inverse of θ.*

Proof. Obvious by direct computation of $\theta \circ \sigma$ and $\sigma \circ \theta$. $\qquad\square$

Corollary 7.6. *The set $B(r)$ of price–income equilibria associated with $r \in \mathbb{R}^\ell$ is a submanifold of $S \times \mathbb{R}^m$ diffeomorphic to $\mathbb{R}^{m-1}$.*

Proof. By 7.3, $B(r)$ is diffeomorphic to $\{r\} \times \mathbb{R}^{m-1}$, submanifold of $\mathbb{R}^\ell \times \mathbb{R}^{m-1}$. $\qquad\square$

Corollary 7.7. *The equilibrium set $E(r)$ is a submanifold of $S \times \Omega(r)$ diffeomorphic to $\mathbb{R}^{\ell(m-1)}$.*

Proof. Apply 7.3 and 7.6. $\qquad\square$

7.3. The Natural Projection Revisited

Corollary 7.7 enables us to apply the smooth apparatus to the natural projection $\pi : E(r) \to \Omega(r)$ that is defined for fixed total resources $r \in \mathbb{R}^\ell$.

Proposition 7.8. *The mapping $\pi : E(r) \to \Omega(r)$ is smooth.*

Proof. Follows from 7.7. $\qquad\square$

Let $\pi : E(r) \to \Omega(r)$. A problem that now arises is whether a singular (resp. regular) value of this smooth mapping is also a singular (resp. regular) value of $\pi : E \to \Omega$.

Proposition 7.9. *The economy $\omega \in \Omega(r)$ is a regular (resp. singular) value of the mapping $\pi : E(r) \to \Omega(r)$ if and only if it is a regular (resp. singular) value of the mapping $\pi : E \to \Omega$.*

Proof. Let us show that the property for (p, ω) of being a critical point for the mapping $\pi : E(r) \to \Omega(r)$ (i.e., for fixed total resources) is equivalent to it being a critical point for the mapping $\pi : E \to \Omega$ defined on the equilibrium manifold E corresponding to variable total resources. There is a technical difficulty due to the lack of a convenient local coordinate system that describes the equilibrium manifold with *fixed total resources* $E(r)$.

Let us take $(\omega_1, \ldots, \omega_{m-1}, r)$, where $r = \Sigma \omega_i$, as a coordinate system for $\Omega = (\mathbb{R}^\ell)^m$. The mapping $\phi : E \to S \times \mathbb{R}^m \times \mathbb{R}^{(\ell-1)(m-1)}$ is a diffeomorphism by (5.17) and enables one to use $S \times \mathbb{R}^m \times \mathbb{R}^{(\ell-1)(m-1)}$ as a coordinate system for E. From Lemma 7.3, we know that the mapping $\theta : S \times \mathbb{R}^m \to \mathbb{R}^\ell \times \mathbb{R}^{m-1}$ is a diffeomorphism. By composing these two diffeomorphisms, it turns out that the parameters $(\bar{\omega}_1, \bar{\omega}_2, \ldots, \bar{\omega}_{m-1}, u_1, \ldots, u_{m-1}, r)$ define a global coordinate system for the manifold E. The mapping π then takes the form $(\bar{\omega}_1, \ldots, \bar{\omega}_{m-1}, u_1, \ldots, u_{m-1}, r) \to (\omega_1, \ldots, \omega_{m-1}, r)$ with these coordinates. This formulation is interesting since the sets $E(r)$ and $\Omega(r)$ are associated with fixed r. Therefore, the Jacobian matrix of $\pi : E \to \Omega$ takes the form,

$$\begin{bmatrix} A & B \\ 0 & I \end{bmatrix},$$

where, unsurprisingly, A is the Jacobian matrix of the natural projection $\pi : E(r) \to \Omega(r)$, which ends the proof of the theorem. $\square$

Let $\Sigma(r)$ and $\mathcal{R}(r)$ denote the set of singular and regular economies for the fixed total resources $r \in \mathbb{R}^\ell$. Then Proposition 7.9 says that we have

$$\Sigma(r) = \Sigma \cap \Omega(r),$$

$$\mathcal{R}(r) = \mathcal{R} \cap \Omega(r).$$

Let $T(r) = T \cap S \times \Omega(r)$ denote the set of no-trade equilibria associated with the total resources $r \in \mathbb{R}^\ell$. Then, the relationship between T and P, the set of Pareto optima, established in Chapter 6 for variable total resources through the natural projection $\pi : T \to P$

yields under the assumption of fixed total resources a mapping $\pi : T(r) \to P(r)$ which is a diffeomorphism.

Furthermore, the set of Pareto optima $P(r)$ (for the fixed total resources $r \in \mathbb{R}^{\ell}$) is contained in one connected component of the set of regular economies $\mathcal{R}(r)$. Equilibrium is unique when ω belongs to this component. In other words, imposing that the total resources be fixed does not change the general picture suggested by the study of the natural projection $\pi : E \to \Omega$ (variable total resources).

We have included the case of fixed total resources because of its economic interest. But, there is also a purely mathematical reason for being interested in this case. We shall see in the next two chapters that in order to go any further in the study of the natural projection, it is necessary to exploit the fiber space structure of the equilibrium manifold. This will lead us to develop two different settings both of which can be given a highly suggestive and powerful geometric formulation in the case of fixed total resources. But, before we develop these topics, we notice that the mapping θ : $S \times \mathbb{R}^m \to \mathbb{R}^{\ell} \times \mathbb{R}^{m-1}$ (which is a diffeomorphism by 7.3) possesses as a (vector) coordinate the sum $\Sigma f_i(p, w_i)$. Therefore, we can expect as by-products of Lemma 7.3 properties of these aggregate demand functions, which we now are going to investigate.

7.4. The Aggregate Demand Function

The individual demand functions exhibit properties which, like 4.11 (diffeomorphism), 4.26 (Slutsky) and 4.27 (revealed preferences), are quite restrictive. What happens to these restrictions when individual demands are summed up in order to yield aggregate demand functions?

An interesting and somewhat disturbing property of the aggregate *excess* demand function has been discovered and elaborated upon in several contributions, the most important ones of which are those of Sonnenschein [86], Mantel [75], and Debreu [57]. Recall that in an economy defined by $\omega \in \Omega$, the aggregate excess demand function is the mapping $z(\cdot, \omega) : S \to \mathbb{R}^{\ell}$ defined by

$z(p, \omega) = \Sigma f_i(p, p \cdot \omega_i) - \Sigma \omega_i$. Because of Walras law, one often drops the last coordinate, considering only the $(\ell - 1)$ first coordinates, i.e., the mapping $\bar{z}(\cdot, \omega) : S \to \mathbb{R}^{\ell-1}$.

The property can be stated as follows. Let $\bar{z} : S \to \mathbb{R}^{\ell-1}$ be an arbitrary continuous function. Let K be an arbitrarily chosen compact subset of S. Then, there exists an economy consisting of ℓ agents such that the aggregate excess demand mapping of this economy $\bar{z}(\cdot, \omega)$ coincides with the arbitrary mapping $\bar{z}$ on the compact set K.

This result has been understood by a few economists as expressing the lack of any specific property of the aggregate excess demand function whenever the number of agents is larger than or equal to the number of commodities. A surprisingly extreme version of this line of thought has taken this result as justification for the use of crude models in economics. In fact, this result does not exclude specific restrictions on aggregate excess demand. Simply, if such restrictions exist, they require having prices tend to the boundary of the price set, i.e., having one or several prices tend either to zero or to infinity. On the other hand, the Sonnenschein–Mantel–Debreu theorem says, among other things, that the local behavior of aggregate excess demand may be absolutely arbitrary. This is particularly interesting in the study of, for example, Walras tatonnement because it implies that the vector field defined by Walras tatonnement can be absolutely arbitrary, at least locally. The linearized version of this property says that there is no restriction on the Jacobian matrix of aggregate excess demand $J(p, \omega)$ at an equilibrium (p, ω), except for the fact that it is a square matrix of order $\ell - 1$.

For a general proof of the Sonnenschein–Mantel–Debreu theorem, the reader is referred to Debreu's [57] paper.

7.4.1. The aggregate demand function

The fact that adding up individual *excess* demand functions destroys their properties (at least locally) may be an indication that excess demand is not necessarily the most interesting aggregate concept. In this regard, the sum of individual demands, which defines a function depending on the price vector $p \in S$ and the m incomes w_i, seems to be a concept even more fundamental than excess demand. The two concepts, of course, are obviously related.

The aggregate demand function $F : S \times \mathbb{R}^m \to \mathbb{R}^\ell$ is defined by the formula,

$$F(p, w_1, \ldots, w_m) = \sum_i f_i(p, w_i).$$

From Walras law, we have

$$p \cdot F(p, w_1, \ldots, w_m) = \sum_i p \cdot f_i(p, w_i) = \sum_i w_i,$$

so that the mapping F is determined by $(\ell - 1)$ coordinates, the ℓth one being computed by the above formula. By convention, we choose the first $(\ell - 1)$ coordinates and denote by $\bar{F}(p, w_1, \ldots, w_m) \in \mathbb{R}^{\ell-I}$ the demand for the first $(\ell - 1)$ commodities, i.e., the demand with the numeraire commodity excluded. Since mapping $\bar{F}$ is smooth, it belongs to the space $C^\infty(S \times \mathbb{R}^m, \mathbb{R}^{\ell-1})$ of smooth mappings from $S \times \mathbb{R}^m$ into $\mathbb{R}^{\ell-1}$.

We denote by $\tilde{\mathfrak{D}}$ the set of *aggregate demand functions* defined on $S \times \mathbb{R}^m$ and taking their values in $\mathbb{R}^{\ell-1}$. As a subset of $C^\infty(S \times \mathbb{R}^m, \mathbb{R}^{\ell-1})$, we have the following:

Proposition 7.10. *The subset $\tilde{\mathfrak{D}}$ is strictly included in $C^\infty(S \times \mathbb{R}^m, \mathbb{R}^{\ell-1})$.*

In other words, there exist smooth mappings from $S \times \mathbb{R}^m$ into $\mathbb{R}^{\ell-1}$ which cannot be interpreted as aggregate demand functions.

Proof. The aggregate function $\bar{F} = \Sigma \bar{f}_i$ is separable with respect to the variables w_i. This implies $\partial \bar{F}/\partial w_i = \partial \bar{f}_i/\partial w_i$. Consequently, the second-order derivatives $\partial^2 \bar{F}/\partial w_i \partial w_j$ are equal to zero for $i \neq j$. $\qquad\square$

7.4.2. Aggregate demand functions and estimation errors

For the time being, let $\bar{F}$ be an arbitrary function from $S \times \mathbb{R}^m$ into $\mathbb{R}^{\ell-1}$. It is practically impossible to specify $\bar{F}$ with perfect accuracy, so that direct measurements cannot distinguish $\bar{F}$ from another mapping $\bar{F}' : S \times \mathbb{R}^m \to \mathbb{R}^{\ell-1}$ that is sufficiently close. This notion of closeness evidently requires the choice of a suitable topology on the space $C^\infty(S \times \mathbb{R}^m, \mathbb{R}^{\ell-1})$, a problem we can safely ignore, at least momentarily.

What is currently at stake is the fact that the properties of the model (any model) associated with the aggregate demand function $\bar{F}$ depend on this function. Some properties may be more important than others, and some may vary more than others depending on the parameters. Consequently, a feature that has to be fulfilled by any model is that its most crucial properties (which undoubtedly include the qualitative ones) are robust to perturbations of the function $\bar{F}$, such as those that would result from measurement inaccuracies or errors. In fact, mathematicians have tended to formalize this necessary invariance as a property of the mapping $\bar{F}$ itself, the idea being that, in order for a mapping to resist minor perturbations, it is necessary and sufficient that one can still use the same formula to describe the perturbed mappings, provided they are placed in a slightly different coordinate system. Within the differentiable framework, changing coordinates amounts to composing mappings with diffeomorphisms of the definition and the image sets.

We reformulate in a mathematically more precise way these concepts before investigating the robustness of aggregate demand functions with respect to perturbations.

7.4.3. The notion of equivalent mappings

Errors in estimating an element in $C^\infty(S \times \mathbb{R}^m, \mathbb{R}^{\ell-1})$ result from inaccurate measures of elements in $S \times \mathbb{R}^m$, the set of prices and incomes, and in $\mathbb{R}^{\ell-1}$, the space of the $(\ell-1)$ first commodities. Measuring incomes seems to be prone to larger errors than the other parameters, which suggests the following definition.

Definition 7.11. The mappings $\bar{F}$ and $\bar{F}'$, elements of $C^\infty(S \times \mathbb{R}^m, \mathbb{R}^{\ell-1})$ are equivalent (which is denoted by $\bar{F} \sim \bar{F}'$) if there exists a diffeomorphism h of $S \times \mathbb{R}^m$ with the property $\bar{F}' = \bar{F} \circ h$.

One readily sees that 7.11 defines an equivalence relation on the space $C^\infty(S \times \mathbb{R}^m, \mathbb{R}^{\ell-1})$. This definition, which is motivated by economic considerations, is stronger than the standard version used in differential topology, although they are closely related (see [18, Chapter 3, Definition 1.1]).

This equivalence relation 7.11 defines equivalence classes that constitute a partition of the set $C^\infty(S \times \mathbb{R}^m, \mathbb{R}^{\ell-1})$. The number of these classes is infinite, with this partition being finer than the standard one.

The next result shows that aggregate demand functions possess a remarkably strong property which can be stated with the help of the equivalence relation.

Proposition 7.12. *All elements of $\tilde{\mathfrak{D}}$ are equivalent.*

In other words, all aggregate demand functions are equivalent. This property implies that very few elements of $C^\infty(S \times \mathbb{R}^m, \mathbb{R}^{\ell-1})$ are aggregate demand functions. Furthermore, all aggregate demand functions can be obtained from just *one* aggregate demand function through compositions with suitable diffeomorphisms of $S \times \mathbb{R}^m$.

Remark. The statement of Theorem 7.12 is true for arbitrary m, hence for $m = 1$, the case where one is simply dealing with an individual demand function. In this sense, 7.12 extends to any number of agents a property of individual demand functions.

7.4.4. The notion of stable mapping

Let then $\bar{F} \in C^\infty(S \times \mathbb{R}^m, \mathbb{R}^{\ell-1})$. It follows from the previous discussion that the most interesting mappings for any practical modeling purpose are those that remain equivalent, in the sense of 7.11, to the mappings $\bar{F}' \in C^\infty(S \times \mathbb{R}^m, \mathbb{R}^{\ell-1})$ when these belong to a neighborhood of $\bar{F}$. But for which topology?

The topology we use is the Whitney C^∞-topology which is the standard one in this function space (see the Mathematical Appendix (Math. Section 4) and the references included there). Let us briefly say that the convergence for this topology of the sequence (f_n) to f where f_n and f are functions defined on some Euclidean space, or, more generally, on *non-compact* manifolds, is a much stronger notion than uniform convergence, especially when dealing with convergence "at infinity," namely, outside compact subsets. The Whitney C^∞-topology is very fine indeed in the sense that it contains many open sets. It is then remarkable (and this makes this topology the most useful and convenient one) that despite its fineness, the space $C^\infty(\mathbb{R}^p, \mathbb{R}^q)$ endowed with this topology is nevertheless a Baire space, i.e., a topological space with the property that any countable intersection of dense open subsets is dense. Such an intersection is called a residual set. Therefore, in Baire spaces, residual sets are dense. In Baire spaces, the notion of residual set provides a convenient formulation of the idea of "large" subset.

We then propose the following definition:

Definition 7.13. A smooth mapping from $S \times \mathbb{R}^m$ into $\mathbb{R}^{\ell-1}$ is stable if there exists a neighborhood for the Whitney C^∞-topology such that any mapping in this neighborhood is equivalent, in the sense of 7.11, to the original mapping.

This definition is clearly the mathematical reformulation of the robustness idea. The empirical relevance of the econometric estimation of an aggregate demand function $\bar{F}$ depends crucially on whether the mapping $\bar{F}$ is stable or not.

Remark. The equivalence class $c\ell(\bar{F})$ of a stable mapping $\bar{F} \in C^\infty(S \times \mathbb{R}^m, \mathbb{R}^{\ell-1})$ is an open subset of $C^\infty(S \times \mathbb{R}^m, \mathbb{R}^{\ell-1})$, and conversely. Indeed, if $\bar{F}$ is stable, then by definition there exists an open neighborhood U of $\bar{F}$ in $C^\infty(S \times \mathbb{R}^m, \mathbb{R}^{\ell-1})$ contained in $c\ell(\bar{F})$. Let now $\bar{F}' \in c\ell(\bar{F})$. By definition of $c\ell(\bar{F})$, there exists a diffeomorphism h of B for which we have $\bar{F}' = \bar{F} \circ h$. Standard properties of the Whitney C^∞-topology imply that the set $U \circ h$ is open in $C^\infty(S \times \mathbb{R}^m, \mathbb{R}^{\ell-1})$ and contains $\bar{F}'$ (see, e.g., (Math 4.5)).

This set $U \circ h$ is clearly contained in $c\ell(F)$, which is therefore open as being a neighborhood of all its elements. The converse property follows from a similar line of reasoning.

This remark implies that the equivalence class $c\ell(\tilde{\mathfrak{D}})$ associated with the (equivalent) elements of $\tilde{\mathfrak{D}}$ is also an open subset of $C^\infty(S \times \mathbb{R}^m, \mathbb{R}^{\ell-1})$. The next result justifies, theoretically at least, the use of aggregate demand functions for the purpose of econometric analysis.

Proposition 7.14. *All aggregate demand functions $\bar{F} \in \tilde{\mathfrak{D}}$ are stable.*

Remark. The mathematical and economic significance of this result can be appreciated more easily if one knows that, depending on the dimensions of the spaces, the stable mappings can be very far from constituting a dense subset of $C^\infty(S \times \mathbb{R}^m, \mathbb{R}^{\ell-1})$. These circumstances have been studied by Mather [79] for the class of proper mappings (i.e., mappings for which the inverse image of every compact subset is compact); see also [18, Chapter 2, Section 6]. A direct application of Mather's conditions to our framework shows that the stable mappings cannot build a dense set for $m \geq 3, \ell \geq 8$ and $m = 2, \ell \geq 7$.

Proof of equivalence 7.12. Let $\bar{F}$ and $\bar{F}'$ be two elements in $\tilde{\mathfrak{D}}$. Let $\theta_{\bar{F}}$ and $\theta_{\bar{F}'}$ denote the diffeomorphisms of $S \times \mathbb{R}^m$ with $\mathbb{R}^\ell \times \mathbb{R}^{m-1}$ associated with $\bar{F}$ and $\bar{F}'$, respectively, by Lemma 7.3. The diagram on this page is easily made commutative by defining $h = \theta_{\bar{F}'}^{-1} \circ \theta_{\bar{F}}$, so that one has $\bar{F} = \bar{F}' \circ h$, where h is a diffeomorphism of $S \times \mathbb{R}^m$. $\qquad\square$

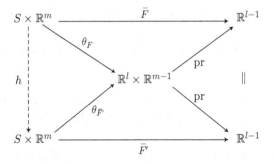

Proof of Stability 7.15. Let F be the aggregate demand function, the sum of the m individual demand functions $f_i : S \times \mathbb{R} \to \mathbb{R}^\ell$. Let $\bar{G}$ be a smooth mapping from $S \times \mathbb{R}^m$ into $\mathbb{R}^{\ell-1}$. Define the mapping $G = (\bar{G}, G^\ell)$, where G^ℓ is given by the formula,

$$G^\ell(p, w_1, \ldots, w_m) = \sum_i w_\ell - p_1 G^1 - \cdots - p_{\ell-1} G^{i-1}.$$

Now, define

$$\theta_{\bar{G}}(p, w_1, \ldots, w_m)$$
$$= (G(p, w_1, \ldots, w_m), u_1(f_1(p, w_1)), \ldots, u_{m-i}(f_{m-i}(p, w_{m-i}))).$$

The mapping $\bar{G} \to \theta_{\bar{G}}$ is clearly continuous for the Whitney C^∞-topology. We know that $\theta_{\bar{F}}$ a diffeomorphism 7.3. The set of diffeomorphisms from $S \times \mathbb{R}^m$ into $\mathbb{R}^\ell \times \mathbb{R}^{m-1}$ is open (Math 4.6). Therefore, there exists an open neighborhood W of $\bar{F}$ such that the mapping $\theta_{\bar{G}}$ is a diffeomorphism whenever $\bar{G}$ belongs to W. The diagram,

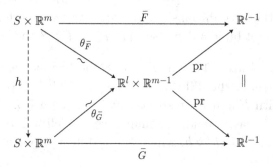

can be made commutative by considering the diffeomorphism $h :$ $S \times \mathbb{R}^m \to S \times \mathbb{R}^m$ defined by the formula $h = \theta_{\bar{G}}^{-1} \circ \theta_{\bar{F}}$. Consequently, we have $\bar{F} = \bar{G} \circ h$, hence $\bar{F}$ and $\bar{G}$ are equivalent for all $\bar{G} \in W$.

$\square$

Remark. The aggregate demand mapping $\bar{F}$, the product of a diffeomorphism with a projection, is a submersion (it would have been possible to establish this result through direct computations). Now, a submersion is stable in the sense of differential topology, a concept closely related if not identical to the one used in 7.11. This property makes the stability of aggregate demand a far less surprising property than it may have seemed at first sight.

7.5. The Class of Aggregate Excess Demand Functions

We have simply mentioned the Sonnenschein–Mantel–Debreu property that aggregate excess demand functions defined on compact subsets of the price set can be arbitrary. We shall show in this section that the behavior of aggregate excess demand functions, when prices tend to the boundary of the price set (namely tend either to zero or to infinity), which is neglected by the compactness assumption, indeed significantly restricts the set of aggregate excess demand functions among the class of mappings defined on the price set S and taking their values in the commodity space $\mathbb{R}^{\ell-1}$.

Let $\omega = (\omega_1, \omega_2, \ldots, \omega_m)$ represent a given economy, i.e., fixed initial endowments. Given $p \in S$, the excess demand mapping of this economy is the mapping $z : S \rightarrow \mathbb{R}^\ell$ defined by the formula,

$$z(p) = \sum_i (f_i(p, p \cdot \omega_i) - \omega_i).$$

We denote by $\bar{z} : S \rightarrow \mathbb{R}^{\ell-1}$ the mapping defined by the first $(\ell-1)$ co-ordinates of z. We have from Walras law

$$z^\ell(p) = -p_1 z^1(p) - \cdots - p_{\ell-1} z^{\ell-1}(p),$$

so that it is sufficient to consider the mapping $\bar{z} : S \rightarrow \mathbb{R}^{\ell-1}$ when dealing with mappings satisfying Walras law.

7.5.1. The set Excess

Let *Excess* denote the set of smooth mappings $\bar{z} : S \rightarrow \mathbb{R}^{\ell-1}$ where z is the aggregate excess demand function of some economy consisting of ℓ commodities and of an arbitrary number of consumers. We are going to show that the set of smooth aggregate excess demand mappings *Excess* is a subset *strictly* contained in the set of smooth mappings from S into $\mathbb{R}^{\ell-1}$. Furthermore, we shall show that this set is "small" in a specific sense for $\ell \geq 3$.

Remark. That there must exist restrictions on the class of aggregate excess demand mappings is obvious for at least the following two reasons: since equilibria always exist, $\bar{z}$ must have zeroes; furthermore, we know that individual demands $f_i(p, p \cdot \omega_i)$ are bounded from below for given ω_i, and $p \in S$, so that excess demands are also bounded from below. These two properties are not shared by every mapping from S into $\mathbb{R}^{\ell-\ell}$. The aim of this section is therefore to translate these restrictions in a precise statement about the degree of mappings that are closely related to excess demand functions.

7.5.2. The aggregate excess demand mapping

Lemma 7.16. *The aggregate excess demand mapping $z : S \to \mathbb{R}^{\ell}$ is proper.*

Proof. **Step 1.** We shall first establish the already mentioned property that z is bounded from below. Let ω_i be the initial endowments of consumer i. Then, for any $p \in S$, one has

$$u_i(f_i(p, p \cdot \omega_i)) \geq u_i(\omega_i).$$

Since every indifference surface is bounded from below, there exists $x_i^* \in \mathbb{R}^{\ell}$ with

$$x_i^* \leq f_i(p, p \cdot \omega_i) \quad \text{for every} \quad p \in S.$$

Consequently, $\Sigma f_i(p, p \cdot \omega_i,)$ and $z(p) = \Sigma f_i(p, p \cdot \omega_i) - \Sigma \omega_i$ are bounded from below for every $p \in S$.

Step 2. Define the set $J(\beta)$ as

$$J(\beta) = \{x \in \mathbb{R}^{\ell} | x^i \leq \beta^i, i = 1, 2, \ldots, \ell\}.$$

Let us prove that the inverse image $z^{-1}(J(\beta))$ is compact for any $\beta = (\beta^i) \in \mathbb{R}^{\ell}$.

For any $p \in z^{-1}(J(\beta))$, one gets

$$\sum f_i(p, p \cdot \omega_i) - \sum \omega_i \leq \beta,$$

which implies

$$\sum f_i(p, p \cdot \omega_i) \leq \beta + \sum \omega_i.$$

Since every $f_i(p, p \cdot \omega_i)$, is bounded from below by Step 1, every demand function is also bounded from above. Therefore, we have established existence of x_i^* and y_i^* in $\mathbb{R}^\ell$ which bound $f_i(p, p \cdot \omega_i)$, i.e.,

$$x_i^* \leq f_i(p, p \cdot \omega_i) \leq y_i^* \quad \text{for } p \in z^{-1}(J(\beta)).$$

Take for example $i = 1$. The set $\{x \in \mathbb{R}^\ell | x_1^* \leq x \leq y_1^*\}$ is compact. Its image by the continuous mapping $x \in \mathbb{R}^\ell \to \text{grad}_n u_1(x) \in S$ is compact. The relationship,

$$\text{grad}_n u_1[f_1(p, p \cdot \omega_1)] = p,$$

implies that the set $z^{-1}(J(\beta))$ is contained in the compact set $\text{grad}_n u_1[\{x \in \mathbb{R}^\ell | x_1^* \leq x \leq y_1^*\}]$, which straightforwardly implies that $z^{-1}(J(\beta))$ is compact. $\qquad\square$

The fact that the aggregate excess demand mapping $z : S \to \mathbb{R}^\ell$ is proper suggests using degree theory. Unfortunately, this is impossible because the sets S and $\mathbb{R}^\ell$ do not have the same dimension. A first attempt at overcoming this difficulty would be to consider $\bar{z} : S \to \mathbb{R}^{\ell-1}$ instead of z. But now, if the dimension requirement is satisfied, the mapping $z : S \to \mathbb{R}^{\ell-1}$ is not proper in general. This can be seen easily in the following example. Take $\ell = 2$ and consider the graph of the mapping $p_1 \to z^1(p_1, 1)$. This set is bounded from below, i.e., there exists x^{1*} such that $x^{1*} \leq z^1(p_1, 1)$ for $p_1 > 0$. Furthermore, from $p_1 z^1(p) + z^2(p) = 0$, one gets

$$p_1 z^1(p) = -z^2(p) \leq k,$$

where k is a constant, hence $z^1(p_1, 1) \leq k/p_1$. Take the compact set $K = [x^{1*}, k]$. Then for $p_1 > 1$, one gets $z^1(p_1, 1) \leq k$, hence $z^1(p_1, 1) \in K$. This proves the inclusion $[1, +\infty) \subset (z^1)^{-1}(K)$, so that $(z^1)^{-1}(K)$ cannot be compact. The lack of properness of the mapping $\bar{z}$ follows from the fact that one coordinate of z has been dropped. Therefore, the following approach aims at transforming $\bar{z}$

into a proper mapping by suitably taking into account the missing coordinate.

Definition of $j(\bar{z})$

More generally, let $\bar{z} : S \to \mathbb{R}^{\ell-1}$ be an arbitrary mapping where $\bar{z}(p) = (z^1(p), z^2(p), \ldots, z^{\ell-1}(p))$. Then, we define $j(\bar{z})$ by the formula,

$$j(\bar{z})(p) = ((1 + p_1)z^1(p), (1 + p_2)z^2(p), \ldots, (1 + p_{\ell-1})z^{\ell-1}(p)).$$

One sees readily from this formula that p is a zero of $\bar{z}$ if and only if it is a zero of $j(\bar{z})$. Therefore, if $\bar{z}$ corresponds to the aggregate excess demand of some economy, then $p \in S$ is an equilibrium price vector of this economy if and only if it is a zero of $j(\bar{z})$.

Properness of $j(\bar{z})$ for $\bar{z} \in$ Excess

Lemma 7.17. *If $\bar{z}$ corresponds to the aggregate excess demand function of an economy, then $j(\bar{z})$ is proper.*

Proof. Let K be a compact subset of $\mathbb{R}^{\ell-1}$. This set is bounded by $a^* = (a^i)$ and $b^* = (b^i)$ in $\mathbb{R}^{\ell-1}$, i.e., $a^i \leq x^i \leq b^i, i = 1, 2, \ldots, \ell - 1$, $x \in K$.

Therefore, the following inequality holds true for every $p \in (j(\bar{z}))^{-1}(K)$:

$$a^i \leq (1 + p_i)z^i(p) \leq b^i, \quad i = 1, 2, \ldots, \ell - 1. \tag{1}$$

This implies

$$z^i(p) \leq \frac{b^i}{1 + p_i} \leq b_i, \quad i = 1, 2, \ldots, \ell - 1, \tag{2}$$

i.e., $z^i(p) \leq b^i$, hence

$$z^i(p) + p_i z^i(p) \leq b_i + p_i z^i(p). \tag{3}$$

Combined with (1), this yields,

$$a^i \leq (1 + p_i)z^i(p) \leq b^i + p_i z^i(p),$$

hence

$$-p_i z^i(p) \leq b^i - a^i = c^i, \quad i = 1, \ldots, \ell - 1. \tag{4}$$

These $(\ell - 1)$ inequalities imply that $z^\ell(p)$ is bounded from above for any $p \in (j(\bar{z}))^{-1}(K)$ because one has

$$z^\ell(p) = -\sum_{i=1}^{\ell-1} p_i z^i(p) \leq \sum_{i=1}^{\ell-1} c^i = c^\ell.$$

We have therefore proved that $(j(\bar{z}))^{-1}(K)$ is a subset of the compact set $z^{-1}(J(c))$ which is compact. The end of the argument is straightforward. □

7.5.3. Degree theory applied to $j(\bar{z})$

Since $j(\bar{z}) : S \to \mathbb{R}^{\ell-1}$ is proper while S and $\mathbb{R}^{\ell-1}$ have the same dimension, it is possible to apply degree theory to classify the mapping $j(\bar{z})$ according to the degree, the computation of which proceeds by first taking a regular value and then by looking at its inverse image.

Lemma 7.18. *The point $0 \in \mathbb{R}^{\ell-1}$ is a regular value of $j(\bar{z})$ if and only if it is a regular value of $\bar{z}$.*

Proof. Let $p \in S$ be a zero of $\bar{z}$. The Jacobian matrix of $j(\bar{z})$ at p is equal to

$$\left((1 + p_i)\frac{\partial z^i}{\partial p_j} + \delta_{ij} z^i \right)_{i,j},$$

where $\delta_{ij} = 1$ if $i = j$, 0 otherwise. From $z^i(p) = 0$ for every i, it follows that the Jacobian determinant of $j(\bar{z})$ is equal to $(1 + p_1)$ $(1 + p_2) \ldots (1 + p_{\ell-1})$ multiplied by the Jacobian determinant of $\bar{z}$. □

Consider now two economies ω and ω' differing only by their initial endowments, everything else like preferences, commodities, etc., being held constant. Let $\bar{z}_\omega$ and $\bar{z}_{\omega'}$ be the mapping associated with these economies ω and ω'. We then have the following:

Lemma 7.19. *The proper mappings $j(\bar{z}_\omega)$ and $j(\bar{z}_{\omega'})$ are properly homotopic.*

Proof. For $t \in [0, 1]$, define

$$\omega(t) = (1 - t)\omega + t\omega'.$$

Let $F : S \times [0, 1] \to \mathbb{R}^{\ell-1}$ be defined by the formula,

$$F(p, t) = j(\bar{z}_{\omega(t)})(p).$$

Clearly, the mapping F is proper and defines a proper homotopy between $j(\bar{z}_\omega)$ and $j(\bar{z}_{\omega'})$ □

Corollary 7.20. *The mappings $j(\bar{z}_\omega)$ and $j(\bar{z}_{\omega'})$ have the same degree.*

Corollary 7.20 implies that to compute the degree of $j(\bar{z}_\omega)$ (either the modulo 2 or the Brouwer degree), one simply has to choose a convenient ω. A good candidate is obviously the ω Pareto optimum.

Proposition 7.21. *The modulo 2 (resp. Brouwer) degree of $j(\bar{z})$ for $\bar{z} \in$ Excess is equal to $+1$ (resp. $(-1)^{\ell-1}$) (assuming that S is identified with $\mathbb{R}^{\ell-1}_{++}$ and $\mathbb{R}^{\ell-1}$ is endowed with its natural orientation).*

Proof. Let ω be Pareto optimal; then from 7.20 and from the invariance of the degree by homotopy, the mappings $j(\bar{z})$ and $j(\bar{z}_\omega)$ have the same degree. Now, ω, being Pareto optimal, is a regular economy. Consequently, $0 \in \mathbb{R}^{\ell-1}$ is a regular value of the mapping $\bar{z}_\omega : S \to \mathbb{R}^{\ell-1}$, hence of $j(\bar{z}_\omega)$. To compute the modulo 2 degree of $j(\bar{z}_\omega)$, one simply counts the number of elements of the inverse image $j(\bar{z}_\omega)^{-1}(0) = (\bar{z}_\omega)^{-1}(0)$; this number is equal to one. To compute the Brouwer degree of $j(\bar{z}_\omega)$, it is necessary to take into account the sign of the Jacobian determinant of $j(\bar{z}_\omega)$ at the unique equilibrium.   □

Remark. The modulo 2 degree splits the set of smooth proper mappings from S into $\mathbb{R}^{\ell-1}$ into two subsets, one consisting of mappings of degree 0, the other of mappings of degree 1. These two subsets are comparable in size (although no rigorous definition of the size is proposed here). Therefore, we have established that the set $j(Excess)$ belongs to only one of these two classes, which therefore provides a measure of the restrictions implied by the fact that a mapping is an aggregate excess demand function. Parenthetically, the construction through the mapping j does not induce any extraneous restrictions on the mappings from S into $\mathbb{R}^{\ell-1}$. In fact, any mapping from S into $\mathbb{R}^{\ell-1}$ can be written in the form $j(\bar{z})$ for a unique $\bar{z}$. We also mention that if the number of commodities ℓ is greater than 3, then the size of the set $j(Excess)$ is small in some properly defined sense. This result requires switching to the Brouwer degree. We know by 7.21 that $j(Excess)$ is contained in the class of mappings having Brouwer degree $(-1)^{\ell-1}$. The question is: For what values of the Brouwer degree are the associated classes non-empty?

If $\ell = 2$, then one is reduced to studying the class of smooth mappings $\psi : \mathbb{R} \to \mathbb{R}$. Properness amounts to having $\lim_{t \to \pm\infty} |\psi(t)| = +\infty$. The definition of the Brouwer degree and Rolle's theorem readily imply that the degree can only take the values $+1, -1$ and 0, values which are indeed obtained for suitable mappings. In this case, the Brouwer degree is not a significant improvement on the topological degree; it is indeed impossible to say that, in this setting, the set $j(Excess)$ is "small."

The picture becomes significantly different for $\ell \geq 3$. Let us start with $\ell = 3$, so that one is reduced to studying smooth mappings $\psi : \mathbb{R}^2 \to \mathbb{R}^2$. We are going to construct for any $n \geq 1$ a smooth proper mapping of degree n. Let us identify $\mathbb{R}^2$ with the complex plane $\mathbb{C}$ and let us consider the mapping $f : z \to z^n$. This mapping is easily seen to be proper. Let us compute the Jacobian determinant $J = ((\partial f_x/\partial x)(\partial f_y/\partial y) - (\partial f_x/\partial y)(\partial f_y/\partial x))$ of f at $z = x + iy$. Using the complex variable formulation, the Jacobian determinant turns out to be equal to the imaginary part of $\overline{(\partial f/\partial x)} \cdot (\partial f/\partial y)$ (where $\overline{(\partial f/\partial x)}$ denotes the complex conjugate of $(\partial f/\partial x)$). But, we have

$$\frac{\partial f}{\partial x} = \frac{\partial}{\partial x}(z^n) = nz^{n-1}\frac{\partial z}{\partial x} = nz^{n-1}\frac{\partial}{\partial x}(x+iy) = nz^{n-1},$$

$$\frac{\partial f}{\partial y} = \frac{\partial}{\partial y}(z^n) = nz^{n-1}\frac{\partial z}{\partial y} = nz^{n-1}\frac{\partial}{\partial y}(x+iy) = inz^{n-1},$$

which imply

$$j = \left(n\bar{z}^{n-1}\right)\left(nz^{n-1}\right) = n^2|z|^{2n-2},$$

which is positive for $z \neq 0$. Consequently, $z \neq 0$ is never a critical point. Furthermore, the sign of J is always strictly positive. There are n nth roots of any non-zero complex number, and since J is positive at these roots, the degree is therefore equal to n. To obtain mappings of degree $-n$ (with $n > 0$), it is sufficient to compose $z \to z^n$ with the symmetry with respect to the real axis (the mapping $z \to \bar{z}$), which changes the sign of the Jacobian determinant.

For $\ell > 3$, one is reduced to studying mappings $\psi : \mathbb{R}^{\ell-1} \to \mathbb{R}^{\ell-1}$. By identifying $\mathbb{R}^{\ell-1}$ with $\mathbb{R}^2 \times \mathbb{R}^{\ell-3}$, one can use the previous argument and consider the Cartesian product of the identity mapping on $\mathbb{R}^{\ell-3}$ with the mapping $z \to z^n$ (resp. $z \to \bar{z}^n$) on $\mathbb{R}^2$ to obtain a smooth proper mapping of degree $n > 0$ (resp. $-n < 0$). Therefore, for $\ell \geq 3$, there exists a *countable* number of *non-empty* classes of mappings defined by the integer value of their Brouwer degree. Invariance of the degree through homotopy (in this regard, see also Hopf's theorem as, for example, in Milnor [29]) hints at the fact (that we shall not elaborate upon here) that these classes have comparable sizes. This means that the set $j(Excess)$ is contained in *one* element of a countable partition of the set of smooth proper mappings from S into $\mathbb{R}^{\ell-1}$. In this sense, the set $j(Excess)$, and hence the set *Excess* itself, is small.

7.5.4. An alternative proof of the existence of equilibria

Proposition 7.21 says that for any $\bar{z} \in Excess$, the modulo 2 degree of $j(\bar{z})$ is equal to $+1$. The proof of this property relies on the concept of Pareto optimality, namely, on the fact that there is uniqueness of equilibrium at a Pareto optimum and that Pareto optima are regular economies, hence regular values of the mapping $j(\bar{z})$. With the same ingredients, we proved existence of equilibria by showing that the natural projection $\pi : E \rightarrow \Omega$ is onto because its degree is non-zero. It is possible to derive from 7.21 an existence result directly in terms of $j(\bar{z})$, therefore avoiding the detour through the equilibrium manifold and the natural projection. The proof goes as follows: Since the degree of $j(\bar{z})$ is equal to one, the mapping $j(\bar{z}) : S \rightarrow \mathbb{R}^{\ell-1}$ is onto, hence the inverse image $j(\bar{z})^{-1}(0)$ is non-empty.

7.6. Conclusion

We have seen in this chapter that imposing fixed total resources does not change the basic features of equilibrium analysis viewed as a study of the natural projection. In doing this study, we have used the concepts of singular and regular values and degree theory. This has already led us to a couple of important properties of the natural projection. But, none of these tools has exploited a remarkable feature of the equilibrium manifold, namely, its fiber space structure. This topic is developed in the next two chapters. It is in particular quite remarkable that the most natural setting for developing the mathematical tools that take advantage of the fiber space structure of the equilibrium manifold requires fixed total resources.

Chapter 8

The Natural Projection
and Envelope Theory

A large part of the results of the previous two chapters can be summarized by saying that equilibrium prices do not show significant qualitative changes as long as the initial endowments vary within the same connected component of the set of regular economies. Discontinuities in terms of prices as well as changes in the number of equilibria can be observed only when initial endowments are varied in order to come across singular economies. The main goal of qualitative comparative statics is therefore one of improving our understanding of the nature of these discontinuities of the price system. This requires a thorough investigation of the singularities of the natural projection, which goes much further than the questions investigated in Chapters 6 and 7 where only the most elementary tools of singularity theory had to be used. More precisely, the properties of equilibria that have been stated so far are consequences of the economic interpretation of such general mathematical concepts as those of critical points, singular values or degree, applied to the natural projection. Almost no use has been made of more specific features among which the fiber bundle structure of the equilibrium manifold should undoubtedly play a prominent role.

We shall show in this chapter that the mathematical tool that will properly exploit the fiber bundle structure is envelope theory. Projecting the fibers of the equilibrium manifold in the space of economies yields a family of linear manifolds. This family of linear subspaces can be identified to some extent with those subspaces having the right dimension that are tangent to a suitable manifold, the envelope, which therefore carries all the relevant properties of this family of subspaces. More precisely, the classical theory of plane curve envelopes suffices to handle the two-agent and two-commodity case for fixed total resources. The more general case for any number of commodities and agents necessitates the extension of envelope theory made by Thom [91]. The main definitions and concepts of envelope theory are explained in the mathematical appendix. A thorough treatment of classical envelope theory from the point of view of singularity theory is available in Bruce and Giblin [55]. As in Chapter 7, total resources are assumed to be fixed and equal to some given vector $r \in \mathbb{R}^\ell$, unless the contrary is explicitly specified.

8.1. A Simple Example: The Case of Two Commodities and Two Agents

Before developing the study of the natural projection in the general setting of any number of agents and commodities, which requires a rather abstract version of envelope theory, let us begin with the simplest case that we have already seen in Chapter 3 and that is defined by two agents and two commodities. As we already mentioned, its main advantage is to need only the classical theory of envelopes of lines in the plane.

8.1.1. The Edgeworth–Bowley revisited box

Let us recall some useful notation. The vector $r = (r^1, r^2) \in \mathbb{R}^2$ represents the total resources. The set of economies $\Omega(r)$ has dimension two and can be identified with a plane. It can be parameterized by two coordinates: the coordinates of ω_1 suffice to locate any economy $\omega = (\omega_1, \omega_2)$, given the relationship $\omega_2 = r - \omega_1$.

We of course recognize the setup introduced in Chapter 3, but there is however a significant difference. We do not impose any more that initial endowments and consumption bundles are strictly positive. These can be either positive, negative or even equal to zero. Nevertheless, the interpretation given in Chapter 3 holds also for this more general case and we are going to use it quite freely. In particular, if $\omega = (\omega_1, \omega_2)$ is a point in the plane representing initial endowments, the price vector $p = (p_1, 1) \in S$ is an equilibrium price vector associated with ω if and only if the line perpendicular to that price vector $p = (p_1, 1)$ and going through the point $\omega = (\omega_1, \omega_2)$ is tangent at the same point $x = (x_1, x_2)$ to the indifference curves of each one of the two agents.

8.1.2. The one-parameter family of lines

The set of Pareto optima $P(r)$ consists of the tangency points, also known as the contact points, of the indifference curves of the two agents. This set $P(r)$ is a one-dimensional submanifold of $\Omega(r)$ diffeomorphic to $\mathbb{R}$; in other words, the set of Pareto optima is a smooth unbounded connected curve and as such can be parameterized by the set of real numbers. One associates with every point M representing a Pareto optimum the tangent $\Delta(M)$ to the indifference curves passing through this point M. This defines a *one-parameter family* of lines that we are going to call the family $\mathfrak{F}$. This leads us to envelope theory at once.

The family $\mathfrak{F}$, i.e., the set of lines $\Delta(M)$, possesses an envelope, namely, a curve (possibly with singularities) such that the tangents to this curve are precisely the lines belonging to the family $\mathfrak{F}$.

8.1.3. Envelope and singular economies

Of paramount importance is the relationship between the fibers of the equilibrium manifold $E(r)$ and the one-parameter family of lines $\mathfrak{F}$ just defined. Each fiber contains a unique no-trade equilibrium. The projection of this no-trade equilibrium is a Pareto optimum. The image of the fiber through the natural projection is simply the tangent line to the indifference curves at the Pareto optimum (Figure 8.1).

We recall that an economy ω is singular if it is the image under the natural projection of a critical equilibrium, an equilibrium being critical if and only if the tangent plane to $E(r)$ at this equilibrium is vertical. This geometric property can be understood analytically by saying that the equilibrium price vector is a multiple "root" of the

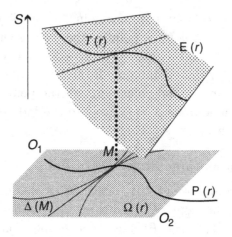

Figure 8.1:   The line $\Delta(M)$ and the equilibrium manifold $E(r)$

equilibrium equation. More precisely, let us consider the equilibrium equation where the unknown is p, namely

$$\bar{z}(p,\omega) = \sum \bar{f}_i(p, p \cdot \omega_i) - \sum \bar{\omega}_i = 0.$$

By definition, an equilibrium price vector of this economy is a solution of the equation $\bar{z}(p,\omega) = 0$. Also by definition, this solution possesses an order of multiplicity at least equal to two if the rank of the linear part of the Taylor expansion of $\bar{z}(\cdot,\omega)$ at p is not maximal. This condition is indeed equivalent to the fact that (p,ω) is a critical equilibrium because both conditions mean that $\det(D\bar{z}/Dp)$ is equal to zero. In other words, one can characterize a critical equilibrium (p,ω) by the property that there exists an equilibrium (p',ω) "infinitely close" to (p,ω). Consequently, ω is a singular economy if and only if the equilibrium equation has a multiple root.

These considerations enable us to relate the set of singular economies $\Sigma(r)$ to the one-parameter family of lines $\mathfrak{F}$. Recall that the price vector $p = (p_1, 1) \in S$ is an equilibrium price vector associated with $\omega \in \Omega(r)$ if there exists a line $\Delta(M) \in \mathfrak{F}$ perpendicular to the price vector p and containing the point ω. The economy ω is singular if, as we have just seen, the equilibrium equation has at least a double root, which can be interpreted in the following way: there exist two lines, namely $\Delta(M)$ and another one, $\Delta(M')$, "infinitely close" to $\Delta(M)$, both containing ω. This condition can be interpreted within the framework of envelope theory as saying that ω is a characteristic point of the line $\Delta(M)$. Therefore, the set of singular economies $\Sigma(r)$ is simply identical to the set of characteristic points of the lines belonging to the family $\mathfrak{F}$, i.e., to the envelope of this family.

8.1.4. Applications to the geometry of $\Sigma(r)$

It is a general property of envelopes of lines that their only generic singularities are cusps and self-intersections. Furthermore, at any regular point of the envelope, i.e., at any point where a tangent to $\Sigma(r)$ can be defined, the curve $\Sigma(r)$ is locally the boundary of a convex set. This can be illustrated as follows. Let L be a regular point of $\Sigma(r)$. The convexity property simply means that every circle centered in L with radius small enough is decomposed by $\Sigma(r)$ into two subsets (the connected components of the complement of $\Sigma(r)$ in the circle), of which one is convex. Geometrically speaking, one finds the equilibria associated with an economy ω by drawing the tangents through ω to the curve $\Sigma(r)$. The local convexity property of $\Sigma(r)$ enables one to monitor the variation of the number of equilibria when ω varies in the set of economies $\Omega(r)$. Everything works locally as if $\Sigma(r)$ was itself the boundary of a circle. If ω lies inside the convex set, there exists no tangent from ω to this part of $\Sigma(r)$; on the other hand, if ω is taken outside the convex set (assuming one remains close enough to $\Sigma(r)$), one can find two distinct tangents. These two tangents coincide when ω is taken on $\Sigma(r)$. Therefore, the set of singular economies $\Sigma(r)$ is exactly the set of economies for which the number of equilibria is not locally constant. Furthermore, the number of equilibria associated with ω increases by two units when ω enters the convex part delimited by $\Sigma(r)$ at a regular point. Going the other way reverses the process: the number of equilibria then decreases by two units.

One can apply this remark to the computation of the number of equilibria of an economy by going from one connected component of the set of regular economies $\mathcal{R}(r)$ to the next one. It suffices to start with the component containing the set of Pareto optima for which we already know that the equilibrium is unique.

8.1.5. The number and the determinateness of equilibria

(A) Consider first the case where the number of equilibria is constant over all of $\Omega(r)$. This constant must be equal to one because equilibrium is unique at a Pareto optimum. In other words, this constancy hypothesis is equivalent to the uniqueness of the equilibrium price vector for every economy. This property surprisingly implies that the equilibrium price vector itself is *constant* over all of $\Omega(r)$.

Let us assume the contrary and, therefore, let us consider two *distinct* equilibrium price vectors associated with two economies that are evidently *distinct* from each other because of the uniqueness assumption. Let us show that this leads to a contradiction. To these economies and their equilibria there must correspond two distinct lines belonging to the family $\mathfrak{F}$. Moreover, these lines are not parallel because they are perpendicular to price vectors which are assumed to be distinct. Therefore, these two lines must intersect at a point ω which has to be located at a finite distance in the plane $\Omega(r)$. Therefore, this economy ω possesses two distinct equilibrium price vectors, which contradicts the uniqueness assumption, and ends this part of the proof. Consequently, the equilibrium price vector is constant and does not depend on the economies in $\Omega(r)$. Note, however, that this does not imply any restriction on the value of the equilibrium price.

(B) Consider now the alternative assumption, namely, that the number of equilibria is *not constant*. This readily implies that there exists an economy which possesses at least two equilibrium price vectors. We recall that the set of singular economies $\Sigma(r)$ is the set of points where the number of equilibria considered as a function of ω is not locally constant. This set $\Sigma(r)$, which is determined by this function, cannot be empty as a result of the multiplicity assumption (otherwise the number of equilibria being everywhere locally constant would be constant and therefore equal to one!).

The family of tangents to $\Sigma(r)$ then defines the family of lines $\mathfrak{F}$. Since knowing that this family is all that is actually required to determine the equilibrium price vectors associated with any economy ω in the plane $\Omega(r)$, it turns out that the knowledge of the number of equilibria for every economy is *sufficient* to determine quantitatively and accurately these equilibria for every economy.

8.1.6. Global properties of economies depending on the number of equilibria

The previous result does not close the subject of the global properties of sets of economies defined in relationship to the number of their equilibria. Indeed, the function describing the number of equilibria is evidently far from being totally arbitrary. We already know that it takes the value one on the connected component of the set of regular economies that contains the whole set of Pareto optima. Before going any further, it might be interesting to point out that the sets defined through singularities of mappings, which include envelopes, do possess important global properties. The already mentioned article by Thom [91] describes some of these global properties; one can also consult the more elementary article by Sasaki [84] for the special case of envelopes of lines in the (projective) plane. These results clearly suggest existence of global properties for sets of economies defined in relationship to the number of their equilibria.

8.1.7. The set of economies with multiple equilibria

In order to study sets of economies with a given number of equilibria, the most convenient construction is to introduce a way for parallel lines to intersect, which is always possible provided one works in the projective plane. A projective line is nothing but a standard line (one says *affine*) to which a point at infinity has been added. Let $P\Omega(r)$ denote the projective plane associated with $\Omega(r)$.

A convenient analytical way of describing the projective plane is to use homogeneous coordinates (x, y, t). The coordinates (x, y, t) and (x', y', t') represent the same point of the projective plane if there exists a real number λ satisfying $x' = \lambda x, y' = \lambda y$ and $t' = \lambda t$.

A projective line is described by a linear equation of the type $ax + by + ct = 0$. The equation of the line at infinity can simply be written $t = 0$.

Recall that $\Delta(M)$ denotes the tangent at M to the indifference curves through M, provided that M represents a Pareto optimum. Let us consider $P\Delta(M) = \Delta(M) \cup \{\infty\}$, the projective line associated with $\Delta(M)$. We recall that $P(r)$ denote the set of Pareto optima. Pick the point $M \in P(r)$ arbitrarily. Let $M' \in P(r)$ be distinct from M. The line $P\Delta(M)$ intersects the set of Pareto optima $P(r)$ only in M. This implies that M' cannot belong to the line $P\Delta(M)$. Consequently, the line $P\Delta(M')$ is distinct from the line $P\Delta(M)$. Let $\theta(M')$ be the necessarily unique intersection point of the lines $P\Delta(M)$ and $P\Delta(M')$. This construction defines a mapping θ on the complement of M in the set of Pareto optima $P(r)$, a mapping taking its values in $P\Delta(M)$ (Figure 8.2). A simple computation of the coordinates of the intersection point enables one to check straightforwardly the continuity of the mapping θ. The most important result of envelope theory characterizes the envelope as the set consisting of the characteristic points, a characteristic point being, loosely speaking, the intersection point of two infinitely close lines of the family. This property of the characteristic points enables one to continuously extend the mapping θ to the set of

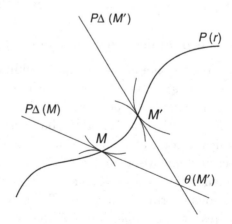

Figure 8.2:   Lines $P\Delta M$ and $P(\Delta(M'))$ and their intersection point

Pareto optima $P(r)$. Let N be the unique characteristic point of the projective line $P\Delta(M)$ (this point is unique for the following reason: the line $P\Delta(M)$ cannot be stationary, otherwise all its points would be part of the envelope $\Sigma(r)$, hence singular economies, which contradicts the fact that all Pareto optima are regular economies); it is the limit of the intersection $P\Delta(M) \cap P\Delta(M')$ when the point $M' \in P(r) \setminus M$ tends to M, which implies the continuity property of θ at M. Therefore, it suffices to define $\theta(M) = N$ for the extension to be continuous.

Let us recall that the set of Pareto optima $P(r)$ is diffeomorphic to $\mathbb{R}$, hence pathconnected. Since the image of a pathconnected set by a continuous mapping is pathconnected, the image set $\theta(P(r))$ is also pathconnected.

Let us now show that $\theta(P(r))$ can be identified with the set of economies with multiple equilibria belonging to the line $P\Delta(M)$ (provided that one takes into account the order of multiplicity of all possible equilibria). Note that the economies at infinity are now considered on the same basis as the other economies. Let ω belong to $\theta(P(r))$. There are two possibilities: either ω is a characteristic point of $P\Delta(M)$, in which case this corresponds to an equilibrium with an order of multiplicity larger than or equal to two, or ω is the intersection of two (projective) lines $P\Delta(M)$ and $P\Delta(M')$ where M and M' are distinct. If the equilibrium prices associated with $P\Delta(M)$ and $P\Delta(M')$ are distinct, then ω possesses at least two equilibria; otherwise, the equilibrium price still has an order of multiplicity at least equal to two. Therefore, the set of economies with multiple equilibria, which has been identified with $\theta(P(r))$, is pathconnected as the image of a pathconnected set by a continuous mapping.

Let now ω and ω' be two economies having multiple equilibria. If ω and ω' belong to the same line $P\Delta(M)$, one can readily apply the connectedness property of $\theta(P(r))$ to link ω and ω' by a continuous path. Otherwise, there exists at least one line $P\Delta(M)$ (i.e., belonging to the family $\mathfrak{F}$) through ω and another one $P\Delta(M')$ through ω'. Let ω'' be the unique intersection point of these two lines: the economy ω'' possesses two distinct equilibria. Then, there exist continuous paths joining ω'' to ω and ω', respectively, and contained in the set of economies with multiple equilibria of $P\Delta(M)$ and $P\Delta(M')$, respectively. This yields a continuous path joining ω to ω' and belonging to the set of economies with multiple equilibria.

Remark. This connectedness property is not true in general if stated in the framework of the affine space $\Omega(r)$ (i.e., without the introduction of economies at infinity).

8.1.8. The set of economies with unique equilibrium

We are now going to show that the set of regular economies possessing a unique equilibrium can be identified with the connected component of the set of regular economies $\mathcal{R}(r)$ that contains the set of Pareto optima $P(r)$. We already know that there is uniqueness in this set. We claim that equilibria are multiple as soon as one takes economies in the other components of the set of regular economies $\mathcal{R}(r)$. But, contrary to the previous results that extend to any number of agents and commodities, this characterization of the set of economies with a unique equilibrium is known to be true only in the case of two agents (and any number of commodities). The general case remains purely conjectural at this stage.

Let us show that the set of economies that belong to the line $\Delta(M)$ and have a unique equilibrium is pathconnected. We recall that the only connected subsets of the line (identified with the set of real numbers $\mathbb{R}$) or of the circle are intervals. Therefore, it suffices to show that the set we investigate is an interval of $\Delta(M)$. We start by considering the image set $\theta(P(r)) = \Im(\theta)$. We already know that it is a connected subset of the projective line $P\Delta(M)$. The projective line $P\Delta(M)$ is homeomorphic to a circle and, as such, can be identified with a circle. The only pathconnected subsets of the circle being the intervals, this implies that $\theta(P(r))$ is also an interval of $P\Delta(M)$. The complement of $\mathrm{Im}(\theta)$ in $P\Delta(M)$, i.e., the subset of $P\Delta(M)$ consisting of economies with a unique equilibrium, is still an interval (being the complement of an interval). Once the point at infinity has been removed, this set defines a subset of $\Delta(M)$ that is an interval of $\Delta(M)$ if and only if the point at infinity is either a boundary point of $\Im(\theta)$ or belongs to $\Im(\theta)$. To establish that this is actually the case, we are going to rely on an argument using the Brouwer degree of the natural projection.

Consider the line $\Delta(M)$; let p be the price vector that supports the Pareto optimal allocation M. Now, let ω describe this line $\Delta(M)$. The equilibrium (p, ω) describes the fiber defined by (p, w_1, w_2) and parameterized by ω_1^1. The Jacobian determinant $J(p, \omega)$ for (p, ω) in this fiber is a linear function $A + B\omega_1^1$ of ω_1^1. This function takes the value zero at the characteristic point of the line $\Delta(M)$. This characteristic point is actually at infinity if B is equal to 0, in which case the point at infinity belongs to $\Im(\theta)$. Now, if B is different from 0, the coordinate of the characteristic point is defined by $\omega_1^1 = -A/B$. Therefore, for $\omega_1^1 > -A/B$ if B is >0, and $\omega_1^1 < -A/B$ if B is <0, we have $\det J(p, \omega) > 0$. This implies that if ω is a regular economy and satisfies these requirements, the economy ω necessarily possesses at least two equilibria p' and p'' with strictly negative Jacobian determinants $\det J(p', \omega)$ and $\det J(p'', \omega)$ in order for the Brouwer degree of the mapping $j(\bar{z})$ (where $\bar{z}$ denotes the aggregate excess demand mapping for the economy ω, while $j(\bar{z})$ has been defined in Section 7.5.2), to be equal to -1. By having ω_1^1 tend to infinity while satisfying the above conditions, one gets to the point at infinity of $P\Delta(M)$ which, therefore, necessarily belongs to the closure of $\text{Im}(\theta)$.

We can now establish from all the preceding developments the pathconnectedness of the set of regular economies with a unique equilibrium. Let ω and ω' be two economies belonging to this set. Let p (resp. p') be the equilibrium price vector associated with ω (resp. ω'). Let M(resp. M') be the equilibrium allocation corresponding to (p, ω) (resp. (p', ω')) and let $\Delta(M)$(resp. $\Delta(M')$) be the tangent at M(resp. M') to the indifference curves through M(resp. M'). Now, the economy identified with M is regular and possesses a unique equilibrium. Therefore, the interval $[M, \omega]$ is contained in the set of regular economies with a unique equilibrium that belongs to $\Delta(M)$, and therefore defines a continuous arc in the space of regular economies with a unique equilibrium linking ω to M. It is the same for ω' and M'. All that remains to be done is to find a path linking M and M'. The set of Pareto optima $P(r)$ itself, being pathconnected and contained in the set of regular economies with a unique equilibrium, defines a suitable path joining M to M'.

8.2. Envelope Theory and the General Equilibrium Model

8.2.1. A family of linear manifolds

We are going to extend to an arbitrary space of economies $\Omega(r)$ the definition of the one-parameter family that we have used in the $(\ell, m) = (2, 2)$ case. To do this, it is convenient to define first the linear manifolds that correspond to the lines in the plane and then, in a second step, to specify those linear manifolds that are suitable among all those that are possible, this part being analogous to the choice of the family $\mathfrak{F}$ among the lines in the plane.

Let us recall that the vector $b = (p, w_1, \ldots, w_m) \in S \times \mathbb{R}^m$ defines a price vector $p \in S$ as well as the income $w_i \in \mathbb{R}$ of the ith agent, with i varying from 1 to m. Since total resources are fixed, the accounting relation,

$$p \cdot r = w_1 + w_2 + \cdots + w_m,$$

is assumed to be satisfied.

Definition 8.1. We denote by $H(r)$ the hyperplane of the set $S \times \mathbb{R}^m$ of price–income vectors that is defined by the equation $p \cdot r = w_1 + w_2 + \cdots + w_m$.

Definition 8.2. For every $b \in H(r)$, the linear manifold $V(b) \subset (\mathbb{R}^\ell)^m$ is defined by the equations:

$$\sum_i \omega_i^k = r^k \quad \text{with} \quad k = 1, 2, \ldots, \ell,$$

$$p \cdot \omega_i = w_i \quad \text{with} \quad i = 1, 2, \ldots, m.$$

It is easy to check that $V(b)$ is indeed a subset of $\Omega(r)$ since b belongs to $H(r)$. For $(\ell, m) = (2, 2), V(b)$ is just the budget line of the plane $\Omega(r)$ associated with the price vector p and the incomes w_1 and w_2.

Remark. The relationship between $V(b)$ and the fibers of the equilibrium manifold $E(r)$ is straightforward and does not require any further comments.

We now have to select a subset of the set of manifolds $V(b)$. The idea is the following one: the vector $b \in H(r)$ parameterizes the manifolds $V(b)$, but there are too many of these manifolds for our purpose. We are therefore going to consider only those manifolds $V(b)$ for b in a suitable subset of $H(r)$. In the case of two goods and two agents, this subset of $H(r)$ is simply the set of triples (p, w_1, w_2) that satisfy the relationship,

$$f_1(p, w_1) + f_2(p, w_2) = r,$$

i.e., the set $B(r)$. Hence the generalization:

Definition 8.3. The family $\mathfrak{F}$ is the set of linear manifolds $V(b)$ parameterized by b belonging to the subset $B(r)$ of $H(r)$.

Once a family of submanifolds of $\Omega(r)$ such as $\mathfrak{F}$ is available, and provided that some technical conditions are verified (see the Mathematical Appendix, or Thom's paper), it is possible to work out a notion of the envelope associated with this family. In fact, two distinct notions of envelopes coexist: the first one is known as the source envelope; the second one corresponds to the more traditional idea of an envelope.

The main theme of this section is to extend to arbitrary dimensions the relationship between the set of singular economies $\Sigma(r)$ and the envelope of the family $\mathfrak{F}$ and to study a few consequences of this relationship. But, beforehand, we have to check several technical conditions.

8.2.2. Envelope theory and the family $\mathfrak{F}$

Let $V(b)$ be the linear submanifold of $\Omega(r)$ associated with the parameter b varying (in a first step) within the set $H(r)$. Let G denote the graph of the correspondence that associates $V(b)$ with b.

It is easy to check that G is a smooth submanifold of $H(r) \times \Omega(r)$. Let $\Phi : G \to H(r)$ and $\Pi : G \to \Omega(r)$ be the restrictions to G

of the natural projections on the coordinate spaces $H(r)$ and $\Omega(r)$, respectively, of the Cartesian product $H(r) \times \Omega(r)$. The mapping Φ is a submersion (i.e., the linear tangent mapping to Φ at any point of G is surjective).

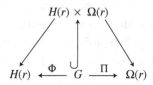

Now let $\bar{E}(r) = \Phi^{-1}(B(r))$ denote the inverse image by Φ of the parameter set $B(r)$, the subset of $H(r)$ defined by the price–income equilibria associated with the total resources $r \in \mathbb{R}^{\ell}$. Clearly, $\bar{E}(r)$ is generated by the set $(b, V(b))$ when b varies in $B(r)$. Using Thom's [91] terminology, we say:

Definition 8.4. The source envelope of the family $\mathfrak{F}$ parameterized by $B(r)$ is the set of critical points of the mapping $\bar{\pi} : \bar{E}(r) \to \Omega(r)$ defined as the restriction of Π to $\bar{E}(r)$. The envelope is the set of singular values of this same mapping $\bar{\pi}$.

By definition, $x \in V(b)$ is a *characteristic point* of $V(b)$ if the pair $(b, x) \in \bar{E}$ is a critical point of the mapping $\bar{\pi}$. The way the envelope is defined here implies that the usual contact or tangency properties one expects from envelopes may not be necessarily satisfied. Still following Thom [91], we can improve the geometrical picture with the following:

Definition 8.5. The envelope is said to be a geometric envelope if the following two conditions are met:

1. The subset of $B(r)$ consisting of $b \in B(r)$ such that $V(b)$ possesses a characteristic point is an open subset.
2. At every regular point of the envelope (i.e., such that the envelope possesses a tangent space at this point), the manifold $V(b)$ is not transverse to the tangent space.

Necessary and sufficient conditions for an envelope to be a geometrical envelope can be given. They take the form of inequalities involving the various dimensions of the manifolds at hand ([91]; see also, (Math 5.1)). We shall make use of one of these conditions in a moment.

8.2.3. The main result

Proposition 8.6. *The set of singular economies $\Sigma(r)$ is the envelope of the family $\mathfrak{F}$.*

This extends the result already obtained for $(\ell, m) = (2, 2)$. The proof relies on the following lemma that does nothing more than to specify the formal relationships existing between $E(r)$ and $\bar{E}(r)$.

Lemma 8.7. *Let $E(r)$ be the equilibrium mainfold. There exists a diffeomorphism $h : E(r) \to \bar{E}(r)$ such that the diagram,*

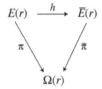

commutes.

Proof of Lemma 8.7. One defines the mapping $i : H(r) \times \Omega(r) \to S \times \Omega(r)$ by

$$i(p, w_1, \ldots, w_m, \omega_1, \ldots, \omega_m), = (p, \omega_1, \ldots, \omega_m)$$

and the mapping $j : S \times \Omega(r) \to H(r) \times \Omega(r)$ by

$$j(p, \omega_1, \ldots, \omega_m) = (p, w_1 = p \cdot \omega_1, \ldots, w_m = p \cdot \omega_m, \omega_1, \ldots, \omega_m).$$

Let h be the restriction of j to $E(r)$. One readily sees that h takes its values in $\bar{E}(r)$ and that the restriction of i to $\bar{E}(r)$ just defines the inverse mapping of h. Finally, the commutation relation $\pi = \bar{\pi} \circ h$ is obvious from the above formulas. $\qquad\square$

Proof of Proposition 8.6. Proposition 8.6 is then a consequence of the fact that considering the commutation relation described in

Lemma 8.7, $(p, \omega) \in E$ is a critical equilibrium, i.e., a critical point of the natural projection, if and only if $h(p, \omega) \in \bar{E}(r)$ is a critical point of $\bar{\pi}$. In other words, the mappings π and $\bar{\pi}$ have the same sets of singular values. $\qquad\square$

Corollary 8.8. *The set of critical equilibria is diffeomorphic by h to the source envelope of the family $\mathfrak{F}$.*

These results enable us to improve significantly our geometric understanding of the set of singular economies $\Sigma(r)$.

Corollary 8.9. *The set of singular values $\Sigma(r)$ is a geometric envelope.*

A sufficient condition stated by Thom [91], for an envelope to be a geometric envelope and applied here to $\Sigma(r)$, is satisfied whenever m and ℓ are both larger than or equal to two (for proof, see (Math 5.1)).

8.3. Applications to the Number of Equilibria

We now go back to the study of the number of equilibria and of related questions with the help of envelope theory. Nevertheless, we shall only outline the related proofs for two reasons. The first one is that, apart from greater mathematical complexity, they follow closely the case $(\ell, m) = (2, 2)$. The second one is that we will come back to these questions in the next chapter following a different and more efficient approach.

8.3.1. The set of economies with a unique equilibrium

Let $\mathcal{U}$ be the set of regular economies $\omega \in \mathcal{R}(r)$ that possesses a unique equilibrium. We already know that a connected component of $\mathcal{U}$ contains the set of Pareto optima. We then have the following:

Proposition 8.7. *For the case of two consumers (i.e., $m = 2$), the set of regular economies with a unique equilibrium $\mathcal{U}$ is identical to the connected component of the set of regular economies containing the set of Pareto optima $P(r)$. Furthermore, the set of economies with a unique equilibrium is contractible.*

As in the case of two agents and two commodities, the proof of this theorem requires beforehand a global result dealing with the economies with multiple equilibria. A sketch of the proof of 8.7 by envelope theory is to be found in the next few pages. Recall that, as previously indicated, we propose an alternative proof of 8.7 in the next chapter (see Section 9.3.5).

Proposition 8.7 solves the problem of characterizing economies with a unique equilibrium in the two-consumer case. An important consequence is that any regular economy that is not in the connected component containing the set of Pareto optima possesses at least three equilibria. The generalization of 8.10 to any number of agents is, for the time being, conjectural.

We mentioned that 8.7 could and would be derived from a global result on economies with multiple equilibria. The suitable framework for such developments is not the space $\Omega(r)$ but, as in the example where $(\ell, m) = (2, 2)$, a variant of this space endowed with enough points at infinity. We introduce them with the help of projective spaces.

8.3.2. The projective framework

The global properties of planar envelopes can be stated rather easily in the setup of the projective plane, the main advantage of this framework being that two lines (even if they are parallel) always intersect (possibly at infinity). Therefore, in order to be able to study the global properties of economies depending on the number of their equilibria, we are led to turn the spaces under consideration into some sort of "projective spaces" by adding points at infinity. Though this extension is motivated mainly by mathematical considerations, we shall see, however, that it is not devoid of economic interest in its own right.

The projective version of $\Omega(r)$

Let $\mathbb{P}^\ell$ be the real projective space of dimension ℓ, i.e., the quotient of $\mathbb{R}^{\ell+1}$ by the equivalence relation $x \sim y$, which means that the vector y is equal to x multiplied by a non-zero real number.

Let $\omega_i \in \mathbb{R}^\ell$ and let $t_i \in \mathbb{R}$. We then interpret the pair (ω_i, t_i) as a system of homogeneous coordinates of a point in $\mathbb{P}^\ell$, the projective completion of $\mathbb{R}^\ell$. We define $P\Omega(r)$, the projective version of $\Omega(r)$, by the system of homogeneous coordinates,

$$(\omega, t) = ((\omega_1, t_1), (\omega_2, t_2), \ldots, (\omega_{m-1}, t_{m-1})),$$

equipped with the following equivalence relation: we have $(\omega, t) \sim (\omega', t')$ if and only if (ω_i, t_i) and (ω'_i, t'_i) represent the same point of $\mathbb{P}^\ell$ for $i = 1, 2, \ldots, m - 1$ (i.e., there exist non-zero real numbers λ_i such that $(\omega'_i, t'_i) = \lambda_i (\omega_i, t_i)$ for $i = 1, 2, \ldots, m - 1$.)

Therefore, $P\Omega(r)$ can be identified with the Cartesian product of the $(m - 1)$ projective spaces $\mathbb{P}^\ell$. In the particular case of $m = 2$, $P\Omega(r)$ is simply the projective space of dimension ℓ. This property does not hold anymore for $m \geq 3$.

The projective version of $V(b)$

We define for every $b \in H(r)$ the projective version $PV(b)$ of the space $V(b)$ by the following equations in $P\Omega(r)$:

$$p \cdot \omega_i = w_i t_i, \quad i = 1, 2, \ldots, m - 1.$$

Envelope theory in the projective setting

In order to extend the envelope theoretic apparatus, we define $P\bar{E}(r)$ as the graph of the correspondence $b \to PV(b)$ restricted to $B(r)$ and $P\bar{\pi} : P\bar{E}(r) \to P\Omega(r)$ the restriction of the natural projection $B(r) \times P\Omega(r) \to P\Omega(r)$ to the set $P\bar{E}(r)$. One checks readily that $P\bar{E}(r)$ is a submanifold of $B(r) \times P\Omega(r)$ and $P\bar{\pi}$ a smooth mapping. Recall that $\Sigma(r)$ is the envelope of the family $V(b)$ parameterized by $b \in B(r)$. Similarly, we denote by $P\Sigma(r)$ the set of singular values of $P\bar{\pi}$. It is also the envelope of the family $PV(b)$ parameterized by $b \in B(r)$.

Remark. The mapping $P\bar{\pi} : P\bar{E}(r) \to P\Omega(r)$ is not onto, contrary to the mapping $\bar{\pi}$. Take an example: for $(\ell, m) = (2, 2)$, the points at infinity of $PV(b)$ for $b = (p, w_1, w_2)$ must be in a direction perpendicular to $p \in S$; therefore, no point at infinity in a direction belonging to the positive quadrant can belong to some $PV(b)$, with the price vector p being strictly positive.

8.3.3. Initial endowments at infinity and the price vector: an economic interpretation

We have introduced vectors of initial endowments at infinity on purely mathematical grounds. But can these initial endowments at infinity be given some kind of economic interpretation?

It is obviously impossible to interpret infinite quantities of commodities directly. It is only after having introduced price vectors that initial endowments at infinity become potentially interesting from an economic viewpoint.

Let us begin with the $(\ell, m) = (2, 2)$ case. If ω is at infinity, the fact that budget lines pass through this point only means that their direction is fixed once and for all. This determines a price vector perpendicular to this direction. In other words, considering ω at infinity is equivalent, from the point of view of equilibrium theory, to fixing the price vector p. The lines $V(b)$ correspond to $b = (p, w_1, w_2)$ which are solutions of the equation,

$$f_1(p, w_1) + f_2(p, w_2) = r,$$

where p and r are fixed, the unknowns being w_1 and w_2. Summarizing, endowments at infinity amount to having equilibria with fixed prices, the unknowns being the income distribution between the economic agents.

This description does extend to the general case of an arbitrary number of consumers and commodities up to some minor changes. Let ω_i be at infinity. This can be described in a homogeneous coordinate system as

$$(\omega_i^1, \ldots, \omega_i^\ell, 0).$$

The budget hyperplane passes through the point at infinity ω_i if, at a finite distance, this hyperplane is parallel to the direction of $\mathbb{R}^\ell$ defined by the vector $(\omega_i^1, \ldots, \omega_i^\ell)$. This amounts to having the price vector satisfy the linear equation,

$$\sum_{j=1}^{\ell} \omega_i^j p_j = 0.$$

The fixed price case turns out to be a special case of this condition. It is observed if the number of consumers is larger than or equal to the number of commodities and if the choice of the ω_is at infinity has been made so as to yield $\ell - 1$ independent linear equations. These equations then have a unique solution, the fixed price vector.

8.3.4. The set of economies with multiple equilibria

We need some new notation. Let $\mathfrak{M}$ be the set of economies ω that possess at least two distinct equilibria or a double equilibrium. This definition implies that $\Sigma(r)$, the set of singular economies, is contained in $\mathfrak{M}$. Furthermore, if a regular economy ω belongs to $\mathfrak{M}$, it follows from the property that the number of equilibria is odd, that the number of equilibria of this economy is at least equal to three.

Let us extend the definition of $\mathfrak{M}$ to the projective case.

Definition 8.11. Let $P\mathfrak{M}$ denote the set of economies $\omega \in P\Omega(r)$ such that there exist several $b \in B(r)$ counted with their order of multiplicity for which ω belongs to $PV(b)$.

We then have the following result that justifies the introduction of the projective framework:

Proposition 8.12. *The set of economies with multiple equilibria in the projective framework $P\mathfrak{M}$ is a pathconnected subset of $P\Omega(r)$.*

Outline of the proof of 8.12

This is merely a sketch, the reason being that the proof parallels the $(\ell, m) = (2, 2)$ case so that we just have to specify some details. An alternative, completely detailed, proof is also provided in Chapter 9.

We parameterize the set $P(r)$ of Pareto optima by $B(r)$. The key to the proof is in the definition of the mapping θ that associates with every $b' \in B(r) \backslash \{b\}$ the intersection $PV(b) \cap PV(b')$. It is no longer true that, as in the $(\ell, m) = (2, 2)$ case, the intersection $PV(b) \cap PV(b')$ is a point. It is usually a projective linear manifold. This difficulty can be overcome by considering, instead of $PV(b)$, a fixed linear subspace D of $PV(b)$ having dimension $m - 1$. Then, $D \cap PV(b')$ is a point, except for possible degeneracies. Of course, D is taken so as to contain the Pareto optimum associated with b.

The second difficulty one encounters in extending the proof of the $(\ell, m) = (2, 2)$ case to the general case concerns the continuous extension of θ at b. As soon as $B(r)$ is not a curve, the continuous extension of θ depends on the direction followed by b' when it tends to b. Therefore, we have to introduce the "blowing-up" of the manifold $B(r)$ at b. Let us just say that this defines a pathconnected manifold which does indeed permit the continuous extension of θ. As in the case $(\ell, m) = (2, 2)$, one finds that the set $\mathrm{Im}(\theta)$ is pathconnected. The end of the proof then proceeds as before. $\qquad\qquad\square$

Outline of the proof of 8.7

It follows from the above proof that, in the projective space defined by D, the set of economies with multiple equilibria is pathconnected. Now, we have $\dim D = m - 1$. Therefore, for $m = 2$, D is a projective line, and we can repeat the argument of the $(\ell, m) = (2, 2)$ case up to the end, including the degree argument because, m being equal to two, the function $\det J(p, \omega)$ is linear with respect to the parameters of the fiber.

8.4. Conclusion

We have seen that the classical theory of line envelopes in the plane provides a framework remarkably well-fitted to the study of general equilibrium theory in the case of two commodities and two agents. A natural step was therefore to look for extensions of envelope theory that could handle more general cases. This role can be played by Thom's [91] formulation. Extremely satisfactory from a purely theoretical point of view, it turns out that although the process of extending proofs from the $(\ell, m) = (2, 2)$ case to the most general one is not infeasible, it requires a lot of mathematical sophistication, to say the least. The proofs of Propositions 8.7 and 8.12 do illustrate these complications. Moreover, extending with the help of envelope theory, the other results proved in the $(\ell, m) = (2, 2)$ case is a major tour de force. This justifies the alternative approach followed in the next chapter, which provides a highly efficient way of dealing with the global properties of the general equilibrium model.

Chapter 9

A Duality Theory

The theorems of welfare economics describe relationships linking equilibrium allocations and Pareto optima. The duality theory that is set out in this chapter can be viewed as a mathematical extension of these theorems. We shall show that there is a duality relationship between general equilibrium theory on one side and the theory of Pareto efficient allocations compatible with *a priori* given budget constraints (also named the B.C.P.E. allocations, where B.C.P.E. stands for budget constrained Pareto efficient) on the other. We shall make use of this duality relationship in two different directions. Firstly, duality provides a powerful means of establishing and proving properties of B.C.P.E. allocations by straightforward translation of the corresponding properties and proofs of general equilibrium theory. We shall illustrate this use of duality in several examples, one of them dealing with the existence of B.C.P.E. allocations. Secondly, this duality relationship possesses the remarkable, although *a priori* unexpected, property of providing a mathematical formulation of general equilibrium theory that lends itself more readily to the study of questions related to the number of equilibria or to singular economies than the original formulation through envelope theory. This potency of the dual formulation stands out most evidently in the several examples investigated in the last part of this chapter.

9.1. The Concept of B.C.P.E. Allocations

This section is devoted to some aspects of the price system that have been largely ignored in the economic literature. Indeed, the neoclassical analysis of the price system has emphasized the role of prices as carriers of information that is necessary and sufficient for individual demands and supplies to coordinate and yield equality of total demand and supply. This point of view has undoubtedly led to some of the most remarkable developments of economic theory. But these achievements can by no means provide a sufficient reason to reject or simply neglect the role played by the price system in all the questions pertaining to income and wealth distributions, the practical importance of which may in fact be as considerable as the coordination of supplies and demands.

9.1.1. The right to the consumption of essential commodities and the price system

The history of mankind tells us that there are commodities which have always been considered essential. As a consequence, their consumption has seemed to be more related to a right than to the logic of maximizing individual utility that is associated with the market. Housing and basic foods account for some obvious examples. But the nature and the quantities of the commodities that can be ascribed to this right may vary with the economic status achieved by one's community. This is best illustrated by the evolution during the last two centuries of the status of labor (more precisely unemployment) and of health when considered as economic entities. Despite the fact that this right to "consume" is defined independently of the market, this does not necessarily mean that the two ideas are antinomic. In fact, it turns out that most commodities considered to be essential are allocated through the market, a role, however, which is often criticized at the first sight of malfunctioning.

Summarizing, if the form and expression of such consumption rights vary depending on the human communities being considered, its existence cannot be denied. Furthermore, if the market holds an established place among the means used to satisfy this right, it has never been the unique one, even in the most economically advanced societies, those that have undergone Polanyi's [81] "great transformation."

Studying the economic consequences resulting from these consumption rights is an important though formidable task. In its full generality, it goes far beyond the rather limited scope of this book. Therefore we shall content ourselves with a formulation that common sense associates with the idea of consumption rights, although this relationship is not always so obvious as one might think. In this version of the problem, it is assumed that the prices of the essential commodities as well as the individual incomes or wealth have been fixed exogenously in order to meet the requirements imposed by these consumption rights. According to this formulation, prices do serve as indicators of individual behavior, but the price fixing mechanism can in no way be formally identified with the market mechanism. It should be noted that the sum of individual demands, given the posted prices, does not equilibrate in general the sum of individual supplies. Therefore, the final allocation of resources requires mechanisms to complement the action of the commodity prices. In one way or another, this must result in forms of quantitative rationing, the influence of which may alter the meaning or the realization of these consumption rights, a subject worthy of further investigation. The analysis which remains to be done involves philosophy, law, economics, etc., and would take us too far afield. Therefore, the simplified version of the consumption right problem we are considering takes the form of exogenously fixed prices and incomes.

9.1.2. Exogenously fixed prices and efficiency

A thesis often propounded by unconditional supporters of the market states that economies where the price system is not regulated by mechanisms that, formally, cannot be reduced to those of the market must be *inefficient*. This statement can be rigorously formalized within the framework of exogenously fixed prices and incomes we are considering, and the analytical tools at our disposal enable us to invalidate it. We shall show that, at least theoretically, there is no inconsistency between economic efficiency and the existence of consumption rights (as formulated through the assumption of fixed prices and incomes).

9.1.3. The price–income system

Let $p \in S$ be a price vector and $(w_1, w_2, \ldots, w_m) \in \mathbb{R}^m$ be the m agents' income distribution. Let us recall that considering incomes independently of the price system is economically unjustified. Indeed, problems related to consumption rights appear only to the extent that, for given incomes, the prices of some of the essential commodities are so high that not all agents have enough income to afford the amounts of these commodities that are considered to be satisfactory in view of this right to consume.

The extreme form of the consumption right problem is one where the price–income vector $b = (p, w_1, w_2, \ldots, w_m) \in S \times \mathbb{R}^m$ is fixed through political considerations independently of any market. With the vector $r \in \mathbb{R}^\ell$ representing the fixed total resources, we assume that individual and total wealth satisfy the accounting relationship,

$$w_1 + w_2 + \cdots + w_m = p \cdot r.$$

In other words, the $(m+1)$-tuple $b = (p, w_1, \ldots, w_m)$ belongs to the space $H(r)$ already defined in (8.1).

9.1.4. The B.C.P.E. allocations

Let us recall that an allocation is nothing but a vector $x = (x_1, x_2, \ldots, x_m)$ belonging to the space $\Omega(r)$, i.e., a vector for which the equality,

$$x_1 + x_2 + \cdots + x_m = r,$$

is satisfied.

Definition 9.1. The allocation $x \in \Omega(r)$ is said to be compatible with the price system $b = (p, w_1, \ldots, w_m) \in H(r)$ if the budget equality $p \cdot x_i = w_i$, is satisfied for i varying from 1 to m. We denote by $A(b)$ the set of all $x \in \Omega(r)$ compatible with a given $b \in H(r)$. We denote by $\mathcal{A}$ the set generated by the spaces $A(b)$ for b varying in $H(r)$.

This definition means that every consumer's budget is entirely spent in the process of acquiring the commodity bundles described by the allocation $x \in \Omega(r)$. One should note, however, that in this definition, the commodity bundle x_i does not necessarily maximize utility $u_i(x_i)$ subject to the budget constraint $p \cdot x_i = w_i$.

Definition 9.2. The allocation $x \in \Omega(r)$ is a B.C.P.E. allocation if simultaneously x is compatible with the price–income vector $(p, w_1, \ldots, w_m) \in H(r)$ and if x is Pareto efficient.

Therefore, a B.C.P.E. allocation is one which, while remaining *compatible* with a price–income system *a priori* given, corresponds nevertheless to an *efficient state* of the economy. To prove the existence of B.C.P.E. allocations would therefore provide a theoretical contradiction to the largely widespread assertion of the inconsistency between economic efficiency and centralized regulation when the latter cannot be formally reduced to some market mechanism. Pareto [80], Barone [53], and Lange [71] have already interpreted the theorems of welfare economics in the framework of socialist economies. But the weak point of their analysis — and it is in this regard that their results differ radically from the existence property of B.C.P.E. allocations just discussed — lies in the fact that they define mechanisms formally identical to the market whose main drawback is simply the lack of any actual support within the framework of a socialist economy.

Some properties of the B.C.P.E. allocations

In this section, we are going to study three properties chosen from among the most important ones of the B.C.P.E. allocations. They are stated in close analogy with similar properties met in the study of general equilibrium. This parallelism cannot be attributed to luck, as we shall see later. They deal with the existence of B.C.P.E. allocations, their property of structural stability, and the sufficient conditions for uniqueness.

Proposition 9.3. *There always exists a B.C.P.E. allocation associated with any arbitrarily given price–income vector.*

Mathematically, this theorem simply says that the intersection set $P(r) \cap A(b)$, where $P(r)$ is the set of Pareto optima associated with the total resources r, is non-empty for every $b \in H(r)$. It establishes the lack of contradiction between economic efficiency and an arbitrarily given price–income vector.

Proposition 9.4. *There exists an open dense subset $\hat{\mathcal{R}}$ of $H(r)$ such that, for every $b \in \hat{\mathcal{R}}$, there exists an open neighborhood U contained in $\hat{\mathcal{R}}$ of b and $2n+1$ smooth mappings $\hat{s}_j : U \rightarrow H(r)$ with the property that the set $\cup_{j=1}^{2n+1} \hat{s}_j(b')$ is the set of B.C.P.E. allocations associated with $b' \in U$.*

This implies that the number of B.C.P.E. allocations is locally constant outside the exceptional set $\hat{\Sigma} = H(r) \backslash \hat{\mathcal{R}}$, exceptional meaning closed with measure zero. Furthermore, these allocations depend smoothly on the price–income vector b as long as it is taken outside $\hat{\Sigma}$.

The number of B.C.P.E. allocations, being locally constant, is therefore constant on every connected component of the set $\hat{\mathcal{R}}$. The next result relates the location of the set of price–income equilibria $B(r)$ with the set $\hat{\mathcal{R}}$ and its partition into connected components.

Proposition 9.5. *The set of price–income equilibria $B(r)$ is contained in only one of the connected components of $\hat{\mathcal{R}}$. Only one B.C.P.E. allocation is associated with every price–income vector b belonging to this component.*

Therefore, the B.C.P.E. allocation is unique if the price–income vector $b = (p, w_1, w_2, \ldots, w_m)$ belongs to the connected component of $\hat{\mathcal{R}}$ containing $B(r)$, which happens to be the case if the excess demand vector,

$$f_1(p, w_1) + f_2(p, w_2) + \cdots + f_m(p, w_m) - r,$$

is small enough. On the other hand, one is likely to observe multiple B.C.P.E. allocations when this vector is large.

Remark. It is possible to give direct proofs of these theorems, and one could even check that their assumptions could somehow be weakened at almost no cost. See, for example, the proof of existence of B.C.P.E. allocations (i.e., Proposition 9.3) by Keiding [69] and Svensson [90]. However, we prefer to establish these results as consequences of a duality relationship between the theory of B.C.P.E. allocations and general equilibrium theory. Statements 9.3–9.5 then come out as simple transpositions of similar statements about general equilibrium. Therefore, the next section is devoted to this duality theory. The hypotheses we have chosen here are justified by the fact they provide the simplest mathematical formulation of this duality theory.

9.2. Duality

This section is devoted to the duality theory between general equilibrium theory and the theory of B.C.P.E. allocations. We begin by specifying the framework by way of recalling the definitions of the spaces and mathematical elements to be put in duality. We therefore have

$\Omega(r)$:	the space of economies (also called initial endowments or allocations)	$H(r)$:	the set of price–income vectors
$x \in \Omega(r)$:	allocation	$b \in H(r)$:	price–income vector
$P(r)$:	the set of Pareto optima	$B(r)$:	the set of price–income equilibria.

The mapping $\rho : P \to S \times \mathbb{R}^m$ defined by the formula,

$$\rho(x) = (g(x), g(x) \cdot x_1, \ldots, g(x) \cdot x_m),$$

where $g(x)$ represents the price vector that supports the Pareto optimum $x \in P$, is going to play an important role. It has been already encountered on several occasions. Let us recall that ρ is a diffeomorphism. Furthermore, we have

$$\rho(P(r)) = B(r).$$

9.2.1. The mathematical theory of B.C.P.E. allocations: Theory $\mathfrak{J}$

Let $b \in H(r)$ be fixed. An allocation $x \in \Omega(r)$ is B.C.P.E. if it belongs to the set $A(b)$ (for the B.C. part) and to the set $P(r)$ (for the P.E. part). In other words, the mathematical theory of B.C.P.E. allocations is equivalent to the study of the intersection set,

$$P(r) \cap A(b),$$

when b varies within the set of price–income vectors $H(r)$, which can be restated as the study of the set $P(r) \cap A$, when A varies within the set $\mathcal{A}$ (cf. Definition 9.1).

9.2.2. The mathematical theory of general equilibrium: Theory $\mathfrak{W}$

With the same notation as in Chapter 8, let $\mathcal{F}$ be the family of sets $A(b)$ generated by having b vary in the set of price–income equilibria $B(r)$. We have already seen that the theory of general equilibrium can be reformulated as the study of the set consisting of those spaces $A \in \mathcal{F}$ that contain $\omega \in \Omega(r)$, i.e., the set,

$$\{A \in \mathcal{F} \quad \text{such that} \quad \omega \in A\}.$$

The quadruple $(\mathcal{A}, \mathcal{F}, \Omega(r), P(r))$ is the only datum that is necessary to define the theories $(\mathfrak{J})$ and $(\mathfrak{W})$.

9.2.3. Duality and equivalent formulations of the general equilibrium and B.C.P.E. allocations theories

We shall start by first defining the components of a new quadruple $(\hat{\mathcal{A}}, \hat{\mathcal{F}}, H(r), B(r))$.

Definition 9.6. The set $\hat{\mathcal{A}}$ is the set of linear subspaces of $H(r)$ having dimension $\ell - 1$ that are not perpendicular to S.

Consequently, the linear subspace $\hat{A}$ of $H(r)$ belongs to $\hat{\mathcal{A}}$ if and only if it can be defined in $S \times \mathbb{R}^m$ by a set of equations of the type,

$$w_i = p \cdot x_i,$$

where i varies from 1 to m, the w_i's and p being the variables, while the x_i's are fixed (and satisfy $\Sigma x_i = r$). Such an equation system is, when it exists, unique.

The mapping $\hat{A} : \Omega(r) \to \hat{\mathcal{A}}$ defined by the formula $\hat{A}(x) = \{b = (p, w_1, \ldots, w_m) \in H(r)|p \cdot x_1 = w_1, p \cdot x_2 = w_2, \ldots, p \cdot x_m = w_m\}$ is in fact, one-to-one and enables one to identify the spaces $\hat{\mathcal{A}}$ and $\Omega(r)$.

Definition 9.7. The set $\hat{\mathcal{F}}$ is the subset of $\hat{\mathcal{A}}$, the elements of which are the subsets $\hat{A}(x)$ generated by x varying in the set of Pareto optima $P(r)$. In other words, we have $\hat{\mathcal{F}} = \hat{A}(P(r))$.

These definitions may seem arbitrary at this stage; nevertheless, the next lemma enables one to expect the forthcoming duality relationships.

Lemma 9.8. *The relationships* $x \in A(b)$ *and* $b \in \hat{A}(x)$ *are equivalent. Furthermore, one has* $A(B(r)) = \mathcal{F}$ *(to be compared to* $\hat{A}(P(r)) = \hat{\mathcal{F}}$*).*

Proof. The first part of the lemma is obvious. Now we turn to the second part. Take $b \in B(r)$. The vector,

$$(f_1(p, w_1), f_2(p, w_2), \ldots, f_m(p, w_m)),$$

belongs to $\Omega(r)$ because of the equality $\Sigma f_i(p, w_i) = r$. Furthermore, this vector is the Pareto optimum allocation supported by the price vector p and the incomes w_i's. Therefore, the linear space,

$$A(b) = \{(x_1, \ldots, x_m) \in \Omega(r)|p \cdot x_1 = w_1, \ldots, p \cdot x_m = w_m\},$$

belongs to the family $\mathcal{F}$. $\qquad\square$

Definition 9.9. The theories $(\hat{\mathfrak{J}})$ and $(\hat{\mathfrak{W}})$ are defined as the study of the following sets:

$(\hat{\mathfrak{J}})$: *study of* $\{\hat{A} \cap B(r)\}$ *for* $\hat{A} \in \hat{\mathcal{A}}$,

$(\hat{\mathfrak{W}})$: *study of* $\{\hat{A} \in \hat{\mathcal{F}}$ *such that* $b \in \hat{A}\}$ *for* $b \in H(r)$.

One should note that, in terms of the quadruple $(\hat{\mathcal{A}}, \hat{\mathcal{F}}, H(r), B(r))$, the theories $(\hat{\mathfrak{J}})$ and $(\hat{\mathfrak{W}})$ are the formal correspondents of the theories $(\mathfrak{J})$ and $(\mathfrak{W})$ stated for the quadruple $(\mathcal{A}, \mathcal{F}, \Omega(r), P(r))$. One can therefore expect that any property of $(\mathfrak{J})$ or $(\mathfrak{W})$ that depends only on the quadruple $(\mathcal{A}, \mathcal{F}, \Omega(r), P(r))$ will be true for $(\hat{\mathfrak{J}})$ or $(\hat{\mathfrak{W}})$ respectively. In principle, it is possible to study the theories $(\hat{\mathfrak{J}})$ and $(\hat{\mathfrak{W}})$ without using any information or result on $(\mathfrak{J})$ or $(\mathfrak{W})$, and conversely. The next proposition extends the standard theorems of welfare economics in a way that specifies the help that theory $(\mathfrak{W})$ can bring to theory $(\hat{\mathfrak{J}})$, and conversely. A similar parallel relationship exists between theories $(\mathfrak{J})$ and $(\hat{\mathfrak{W}})$. This approach enables us to establish the properties of B.C.P.E. allocations $(\mathfrak{J})$ from those of general equilibrium $(\mathfrak{W})$, after using theory $(\hat{\mathfrak{W}})$ as an intermediary formulation.

Proposition 9.10. *The theories* $(\mathfrak{J})$ *and* $(\hat{\mathfrak{W}})$ *are equivalent. Similarly, the theories* $(\mathfrak{W})$ *and* $(\hat{\mathfrak{J}})$ *are equivalent.*

Proof. Let us start with the relationship $\mathcal{A} = A(H(r))$. Then, $(\mathfrak{J})$ becomes the study of the set $P(r) \cap A(b)$, where b varies in $H(r)$. It follows from Lemma 9.8 that the relationship $x \in A(b)$ is equivalent to $b \in \hat{A}(x)$. Furthermore, one sees readily that $x \in P(r)$ is equivalent to $\hat{A}(x) \in \hat{A}(P(r)) = \hat{\mathcal{F}}$. Therefore, we can reformulate $(\mathfrak{J})$ as the study of the set,

$$\{\hat{A}(x) \in \hat{\mathcal{F}} \quad \text{such that} \quad b \in \hat{A}(x)\},$$

which is precisely what theory $(\hat{\mathfrak{W}})$ is about. A similar argument would show the equivalence of $(\mathfrak{W})$ and $(\hat{\mathfrak{J}})$. □

It follows from 9.10 that the study of theory $(\mathfrak{W})$, i.e., general equilibrium theory, is equivalent to the study of $(\hat{\mathfrak{J}})$. We shall develop this approach to general equilibrium theory in the next section because it turns out that the direct study of $(\hat{\mathfrak{J}})$ is seemingly easier with regard to questions concerning the number of equilibria or singular economies. But in the meantime, we are going to highlight a complete mathematical symmetry between the elements defining the two quadruples $(\mathcal{A}, \mathcal{F}, \Omega(r), P(r))$ and $(\hat{\mathcal{A}}, \hat{\mathcal{F}}, H(r), B(r))$, which fully justifies the duality terminology and, incidentally, explains its power.

To work out this full duality concept, we shall first define "*utility functions*" on the set of prices and incomes, i.e., on the space $H(r)$. In a second step, we shall relate the set $B(r)$ to the set of "*Pareto minima*" associated with the "utility" functions defined on $H(r)$.

Let $\hat{u}_i : S \times \mathbb{R} \to \mathbb{R}$ be the indirect utility function associated with u_i. In other words, we define

$$\hat{u}_i(p, w_i) = u_i(f_i(p, w_i)),$$

as the utility of agent i for the demand $f_i(p, w_i)$. We denote by $\hat{v}_i : H(r) \to \mathbb{R}$ the mapping defined by the formula,

$$\hat{v}_i(p, w_1, w_2, \ldots, w_m) = \hat{u}_i(p, w_i).$$

We then extend the definition of efficiency for the functions $\hat{v}_i$ as follows:

Definition 9.11. The price–income vector $b = (p, w_1, w_2, \ldots, w_m) \in H(r)$ is a Pareto minimum (with respect to the indirect utility functions $\hat{u}_i$) if there exists no vector $b' \in H(r)$ such that the inequalities $\hat{v}_i(b') \le \hat{v}_i(b)$ are all satisfied, with at least one of these being a strict inequality.

The functions $\hat{v}_i$ defined on the space $H(r)$ make the picture comparable to what happens in $\Omega(r)$ with the functions $v_i : \Omega(r) \to \mathbb{R}$ defined by the formula,

$$v_i(x_1, x_2, \ldots, x_i, \ldots, x_m) = u_i(x_i).$$

The next result builds up, in an essential way, the equivalence relationship described in 9.10.

Proposition 9.12. *The set $B(r)$ of price–income equilibria is also the set of Pareto minima for the functions $\hat{v}_i$, defined on $H(r)$.*

To prove 9.12, we are going to use a characterization of Pareto minima through a geometric formulation of the first-order conditions.

Let $b \in H(r)$ be some price–income vector. We denote by $\hat{T}_i(b)$ the hyperplane which is tangent at b to the hypersurface,

$$\{b' \in H(r) | \hat{v}_i(b') = \hat{v}_i(b)\}.$$

A simple straightforward computation shows that the equation of the tangent hyperplane is

$$w'_i = p'_i \cdot f_i(p, w_i),$$

where p' and w'_i are variable, p and w_i are fixed.

The intersection of these m tangent hyperplanes is a linear subspace denoted $\hat{D}(b)$. It is defined in $S \times \mathbb{R}^m$ by the following systems of linear equations:

$$p' \cdot f_1(p, w_1) - w'_1 = 0,$$

$$p' \cdot f_2(p, w_2) - w'_2 = 0,$$

$$\vdots$$

$$p' \cdot f_m(p, w_m) - w'_m = 0$$

and

$$p' \cdot r - w'_1 - w'_2 - \cdots - w'_m = 0,$$

where the last relationship is just the equation of $H(r)$. The matrix defined by the coefficients of these linear equations is equal to

$$M = \begin{bmatrix} f_1^1 & \cdots & f_1^{\ell-1} & -1 & 0 & \cdots & 0 \\ f_2^1 & \cdots & f_2^{\ell-1} & 0 & -1 & \cdots & 0 \\ \vdots & \vdots & \vdots & \vdots & \vdots & \vdots & \vdots \\ f_m^1 & \cdots & f_m^{\ell-1} & 0 & 0 & \cdots & -1 \\ r^1 & \cdots & r^{\ell-1} & -1 & -1 & \cdots & -1 \end{bmatrix}$$

and we have

$$\dim \hat{D}(b) = \dim(S \times \mathbb{R}^m) - \text{rank}(M).$$

From an examination of the last m columns made of -1's and 0's, it is clear that the rank of M is *larger than or equal* to m. This implies for $\hat{D}(b)$ the possibilities $\dim \hat{D}(b) = \ell - 1$ or $\ell - 2$, in which cases the codimension of $\hat{D}(b)$ in $H(r)$ is equal to $m - 1$ and m, respectively.

Lemma 9.13. *The vector $b \in H(r)$ is a Pareto minimum if and only if* $\dim \hat{D}(b) = \ell - 1$.

We prove this lemma simultaneously with Proposition 9.12 by following the logical scheme:

b Pareto minimum $\Rightarrow \dim \hat{D}(b) = \ell - 1 \Rightarrow$

b price–income equilibrium $\Rightarrow b$ Pareto minimum.

Proof.

(1) The necessary first-order conditions imply that the codimension of $\hat{D}(b)$ in H must be less than or equal to $m - 1$, which entails the inequality $\dim \hat{D}(b) \geq \ell - 1$. From what we already know, this implies

$$\dim \hat{D}(b) = \ell - 1.$$

(2) Take matrix M. Its rank is equal to m (which is equivalent to $\dim \hat{D}(b) = \ell - 1$) if and only if its last row is the sum of the m other rows (considering the structure of the m last columns), i.e., if the equality,

$$r^k = \sum_{i=1}^{m} f_i^k,$$

holds true for $k = 1, 2, \ldots, \ell - 1$.

The vector equality,

$$r = \sum_i f_i(p, w_i),$$

then follows from Walras law. This shows that b is indeed a price–income equilibrium.

(3) To establish the last logical implication, let us take $b \in B(r)$ and assume that b is not a Pareto minimum. Then there exists some Pareto minimum b' satisfying the inequalities,

$$\hat{v}_i(b') \le \hat{v}_i(b)$$

for $i = 1, 2, \ldots, m$, at least one of these inequalities being strict. Furthermore, we now know that, being a Pareto minimum, b' necessarily belongs to $B(r)$. Let us take the inverse image of b and b' by the mapping $\rho : P \to S \times \mathbb{R}^m$ for which $B(r) = \rho(P(r))$. The allocations $\rho^{-1}(b)$ and $\rho^{-1}(b')$ belong to $P(r)$ and, therefore, are Pareto optima. But, the relationships,

$$v_i(\rho^{-1}(b)) = \hat{v}_i(b),$$

$$v_i(\rho^{-1}(b')) = \hat{v}_i(b'),$$

imply that we have $v_i(\rho^{-1}(b)) \ge v_i(\rho^{-1}(b'))$ for every i, at least one of these inequalities being strict. Therefore, $\rho^{-1}(b)$ Pareto dominates $\rho^{-1}(b')$, which contradicts the fact that $\rho^{-1}(b')$ is a Pareto optimum.

$\square$

Remark. By now, we have completely described the duality relationship between $(\mathfrak{J})$ and $(\mathfrak{W})$. Summarizing, this duality is based on the equivalence between $(\mathfrak{J})$ and $(\hat{\mathfrak{W}})$. We can apply this to proving Propositions 9.3–9.5. One just needs to formulate them as statements of the theory $(\hat{\mathfrak{W}})$, which become formally identical to statements of the theory $(\mathfrak{W})$. The assumptions underlying $(\mathfrak{W})$ and $(\hat{\mathfrak{W}})$ have slight differences, however. As far as rigor is concerned, these differences are sufficient to justify reworking the proofs; more precisely, a careful adaptation of the proofs of $(\mathfrak{W})$ to the setting of $(\hat{\mathfrak{W}})$ as defined by the space $H(r)$, the functions $\hat{v}_i$, and the price–income vector $b \in H(r)$. We leave this rather formal exercise to the interested reader who may, however, consult the article of Balasko [48] for explicit proofs.

9.3. The Direct Study of $(\hat{\mathfrak{J}})$ with Applications to General Equilibrium Theory

In the previous sections, starting from the idea of B.C.P.E. allocations, we were led to define theory $(\mathfrak{J})$, which turned out to be equivalent by duality to theory $(\mathfrak{W})$, itself formally identical to general equilibrium theory. It was then easy and convenient to transpose the results about general equilibrium obtained in the first eight chapters to properties of the B.C.P.E. allocations. This is what we have done for existence, structural stability and sufficient uniqueness conditions.

But it is in the opposite direction that we are now going to apply this duality theory. We know that the theories $(\mathfrak{W})$ and $(\hat{\mathfrak{J}})$ are equivalent, but it turns out that the direct study of $(\hat{\mathfrak{J}})$ (which is formally identical to the theory of B.C.P.E. allocations) is much easier than the study of $(\mathfrak{W})$ for problems dealing with the number of equilibria and with singular economies. One explanation is to be found in the fact that theory $(\mathfrak{W})$ requires envelope theory, the use of which is always intricate, contrary to the direct formulation of theory $(\hat{\mathfrak{J}})$, which deals with intersections of sets and manifolds.

The properties that we are going to investigate in the framework of theory $(\hat{\mathfrak{J}})$ are the following ones:

— Connectedness of the set of economies with multiple equilibria;
— Connectedness of the set of economies with a unique equilibrium;
— Structure of the set of critical equilibria;
— Relationship between the number of equilibria and the global determinateness of the equilibria;
— Definition and existence of "maximal" definition sets for the equilibrium price selection mappings.

In Chapter 8, only the first two themes were investigated at a general level; the fourth one was tackled only for the special case of two commodities and two agents. One of the definitive advantages of the $(\hat{\mathfrak{J}})$ formulation as compared to the standard Walrasian approach consists of being easily accessible to geometric intuition, a feature of which we are going to take advantage in the forthcoming presentation.

9.3.1. Main definitions and concepts of $(\hat{\mathfrak{J}})$: A reminder

The space $H(r)$ is the set of price–income vectors $(p, w_1, w_2, \ldots, w_m)$ $\in S \times \mathbb{R}^m$ which satisfy the equality,

$$p \cdot r = w_1 + w_2 + \cdots + w_m.$$

This space $H(r)$ is parameterized by the price vector $p \in S$ and the incomes $w_1, w_2, \ldots, w_{m-1}$, of the first $m-1$ consumers, with the income w_m being determined by the above relationship. We therefore identify $H(r)$ with $S \times \mathbb{R}^{m-1}$. The price set S can be identified with $S \times \{0\}$ and as such be considered as embedded in $H(r)$. The dimension of $H(r)$ is $\ell + m - 2$.

We also recall that $B(r)$ is the subset of $H(r)$ generated by the price–income equilibria. Let $\omega \in \Omega(r)$. We define $\hat{A}(\omega)$ as the set of $(m+1)$-tuples $(p, w_1, w_2, \ldots, w_m) \in S \times \mathbb{R}^m$ which satisfy the m equalities,

$$w_i = p \cdot \omega_i \quad \text{for } i = 1, 2, \ldots, m.$$

Clearly $\hat{A}(\omega)$ is embedded in $H(r)$, has dimension $(\ell - 1)$, and is not perpendicular to the subspace $S \times (0)$ of $S \times \mathbb{R}^{m-1}$, with which $H(r)$ has been identified. Conversely, every linear subspace satisfying these conditions can be identified with some $\hat{A}(\omega)$ for a suitable $\omega \in \Omega(r)$.

When the initial endowment vector ω varies in $\Omega(r)$, the subspace $\hat{A}(\omega)$ of $H(r)$ generates the set denoted $\hat{\mathcal{A}}$ consisting of the dimension $(\ell - 1)$ linear subspaces of $H(r)$ not perpendicular to $S \times (0)$. The set $\hat{\mathcal{A}}$ is naturally equipped with a manifold structure (as an open subset of the suitable Grassmann manifold) and the mapping $\hat{A} : \Omega(r) \to \hat{\mathcal{A}}$ is, in fact, a diffeomorphism.

The equilibrium price vectors $p \in S$ associated with the economy $\omega \in \Omega(r)$ are the solutions of the equation,

$$\sum f_i(p, p \cdot \omega_i) = \sum \omega_i (= r).$$

Let $w_i = p \cdot \omega_i$. Then, the price–income vector $b = (p, w_1, \ldots, w_m)$ associated with the equilibrium price vector p is a solution of the equation system,

$$\begin{cases} \sum f_i(p, w_i) = r, \\ w_i = p \cdot \omega_i, \quad i = 1, 2, \ldots, m. \end{cases}$$

Geometrically, this just means that $b = (p, w_1, \ldots, w_m)$ belongs to the intersection of the manifolds $B(r)$ and $\hat{A}(\omega)$. Note that the manifolds $B(r)$ and $\hat{A}(\omega)$ have complementary dimensions in $H(r)$, namely, $m + \ell - 2 = (m - 1) + (\ell - 1)$.

These elementary considerations should prove sufficient to explain the definitions to come. A rigorous approach, however, would require a more formal treatment.

Let $\sigma : S \times \Omega(r) \to H(r) \times \hat{A}$ be the mapping defined by the formula,

$$\sigma(p, \omega_1, \omega_2, \ldots, \omega_m) = (p, p \cdot \omega_1, \ldots, p \cdot \omega_m, \hat{A}(\omega)).$$

The image of an equilibrium $(p, \omega) \in E(r)$ by the mapping σ is a pair $(b, \hat{A})$ such that b belongs to $B(r) \cap \hat{A}$. Let $\mathcal{E}$ be the subset of $H(r) \times \hat{A}$, the elements of which are all the pairs $(b, \hat{A})$ with $b \in B(r) \cap \hat{A}$. The mapping is one-to-one from $E(r)$ into $\mathcal{E}$. More precisely, one readily sees that σ is an embedding (i.e., a proper immersion) from $E(r)$ into $H(r) \times \hat{A}$. Its image $\mathcal{E}$ is therefore a submanifold of $H(r) \times \hat{A}$, which is diffeomorphic to $E(r)$.

Formulated in this framework, the natural projection $\pi : (p, \omega) \to \omega$ becomes the mapping from $\mathcal{E}$ into $\hat{A}$ which associates with the pair $(b, \hat{A})$ (where b belongs to $B(r) \cap \hat{A}$) the element $\hat{A}$, which mapping we still denote π (confusion is unlikely and, in any event, harmless) and which of course is proper just as the natural projection $\pi : E(r) \to \Omega(r)$ is. It becomes true, at least intuitively true (and we leave this as an exercise for the expert reader) that the equilibrium $(b, \hat{A})$ is a critical one if the manifolds $B(r)$ and $\hat{A}$ are not transverse in b, which implies that we must then have

$$\dim(\hat{A} \cap T_b(B(r))) \geq 1.$$

Consequently, the economy ω is regular if $\hat{A}(\omega)$ is transverse to $B(r)$. The fiber bundle structure of the equilibrium manifold is easy to put forth with the mapping $\mathcal{E} \rightarrow B(r)$ that associates with the pair $(b, \hat{A}) \in \mathcal{E}$ the point $b \in B(r)$. The inverse image of $b \in B(r)$ consists indeed of the pairs $(b, \hat{A})$, where the sets $\hat{A} \in \hat{\mathcal{A}}$ contain $b \in B(r)$. We must have $\hat{A} = \hat{A}(\omega)$ for some $\omega \in \Omega(r)$, which satisfies the relationships $p \cdot \omega_i = w_i$ for every i. One recognizes, in this form, the fibers of E. From now on, the manifolds $E(r)$ and $\mathcal{E}$ will indifferently be called equilibrium manifolds.

9.3.2. The notion of geometric equilibrium

Let us consider, instead of $\hat{A}$, the set $P\hat{A}$ consisting of all the linear subspaces $\hat{A}$ of $H(r)$ having dimension $\ell - 1$. The previous developments lead to the following extensions of the definition of an equilibrium and of a critical equilibrium.

Definition 9.14. The pair $(b, \hat{A}) \in H(r) \times P\hat{A}$. is a geometric equilibrium if b belongs to the intersection $B(r) \cap \hat{A}$. Let $P\mathcal{E}$ denote the set of geometric equilibria.

The structure of the intersection set $B(r) \cap \hat{A}$ obviously depends on the relative positions of $B(r)$ and of $\hat{A}$, which motivates the next two definitions.

Definition 9.15. The space $\hat{A} \in P\hat{A}$ is regular if it is transverse to the manifold $B(r)$.

Let $T_b(B(r))$ be the tangent space to $B(r)$ at b. Since the manifold $B(r)$ is embedded in $H(r)$, the tangent space $T_b(B(r))$ can be identified with a linear subspace of $H(r)$ of dimension $m - 1$. A geometric equilibrium $(b, \hat{A})$ is critical if the manifolds $\hat{A}$ and $B(r)$ are not transverse in b, which is equivalent to the condition,

$$\dim(\hat{A} \cap T_b(B(r))) \geq 1.$$

This leads to the following classification of critical equilibria.

Definition 9.16. The geometric equilibrium $(b, \hat{A})$ is critical of type i, with $i \geq 1$, if $\dim(\hat{A} \cap T_b(B(r))) = i$.

This definition enables one to partition the set of critical equilibria according to their type. We shall study the structure of these sets in Section 9.3.6.

Remark. Considering $P\hat{A}$ instead of $\hat{A}$ amounts to having in the picture, as in Chapter 8, economies located "at infinity," but the need for and the mathematical interest for such an introduction is even more obvious in the current framework. We refer to Chapter 8 for an economic interpretation.

9.3.3. The set of economies with multiple equilibria

The search for global properties of economies in relationship to the number of their equilibria begins with the study of the set of economies with multiple equilibria,

$$\mathfrak{M}(b) = \{\hat{A} \in P\hat{A} \mid b \in \hat{A} \text{ and either } \#(\hat{A} \cap B(r)) \geq 2$$
$$\text{or } \dim(\hat{A} \cap T_b(B(r))) \geq 1\},$$

where b belongs to $B(r)$ and is fixed.

The set $\mathfrak{M}(b)$ corresponds therefore to the economies with multiple equilibria belonging to the fiber associated with b including the adjunction of economies at infinity corresponding to $\hat{A}$ perpendicular to $S \times \{0\}$.

Proposition 9.17. *The set $\mathfrak{M}(b)$ is pathconnected.*

Proof. Case $\ell = 2$. Let us specify the dimensions at stake in this example. We have $\dim H(r) = m$, $\dim B(r) = m - 1$, $\dim \hat{A} = 1$. The elements $\hat{A}$ belonging to $P\hat{A}$ are therefore the *lines* of $H(r)$. These lines are determined either by two distinct points of $H(r)$ or by a point and a vector. To prove the pathconnectedness of $\mathfrak{M}(b)$ amounts to proving that the set of lines in $H(r)$ that pass through b and that are either tangent in b to $B(r)$ or intersect $B(r)$ in another point $b' \neq b$ is pathconnected.

This problem can be given an intuitive illustration: the set $\mathfrak{M}(b)$ can be identified with the "view" one gets from the surface $B(r)$ at the point b; we are going to show that this "view," or space, is pathconnected because $B(r)$ is pathconnected.

Step 1. Let $\hat{A} \in \mathfrak{M}(b)$. Let us show first that if $\hat{A}$ intersects $B(r)$ in a point b' different from b, one can construct some $\hat{A}'$ tangent in b to $B(r)$ and link $\hat{A}$ to $\hat{A}'$ by a continuous path contained in $\mathfrak{M}(b)$.

We shall begin by defining a smooth path $h : [0,1] \to B(r)$ with the properties:

$$h(0) = b,$$
$$h(1) = b',$$
$$h(t) \neq b \quad \text{for every } t \neq 0.$$

Recall that $B(r)$ is diffeomorphic to $\mathbb{R}^{m-1}$. Let β and β' be the image of b and b' in $\mathbb{R}^{m-1}$ by some diffeomorphism. Take in $\mathbb{R}^{m-1}$ the segment $[\beta, \beta']$ parameterized by $t \in [0,1]$ by the formula $\beta(t) = (1-t)\beta + t\beta'$. Its inverse image by the same diffeomorphism defines a smooth path in $B(r)$ with the suitable properties. This path defined by the mapping h enables one to associate with every $t \neq 0$ the line denoted $\hat{A}(t)$ and defined by the two different points b and $h(t)$. This continuous mapping from $(0,1]$ into $P\hat{A}$ can be continuously extended to $t = 0$ as follows: the image of $t = 0$ is the tangent at b to the curve $t \to h(t)$ because it is the limit position of the lines $\hat{A}(t)$ when t tends to zero.

The line $\hat{A}(t)$ belongs, by construction, to $\mathfrak{M}(b)$ for $t \in (0,1]$. To end the proof of Step 1, it suffices to define $\hat{A}(0)$ by $\hat{A}(0) = \hat{A}$!

Step 2. It follows from the observation that the set of tangents to $B(r)$ at b is identical to the set of lines of the tangent space $T_b(B(r))$ passing through b (Figure 9.1). This latter set can be identified with the real projective space of dimension $m-2$. It is pathconnected (see, e.g., (Math 4.2) or Dieudonné [17, (16.11.9)]).

Case $\ell \geq 3$. We have to adjust the previous proof to take into account the fact that two distinct points in $B(r)$ no longer define a unique element of $P\hat{A}$, because $\hat{A}$ has now dimension $\ell - 1$, which, in this case, is larger than or equal to two. We therefore introduce the property for a line D passing through b to be a *"multiple" line* if D is either tangent to $B(r)$ at b or intersects $B(r)$ at some point

b' distinct from b. It is obvious that $\hat{A} \in P\hat{A}$ belongs to $\mathfrak{M}(b)$ if and only if $\hat{A}$ contains a multiple line.

Let us take $\hat{A}'$ and $\hat{A}''$ belonging to $\mathfrak{M}(b)$ and let us show that it is always possible to construct a continuous path in $\mathfrak{M}(b)$ linking $\hat{A}'$ to $\hat{A}''$. To perform this construction, we distinguish two possibilities.

First case: the intersection $A' \cap A''$ contains a multiple line. Let D denote this line, and let us take one of its point as an origin. Let V be a hyperplane (of $H(r)$) supplementary to D through the origin (it is sufficient to take, for example, the hyperplane V perpendicular to D).

Every dimension n subspace W of $H(r)$ that contains D intersects V along $V \cap W$, which itself is a dimension $(n-1)$ subspace. Conversely, every dimension $(n-1)$ subspace of V passing through the origin defines with the line D some dimension n subspace of $H(r)$. This establishes a bijection mapping between the set of dimension n subspaces of $H(r)$ containing D and the set of dimension $(n-1)$ subspaces of V. With this mapping and its inverse both being continuous (straightforward verification), these spaces are homeomorphic. The proof therefore reduces to showing that the set of dimension $(n-1)$ vector subspaces is pathconnected. This set can be identified with a Grassmann manifold, here $G_{\ell+m-3,\ell-2}$ (since dim $V = \ell + m - 3$), which are all pathconnected (see (Math 4.2) or Dieudonné [17, (16.11.9)]). Let $W' = \hat{A}' \cap V$ and $W'' = \hat{A}'' \cap V$ be the intersections of $\hat{A}'$ and $\hat{A}''$ with V. It follows from the path-connectedness property of $G_{\ell+m-3,\ell-2}$ that there exists a continuous

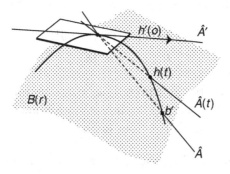

Figure 9.1:   Lines through $b \in B(r)$

arc joining W' to W''. Its inverse image defines a continuous arc $t \to \hat{A}(t)$ joining $\hat{A}'$ to $\hat{A}''$, and such that the multiple line D is contained in $\hat{A}(t)$. This implies that $\hat{A}(t)$ belongs to $\mathfrak{M}(b)$ for every $t \in [0, 1]$.

Second case: The intersection $\hat{A}' \cap \hat{A}''$ does not contain any multiple line. Let D' (resp. D'') be an arbitrary multiple line contained in $\hat{A}'$ (resp. $\hat{A}''$). Since b belongs to D' and D'' and since these lines are distinct by assumption, they generate a plane itself contained in at least a linear manifold $\hat{A}$ of dimension $(\ell - 1)$ (recall that we have $\ell - 1 \geq 2$). Since D' and D'' are multiple lines, this implies that $\hat{A}$ belongs to $\mathfrak{M}(b)$. Now, the linear spaces $\hat{A}$ and $\hat{A}'$ on the one hand, and $\hat{A}$ and $\hat{A}''$ on the other, respectively, contain a multiple line, which enables us to apply to $\hat{A}$ and $\hat{A}'$, and to $\hat{A}$ and $\hat{A}''$, respectively, the property established for the first case. This defines two continuous arcs, the first one joining $\hat{A}'$ to $\hat{A}$, the second one $\hat{A}$ to $\hat{A}''$, which solves the problem of joining $\hat{A}'$ to $\hat{A}''$. $\square$

Remark. One immediately infers from 9.17 that the union,

$$\mathfrak{M} = \bigcup_{b \in B(r)} \mathfrak{M}(b),$$

is also pathconnected.

9.3.4. The set of economies with a unique equilibrium

We define $\mathcal{U}(b)$ as the set of linear spaces $\hat{A} \in P\hat{A}$ that intersect $B(r)$ only in b and that are transverse to $B(r)$. In other words, we impose

$$\begin{cases} T_b(B(r)) \cap \hat{A} = \{b\}, \\ B(r) \cap \hat{A} = \{b\}. \end{cases}$$

The set $\mathcal{U}(b)$ can be interpreted as corresponding to the set of economies (where economies at infinity are allowed) with a unique equilibrium belonging to the fiber defined by $b \in B(r)$ (Figure 9.2).

Proposition 9.18. *The space $\mathcal{U}(b)$ is pathconnected in the case of two agents (i.e., $m = 2$).*

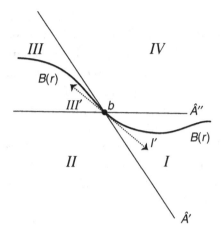

Figure 9.2: Economies with a unique equilibrium

Proof. Let us begin by specifying the dimensions of the spaces being considered. The manifold $B(r)$ has dimension $m - 1$: it is a curve diffeomorphic to $\mathbb{R}$. The linear spaces $\hat{A} \in P\hat{A}$ have dimension $\ell - 1$: these are hyperplanes of the space $H(r)$, itself of dimension ℓ. Let us consider two distinct hyperplanes belonging to $\mathcal{U}(b)$, i.e., passing through b, transverse to the curve $B(r)$, and intersecting $B(r)$ only in $\{b\}$. We denote these hyperplanes by $\hat{A}'$ and $\hat{A}''$; let L be their intersection. We have dimension $L = \ell - 2$.

The space $H(r)$ is partitioned by $\hat{A}'$ and $\hat{A}''$ into four quadrants. The idea of the proof is to locate the curve $B(r)$ with respect to these quadrants. Consider the tangent at b to the curve $B(r)$. The transversality assumption implies that this tangent is contained neither in $\hat{A}'$ nor in $\hat{A}''$. Consequently, with the exception of point b, the tangent is contained in the complement in $H(r)$ of the union $\hat{A}' \cup \hat{A}''$. This tangent is made of two opposite half-lines that belong, therefore, to two opposite quadrants among the four possible ones. By convention, we call these quadrants I and III. Let us show that the curve $B(r)$ is entirely contained in the union of these two quadrants and the point b. The complement of b in $B(r)$ is made of two continuous arcs. One, denoted by (I'), is defined by the property that the half-tangent to (I') at b is contained in quadrant I. The other one, denoted respectively by (III'), is defined by having its half-tangent contained in III. It follows from these definitions and from the transversality property, that all the points of arc (I') taken in a small *neighborhood* of b belong to quadrant I. A similar property holds true for arc (III') and quadrant III.

Now, let us show that *all* the points of arc (I') are contained in quadrant I (and not only those belonging to some small neighborhood of b). Assume the contrary, i.e., that arc (I') contains a point M' not in quadrant I, i.e., in one of the three other quadrants. Let M be a point of arc (I') close enough to b to belong to I. The part of arc (I') between the points M and M' defines a continuous path linking these two points. Since these two points do not belong to the same quadrants defined by $\hat{A}'$ and $\hat{A}''$, arc (I') must necessarily intersect at least one of the two hyperplanes $\hat{A}'$ and $\hat{A}''$ (see Figures 9.3 and 9.4). Since arc (I') does not contain b, this intersection point must necessarily be different from b. Therefore, either $\hat{A}'$ or $\hat{A}''$ intersect $B(r)$ in at least two different points, which contradicts the assumptions. The same argument would show that arc (III') is contained in quadrant III. Therefore, the two other quadrants, namely II and IV, do not contain any point of $B(r)\backslash\{b\}$. Consequently, any hyperplane containing $L = \hat{A}' \cap \hat{A}''$ and contained in the two opposite quadrants II and IV intersects $B(r)$ only in b, is transverse to $B(r)$, and therefore belongs to $\mathcal{U}(b)$.

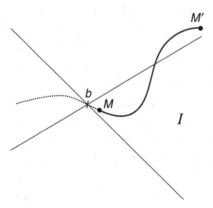

Figure 9.3:   A counterexample to the uniqueness of equilibrium

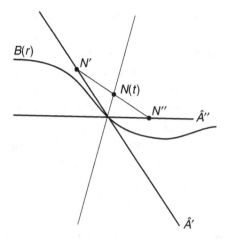

Figure 9.4: Connectedness in the case of a unique equilibrium

All that remains to be done is to join $\hat{A}'$ and $\hat{A}''$ by a continuous family of planes $\hat{A}(t)$ containing L and being contained in the quadrants *II* and *IV*.

Let us choose points $N' \in \hat{A}'$, $N'' \in \hat{A}''$ such that the segment $N'N''$ belongs to quadrant *II*, for example.

Set $N(t) = (1-t)N' + tN''$ with $t \in [0,1]$. The point $N(t)$ and the codimension 2 space L define a hyperplane $A(t)$. It is straightforward that this construction possesses the desired properties. □

Remark. There is as yet no proof of the connectedness of the set of regular economies with unique equilibrium in the case of any number of agents, preferences satisfying the general assumptions of Chapter 4. This is because the proof of 9.18, which works for $m = 2$, simply does not extend to $m \geq 3$.

9.3.5. The structure of the set of critical equilibria

Let us consider the set of critical equilibria of type i, i.e.,

$$PS_i = \{(b, \hat{A}) \in P\mathcal{E} | (b, \hat{A}) \text{ is critical of type } i\}.$$

By definition, the set of critical equilibria is the disjoint union

$$\bigcup_{i \geq 1} PS_i.$$

The next result clarifies the structure of these strata. Its proof requires technical notions related to vector and Grassmann bundles. Luckily, these notions can be made natural by relying heavily on geometric intuition. The knowledgeable reader will have no problem completing the rather intuitive geometrical considerations presented here by the formal arguments that make a proof rigorous.

Recall that $B(r)$, the manifold of price–income equilibria, is diffeomorphic to $\mathbb{R}^{m-1}$. We denote by $T(B(r))$ the tangent bundle to $B(r)$. It can be identified with the "disjoint" union,

$$\bigcup_{b \in B(r)} T_b(B(r))$$

of the tangent spaces to $B(r)$. One defines a mapping $T(B(r)) \to B(r)$ by associating with every element of $T(B(r))$ the corresponding point $b \in B(r)$. The inverse image of $b \in B(r)$ is of course $T_b(B(r))$. To sum up, the tangent bundle $T(B(r))$ is a vector bundle over $B(r)$.

We are now going to extend to the framework of vector bundles the construction of Grassmann manifolds. Let us fix $b \in B(r)$ and take it as the origin of the tangent space $T_b(B(r))$ considered as embedded in $H(r)$. This enables us to identify $T_b(B(r))$ with a dimension $m - 1$ vector space. The vector subspaces of $T_b(B(r))$ having dimension i generate a Grassmann manifold diffeomorphic to $G_{m-1,i}$, the set of vector subspaces of dimension i in $\mathbb{R}^{m-1}$. Let us vary $b \in B(r)$. Let $\mathcal{G}_i$, be the "disjoint" union of the above manifolds. One defines a mapping,

$$\mathcal{G}_i \to B(r),$$

by associating with every element of $\mathcal{G}_i$, the corresponding point b of $B(r)$. The inverse image of b by this mapping is the set of vector subspaces of $T_b(B(r))$ having dimension i. In other words, the manifold $\mathcal{G}_i$ is a Grassmann bundle on $B(r)$, the typical fiber being diffeomorphic to $G_{m-1,i}$. One shows that this bundle is diffeomorphic to $\mathbb{R}^{m-1} \times G_{m-1,i}$. The mapping $\mathcal{G}_i \to B(r)$ is the projection of the bundle.

Now, fix some element G in $\mathcal{G}_i$: It is a vector subspace of dimension i of some $T_b(B(r))$. Recall that $T_b(B(r))$ is a linear manifold embedded in $H(r)$.

Therefore, one can consider the linear subspaces of $H(r)$, having dimension $\ell - 1$, that contain the subspace G. They generate a manifold diffeomorphic to the Grassmann manifold $G_{\ell+m-2-i,\ell-i-1}$. This can easily be checked out by projecting $H(r)$ and its subspaces parallel to G onto a complement of G. Let $\mathcal{H}_i$ be the set of these linear subspaces when G varies in $\mathcal{G}_i$. It is clear that $\mathcal{H}_i$ is a fiber bundle on $\mathcal{G}_i$, the typical fiber being diffeomorphic to the Grassmann manifold $G_{\ell+m-2-i,\ell-1-i}$.

Proposition 9.19. *The set* PS_i, *of critical equilibria of type* i *can be identified with the manifold* $\mathcal{H}_i$, *fibered on* $\mathcal{G}_i$, *itself fibered on* $B(r)$.

Proof. The only difficulty is to construct and interpret the fibered manifolds $\mathcal{G}_i$ and $\mathcal{H}_i$. From there, everything becomes simple. Indeed, the equilibrium $(b, \hat{A})$ is critical of type i if and only if $\hat{A} \cap T_b(B(r))$ is a subspace of dimension i, i.e., belongs to $\mathcal{G}_i$; then $\hat{A}$ belongs to $\mathcal{H}_i$, and conversely. $\qquad\square$

This proposition is remarkable, because it is rather exceptional that sets analogous to PS_i are manifolds in more general frameworks. Furthermore, 9.19 provides a description of the global structure of the manifolds PS_i. Therefore, 9.19 can be considered as pointing to a detailed study of the singularities of the natural projection, a necessary step towards understanding the discontinuous behavior of the equilibrium prices.

Corollary 9.20. *We have*

$$PS_i = \varnothing \quad for \ i > \inf(\ell - 1, m - 1),$$
$$PS_i \neq \varnothing \quad for \ i \leq \inf(\ell - 1, m - 1).$$

Proof. For $\hat{A} \in PS_i$, we necessarily have

$$i = \dim(T_b(B(r)) \cap \hat{A}) \leq \inf(\dim T_b(B(r)), \dim \hat{A}),$$

which implies $i \leq \inf(\ell - 1, m - 1)$. Furthermore, the proof of 9.19 shows how to construct an example of critical equilibria of type i as long as i is less than or equal to $\inf(\ell - 1, m - 1)$. $\qquad\square$

Corollary 9.21. *For $i \leq \inf(\ell - 1, m - 1)$, one has*

$$\dim PS_i = (\ell - 1)(m - 1) - i^2.$$

Proof. The dimensions of the Grassmann manifolds $G_{m-1,i}$ and $G_{\ell+m-2-i,\ell-1-i}$ are respectively equal to $i(m - 1 - i)$ and $(\ell - 1 - i)(m - 1)$ (Math 5.2). It follows from 9.19 that $\dim PS_i$, is therefore the sum,

$$i(m - 1 - i) + (\ell - 1 - i)(m - 1) = (\ell - 1)(m - 1) - \ell^2. \qquad \square$$

9.3.6. The relationship between the number and the determinateness of equilibria

This section takes up again the question of the relationship between the knowledge of the number of equilibria for *all* economies and the determination of these equilibria. We have already investigated this question with the help of envelope theory in the case of two commodities and two agents. We now address the general case with the formalism of theory $(\hat{\mathfrak{J}})$.

Recall that $W : \Omega(r) \to S$ denotes the equilibrium correspondence, i.e.,

$$W(\omega) = \{p \in S | (p, \omega) \text{ is an equilibrium}\}.$$

Let $N(\omega) = \#W(\omega)$ be the number of elements of the set $W(\omega)$. If this number is infinite, one simply sets $N(\omega) = \{\infty\}$. It is obvious that if the equilibrium correspondence W is known, then the function $N : \Omega(r) \to \mathbb{N} \cup \{\infty\}$ giving the number of equilibria is also known. It is the inverse problem that we are going to investigate.

Proposition 9.22.

(1) *If there exists $\omega \in \Omega(r)$ for which one has $N(\omega) \geq 2$, then the function N determines the equilibrium correspondence W.*

(2) *If for every $\omega \in \Omega(r)$ there is uniqueness of equilibrium (i.e., $N(\omega) = 1$), the equilibrium correspondence (which is actually a function in that case) is constant: the equilibrium price vector p associated with ω does not depend on ω.*

Remark 1. This result is remarkable on more than one account. After its proof, we shall come back to its implications for economic theory. For the time being, we shall content ourselves to illustrate the peculiarity of this result from the mathematical point of view.

The first part of Proposition 9.22 basically says that the equilibrium equation parameterized by $\omega \in \Omega(r)$, i.e.,

$$\sum f_i(p, p \cdot \omega_i) = \sum \omega_i,$$

where the unknown is the equilibrium price vector $p \in S$, is such that the knowledge of the number of its solutions for all possible values of the parameter ω is just equivalent to knowing the precise values of these solutions. Not many equations share this property. This peculiarity of the equilibrium equation is a far-reaching consequence of the purely qualitative assumptions described in Chapter 4 that underly the general equilibrium model.

Proof of 9.22. We are going to start with part (2), the easier one, by showing that the projection of $B(r)$ on the coordinate space S (recall that $B(r)$ is embedded in $H(r)$ which itself is identified with $S \times \mathbb{R}^{m-1}$) is some point $\{p\}$. Since $B(r)$ is diffeomorphic to $\mathbb{R}^{m-1}$, it is always possible to find at least two points b and b' in this manifold. Let $\hat{A}$ be some linear subspace of $H(r)$ having dimension $\ell - 1$ and containing these two points b and b'. It intersects $B(r)$ at least in b and in b'. But, it follows from the uniqueness assumption that if there exists $\omega \in \Omega(r)$ such that $\hat{A} = \hat{A}(\omega)$, then the intersection $\hat{A} \cap B(r)$ reduces to one point. Therefore, existence of such ω at finite distance is impossible, which is equivalent to having $\hat{A}$ perpendicular to S. This perpendicularity property is therefore satisfied by all subspaces $\hat{A}$ of dimension $\ell - 1$ containing the line bb'. It is therefore the line bb' itself which must be perpendicular to S. Let us fix $b = (p, w_1, \ldots, w_m) \in B(r)$. Its projection on S is the price vector p. Any other point $b' \in B(r)$ being such that bb' is perpendicular to S also projects in b, which ends the proof of part (2) of the proposition.

For part (1), we shall stick to the point of view provided by theory $(\hat{\mathfrak{J}})$. We recall that $\hat{\mathcal{A}}$ designates the set of linear subspaces $\hat{A}$ of

$H(r)$ having dimension $\ell - 1$ and not perpendicular to S. Therefore, a formulation that is equivalent to 9.22 would be to say that the knowledge of the number of points of the intersection $\hat{A} \cap B(r)$ for all spaces $\hat{A} \in \hat{\mathcal{A}}$ is sufficient to determine the manifold $B(r)$ embedded in $H(r)$.

Assume that this result is not true. This means that there exist for the same function N two distinct manifolds $B(r)$ and $B'(r)$. To get a contradiction, it suffices to establish the existence of some $\hat{A} \in \hat{\mathcal{A}}$ for which the number of points of the sets $\hat{A} \cap B(r)$ and $\hat{A} \cap B'(r)$ are distinct.

This property follows from (Math 4.3), the manifolds $B(r)$ and $B'(r)$ being *properly* embedded in $H(r)$ relatively to $\hat{A}$, since the mapping $(b, \hat{A}) \to \hat{A}$ defined on the set of equilibria $\mathcal{E}$ and taking its values in $\hat{\mathcal{A}}$ is proper, a result established for the manifold $B(r)$, but which therefore also applies to $B'(r)$.   □

Remark 2. Proposition 9.22 enables one to better recognize the importance of the role played by the number of equilibria. Very early on, we have seen that multiple equilibria were necessary for discontinuous behavior of the equilibria to occur. With the proof of the uniqueness of equilibrium at Pareto optima given in Chapter 6, this multiplicity has turned out to be a sufficient condition also. Proposition 9.22 goes considerably further, since it is the quantitative behavior of the equilibria that is in fact determined by their number. In other words, the properties usually associated with comparative statics directly depend, in fact, on the number of equilibria.

The "correspondence principle" stated by Samuelson [83], which relates uniqueness, stability and the comparative statics of equilibria, anticipates in some sense the results of Proposition 9.22.

9.3.7. Domains of definition of selections of price equilibria

We recall that if $\omega \in \Omega(r)$ is a regular economy, there exist an open neighborhood U of ω and smooth mappings $s_i : U \to S$ such that the union $\bigcup s_i(\omega)$ is the set $W(\omega)$ consisting of the equilibrium price vectors associated with the economy ω by Proposition 6.11. We are going to extend this result by describing a method of defining these definition sets U in a way such that, in some sense, make them the biggest possible. The theoretical and econometric implications of such a result are obvious.

We illustrate the mathematical nature of the problem raised by the search for maximal definition sets by the following example. Consider the helix in $\mathbb{R}^3$ defined in parametric form by the equations $x = \cos\theta$, $y = \sin\theta$, $z = \theta$ with $\theta \in \mathbb{R}$. The circle centered at the origin and with radius one in the plane xy plays the role of $\Omega(r)$, the helix curve the role of $E(r)$. The only difference with the framework of the natural projection π is that the projection from the helix onto the circle is not proper, but this is inessential in order to get the flavor of the problem. A selection is a function θ depending on the coordinates (x, y) of a point on the circle such that $x = \cos\theta$, $y = \sin\theta$. Therefore, these selections are defined up to an angle of 2π radians. Consequently, the biggest definition set of any one of these selections can be the base circle with one arbitrary point deleted. On the other hand, there exists no smooth selection defined on the whole circle. The maximal definition sets are the circle minus one point.

Summarizing, the problem raised is the determination of definition sets for the equilibrium price selections that are the largest possible ones. We investigate first the case $\ell = 2$, then the case $m = 2$ and finally the general case.

First case: $\ell = 2$. We begin with the easiest case where there are only two commodities, which can, in fact, be solved within the elementary framework of the natural projection π.

The set of prices S can be identified with $\mathbb{R}_{++}$. Let then $\omega_0 \in \mathcal{R}$ be a regular economy. Let us show that we can take for U the connected component of $\mathcal{R}$ that contains ω_0. Indeed, we know that every economy $\omega \in U$ possesses a finite constant number n of equilibrium price vectors. Define $s_1(\omega), s_2(\omega), \ldots, s_n(\omega)$ by the convention that the coordinates $p_1(s_i(\omega))$ of the price vector $s_i(\omega)$ (because we have $s_i(\omega) = (p_1(s_i(\omega)), 1)$) satisfy the inequalities,

$$p_1(s_1(\omega)) < p_1(s_2(\omega)) < \cdots < p_1(s_n(\omega)).$$

We thus define n mappings by $s_i : U \to S$. It is therefore sufficient to show that each one of these mappings is smooth. This is straightforward: take any $\omega \in U$; there exists by 6.11 an open neighborhood V of ω and n smooth mappings denoted by $\bar{s}_i$ defined on V and taking their values in S for which we have

$$W(\omega) = \bigcup \{\bar{s}_i(\omega)\}.$$

It is of course possible to choose the i's so that $\bar{s}_i(\omega) = s_i(\omega)$. It follows from the continuity of the mappings $\bar{s}_i$ that it is always possible to take V small enough for the following properties to be true:

(1) V is contained in U;
(2) the inequalities $p_1(\bar{s}_i(\omega')) < p_1(\bar{s}_j(\omega'))$ are satisfied for $i < j$

and every $\omega' \in V$.

This implies that the restriction of s_i, to the open set V is identical to $\bar{s}_i$, which ends the proof of this simple case.

This proof, however, does not easily extend to the case of more than two commodities simply because no such continuous order can then be defined on S. We are therefore going to reformulate the problem within the framework of theory $(\hat{\mathfrak{J}})$. It is clear that defining a smooth mapping $s : U \to S$ where $s(\omega)$ is an equilibrium price vector associated with the economy $\omega \in U$ is simply equivalent to defining a smooth mapping $\sigma : U \to B(r)$ where $\sigma(\omega)$ belongs to the intersection $\hat{A}(\omega) \cap B(r)$. It is in this form that we now are going to study the problem of the selections of price equilibria.

Second case: $m = 2$. We already know that the manifold $B(r)$ is diffeomorphic to $\mathbb{R}$, which enables one to define on $B(r)$ a continuous ordering relation denoted by $\leq$ simply by transferring the structure of $\mathbb{R}$ to $B(r)$. It then becomes possible to repeat the argument of the first part and to define mappings σ_i where the relationship $\sigma_i(\omega) < \sigma_j(\omega)$ is equivalent to inequality $i < j$. These mappings are defined on the connected component of $\mathcal{R}$ that contains the economy ω as in the first case. Unfortunately, this result does not extend to the more general case either.

Third case: ℓ and m arbitrary. The idea is to follow the same approach as in the second case by considering on $\mathbb{R}^{m-1}$ (to which $B(r)$ is diffeomorphic) a *preordering* that possesses sufficient continuity properties. Let us consider to this effect the preorder $\leq$ on $\mathbb{R}^{m-1}$ where $x = (x_1, \ldots, x_{m-1}) \leq x' = (x'_1, \ldots, x'_{m-1})$ is equivalent to the inequality $x_1 \leq x'_1$. By transferring the structure of $\mathbb{R}^{m-1}$ to $B(r)$, one thus defines a preorder on $B(r)$ still denoted by $\leq$. Let us denote by $\sim$ the equivalence relation associated with the preorder (i.e., $b \sim b'$ is equivalent to $b \leq b'$ and $b' \leq b$). For the sake of convenience, let $x_1(b)$ denote the first coordinate of the point $x = (x_1, \ldots, x_{m-1}) \in \mathbb{R}^{m-1}$ which is associated with $b \in B(r)$ through the diffeomorphism of $B(r)$ with $\mathbb{R}^{m-1}$. Define the subset $\mathcal{R}'$ of the set of regular economies $\mathcal{R}$ by the following property:

$$\mathcal{R}' = \left\{ \omega \in \mathcal{R} \,\middle|\, \begin{array}{l} \text{all the elements of } B(r) \cap \hat{A}(w) \\ \text{belong to distinct equivalence classes} \end{array} \right\}.$$

In other words, we have

$$\mathcal{R}' = \left\{ \omega \in \mathcal{R} \,\middle|\, \begin{array}{l} \text{the } x_1(b)\text{'s are pairwise} \\ \text{distinct for all } b \in B(r) \cap \hat{A}(\omega) \end{array} \right\}.$$

We then have the following:

Proposition 9.23. *The set $\mathcal{R}'$ is open dense in $\Omega(r)$. For every regular economy $\omega \in \mathcal{R}'$, one can take as the domain of definition of the selections of price equilibria the connected component of $\mathcal{R}'$ that contains ω.*

Proof. It proceeds in three steps.

(1) First, we show that $\mathcal{R}'$ is open in $\Omega(r)$. Let $\omega \in \mathcal{R}'$. It is clear that every ω' close enough to ω belongs to $\mathcal{R}$ and that the selections of equilibrium prices s_i are also defined at ω'. Let us set $b_i(\omega') = (s_i(\omega'), s_i(\omega') \cdot \omega'_1, \ldots, s_i(\omega') \cdot \omega'_m)$. By composing these mappings defined for $i = 1, 2, \ldots, n$ with x_1, we get n continuous mappings denoted by $B_i : U \to \mathbb{R}$ where U is an open neighborhood of ω. Since the mappings B_i are continuous, it is possible to choose U small enough so that all the $B_i(\omega')$'s are pairwise distinct for

every $\omega' \in U$. Consequently, the open set U is contained in $\mathcal{R}'$, which is therefore a neighborhood of all its points, hence is open.

(2) Let us show that it is possible to take the connected component of $\mathcal{R}'$ that contains ω as the definition set of all the equilibrium price selections. Indeed, since none of the points of $B(r) \cap \hat{A}(\omega')$ for $\omega' \in \mathcal{R}'$ are equivalent, it is possible to rank them as follows:

$$b_1 < b_2 < \cdots < b_n,$$

which enables us to define as in the first two cases, i.e., either $\ell = 2$ or $m = 2$, n smooth selections on the whole connected component under consideration.

(3) The part that remains is the most difficult one: to show that $\mathcal{R}'$ is dense in $\mathcal{R}$. Consider the set F, the elements of which are the triples $(b, b', \hat{A})$ where $\hat{A} \in \hat{\mathcal{A}}$ contains both points b and b' assumed to be distinct (one does not require that b and b' belong to $B(r)$; they are simply in $H(r)$). The projection $(b, b', \hat{A}) \to (b, b')$ defines a mapping from F onto $H(r) \times H(r)\backslash\Delta$, the complement of the diagonal Δ in $H(r) \times H(r)$. The inverse image of any point by this projection $(b, b', \hat{A}) \to (b, b')$ can be identified with the set consisting of subspaces $\hat{A} \in \hat{\mathcal{A}}$ that contain the line defined by the two points b and b': this inverse image can be identified with the Grassmann manifold $G_{m+\ell-3, \ell-2}$. A routine technique shows that F is a Grassmann fiber bundle on $H(r) \times H(r)\backslash\Delta$, with fibers diffeomorphic to $G_{m+\ell-3, \ell-2}$.

Let us now consider the manifold $B(r) \times B(r)\backslash\Delta$ embedded in $H(r) \times H(r)\backslash\Delta$. The fiber bundle F defined by restriction of the base $H(r) \times H(r)\backslash\Delta$ to $B(r) \times B(r)\backslash\Delta$ is a Grassmann fiber bundle denoted by G. The dimension of G is equal to

$$\dim(B(r) \times B(r)\backslash\Delta) + \dim G_{m+\ell-3, \ell-2} = (m-1).$$

It is, incidentally, equal to the dimension of $\hat{\mathcal{A}}$.

The mapping $(b, b', \hat{A}) \to \hat{A}$ is a smooth mapping defined on G and taking values in $\hat{\mathcal{A}}$. Both spaces have the same dimension. Let D be the subset of $B(r) \times B(r)\backslash\Delta$ consisting of the pairs (b, b') with $b \neq b'$ and $b \sim b'$. The diffeomorphism between $B(r)$ and $\mathbb{R}^{m-1}$

extends to a diffeomorphism of $B(r) \times B(r) \backslash \Delta$ with $\mathbb{R}^{m-1} \times \mathbb{R}^{m-1} \backslash \Delta$. The image of the set D by this diffeomorphism is the set of $(m-1)$-tuples,

$$(x_1, \ldots, x_{m-1}, x_1', \ldots, x_{m-1}') \in \mathbb{R}^{m-1} \times \mathbb{R}^{m-1},$$

that satisfy the equality $x_1 = x_1'$, while $x_j \neq x_j'$ for at least one $j \geq 2$. This set is a smooth submanifold of $\mathbb{R}^{m-1} \times \mathbb{R}^{m-1} \backslash \Delta$ of codimension one (because of the equation $x_1 = x_1'$). Consequently, D, which is diffeomorphic to this manifold, is also a codimension one submanifold of $B(r) \times B(r) \backslash \Delta$. Let G' be the Grassmann fiber bundle on D obtained through the restriction of the base $B(r) \times B(r) \backslash \Delta$ of G to the submanifold D. This manifold G' is therefore a codimension one submanifold of G, which implies the inequality,

$$\dim G' < \dim G = \dim \hat{\mathcal{A}}.$$

Therefore, the image of G' by the mapping $(b, b', \hat{A}) \to \hat{A}$ is a subset of measure zero of $\hat{\mathcal{A}}$ (Math 1.7).

Let us now show that $\hat{A}(\Omega(r) \backslash \mathcal{R}')$ is a subset of G'. Let $\hat{A} \in \Omega(r) \backslash \mathcal{R}'$. This means that $\hat{A}$ intersects $B(r)$ in at least two distinct points (in fact an odd number ≥ 3) of which at least two are equivalent. Therefore (b, b', A) belongs to G' by the definition of G'.

It follows from the inclusion $\hat{A}(\Omega(r) \backslash \mathcal{R}') \subset G'$ just proved that the measure of $\hat{A}(\Omega(r) \backslash \mathcal{R}')$ is zero. The mapping $\hat{A}: \Omega(r) \to \hat{\mathcal{A}}$ being a diffeomorphism, it follows that $\Omega(r) \backslash \mathcal{R}'$ also has measure zero. We have therefore proved that $\mathcal{R}'$ is an open dense subset of Ω.   □

Remark 1. The so-called "maximal" feature associated with the definition set defined through $\mathcal{R}'$ is expressed by the property that it is an open *dense* set. One will note that this construction does depend on the choice of a diffeomorphism from $B(r)$ onto $\mathbb{R}^{m-1}$, and on a continuous preordering of $B(r)$. Therefore, there is no uniqueness of the maximal set $\mathcal{R}'$.

Remark 2. It is also possible to infer from 9.23 a proof of Proposition 6.20 that does not require using an open covering of $\mathcal{R}$ by balls or cubes, i.e., simply connected open subsets (up to some set of measure zero). Let us take again the assumptions and notation of Proposition 6.20.

Alternative proof of 6.20. Let U_j be the connected components of the open set $\mathcal{R}'$ that have non-empty intersection with the compact set K. Let J' be the set of indices j for which there exist at least n equilibria associated with an economy $\omega \in U_j$. It is therefore clear that:

$$\text{(i)} \ \ K \cap U_j \subset \Omega_n(K),$$
$$\text{(ii)} \ \ \mu(\Omega_n(K)) = \sum_{j \in J'} \mu(K \cap U_j).$$

The inverse image $\pi^{-1}(K \cap U_j)$ is the disjoint union of at least n sets $V_{j,\alpha}$ all diffeomorphic to $K \cap U_j$. We have

$$\lambda(\pi^{-1}(K \cap U_j)) = \sum_{\alpha} \lambda(V_{j,\alpha}).$$

As a result of orthogonal projection, one gets

$$\mu(K \cap U_j) = \mu(\pi(V_{j,\alpha})) \leq \lambda(V_{j,\alpha}).$$

Since there exist at least n sets $V_{j,\alpha}$ contained in $\pi^{-1}(K \cap U_j)$, these two inequalities yield

$$n\mu(K \cap U_j) \leq \lambda(\pi^{-1}(K \cap U_j)).$$

Summing up all these inequalities for $j \in J'$ implies

$$n \sum_{j \in J'} \mu(K \cap U_j) \leq \sum_{j \in J'} \lambda(\pi^{-1}(K \cap U_j)).$$

The right-hand side term of this inequality is less than or equal to $\lambda(\pi^{-1}(K))$; combined with equality (ii) this implies the inequality,

$$n\mu(\Omega_n(K)) \leq \lambda(\pi^{-1}(K)).$$

Since the natural projection π is proper, the set $\pi^{-1}(K)$ is compact. Its Lebesgue measure $c(K) = \lambda(\pi^{-1}(K))$ is finite, which enables us to write

$$\mu(\Omega_n(K)) \leq \frac{c(K)}{n}. \qquad \qquad \square$$

9.4. Conclusion

The results in this chapter extend or develop general equilibrium theory in several directions, First, the theory of B.C.P.E. allocations has the price vector play a totally different role from the usual one in general equilibrium theory. That this framework is not inconsistent with the idea of economic efficiency as formalized by Pareto optimality is indeed remarkable and certainly challenges many standard ideas. But our aim was not to examine in this book the ultimate consequences of this result as far as economic theory and practice are concerned. This would have undoubtedly taken us too far away from general equilibrium theory. Much room remains for some original thinking on the subject. The other direction belongs to the body of general equilibrium theory. But the mathematics used in this formulation is different from that used in the direct approach through the natural projection. The link between the theory $(\hat{\mathfrak{J}})$ and the theory of B.C.P.E. allocations imposes itself most naturally and explains our choices to begin this chapter by an autonomous presentation of the idea of a B.C.P.E. allocation. Nevertheless, the most spectacular results of this chapter deal with theory $(\hat{\mathfrak{J}})$, i.e., with general equilibrium theory. They include the study of the sets of economies with unique or multiple equilibria, respectively, the determinateness of the equilibria, and finally the size of the set of economies having more than a given number of equilibria. One should have noticed, however, that, with one exception, we have not tried to establish directly within the framework of $(\hat{\mathfrak{J}})$ the results that have been proved in Chapter 6, which include the proof of existence of equilibria. This choice is easy to explain: the proofs given in Chapter 6 of these results are undoubtedly the shortest ones; though they can be reformulated straightforwardly within the framework of $(\hat{\mathfrak{J}})$, this would require calling on the theory of manifold intersections. A major tool in this theory is a form of a transversality theorem due to Thom, the statement of which is inevitably less immediate than Sard's remarkable theorem. Nevertheless, a knowledgeable reader would have absolutely no difficulty in establishing the basic properties of general equilibrium while remaining only within the framework of $(\hat{\mathfrak{J}})$.

To conclude, the point of view proposed by theory $(\hat{\mathfrak{J}})$, namely, the formulation of equilibrium as an intersection of sets, is potentially more important for the mathematical formulation of economic theory in the large than the properties, however remarkable, that the formulation through $(\hat{\mathfrak{J}})$ enables one to reach. Recent progress, some of which is mentioned in Chapter 10, has made decisive use of this approach. Besides the significant simplification brought about by considering intersections of sets instead of envelopes, another reason for the fertility of the formulation through $(\hat{\mathfrak{J}})$ stems from the fact that the two sets that are being intersected, namely $B(r)$ and $\hat{A}(\omega)$, possess definitions where preferences, individual and total resources play well-separated roles. More precisely, $B(r)$ is defined by preferences and total resources, while $\hat{A}(\omega)$ depends only on the individual endowments. More general versions of the general equilibrium model which succeed in keeping this dichotomy between analogs of $B(r)$ and $\hat{A}(\omega)$, though more complex than the model of pure exchange, should preserve the main properties of theory $(\hat{\mathfrak{J}})$ and permit one to generalize the results obtained here for pure-exchange economies with a finite number of agents and commodities.

Chapter 10

Several Extensions of the General Equilibrium Model

10.1. Introduction

Up to now, we have studied only one member of the large family of general equilibrium models, namely, the pure exchange economy with finite numbers of agents and commodities. Furthermore, this model has been investigated under a number of assumptions which, certainly for some, may have seemed to be of a rather restrictive nature. Therefore, there is undoubtedly need and room for further extension. We have neither the ambition nor the possibility to propose in one chapter a thorough investigation of developments which would be arduous, to say the least, and would require a book of its own for any satisfactory treatment. Therefore, we shall sketch just a few important extensions to the basic model that have been developed through the years.

Most developments of the basic pure exchange model result from reformulations that attempt to increase the economic relevance of one or of several hypotheses used in defining the model of the exchange economy. These extensions belong to two categories. In the first, the goal of greater relevance is achieved through more complex and sophisticated assumptions bearing on commodities and preferences, but without altering the fundamental pure exchange character of the general equilibrium model. In the second category, it is the modeling of the exchange process itself that is being further developed, for example, by the introduction of new types of agents, or by considering commodities with very specific features. But, whatever the category, the price one pays for these extensions is always an increased complexity of the model, in parallel with increased mathematical difficulty.

Let us illustrate this by way of examples. In the first category we would put extensions dealing with the following themes:

— incorporating into the model the fact that, in some cases, the numbers of agents and of commodities may be quite large;
— defining among properties of the commodity space specific algebraic structures that may reflect time, uncertainty or other relevant features;
— weakening the convexity assumption on preferences, for example, by recognizing that some goods are in fact indivisible.

In the second category, we would find:

— the modeling of production within the general equilibrium model;
— adding money and, more generally, financial instruments and institutions within the equilibrium framework.

These themes are far from being independent of one another. For example, we shall see that taking into account uncertainty in the definition of commodities amounts to defining a specific algebraic structure on the commodity space. Evidently, these themes are far from constituting a complete catalog of all the possible extensions of the general equilibrium model, developments whose necessity is considered imperative in the many fields where economic theory or, more precisely, equilibrium theory is tentatively applied. Except for production, which is obviously impossible to ignore, but for which we believe a brief presentation is sufficient, we have chosen to present developments which still seem to us to have promising prospects. This bias explains, for example, the absence of an important theme of mathematical economics in the forthcoming developments: the study of economies with a large number of agents. Since the remarkable results about the core of an economy, due mainly to Aumann [46, 47], Debreu and Scarf [59], and Vind [92], this subject has benefited from an extensive literature. The grand topic is exposed by Hildenbrand [66], the latest contributions given by Mas-Colell [77]. Let us simply say that this development has clarified the following facts:

(1) The larger the number of agents, the less the convexity assumption on preferences is crucial to the properties of equilibria.
(2) The larger the number of agents, the closer the equilibrium allocations are to the core solution (whose game-theoretic definition conveys the idea that economic agents may form coalitions).

The chapter deals more specifically with the following topics:

— modeling and introducing production within the general equilibrium model;
— incorporating uncertainty;
— incorporating time;
— introducing money.

10.2. Production

It is hardly necessary to underline the importance of production to economic analysis; it is impossible to ignore this subject. Therefore, this section is devoted to modeling the production process and to integrating it into the framework of the general equilibrium model. But, the version of the neoclassical view of the producer we present in this book is undoubtedly among the simplest ones. In making this choice we have been biased by the intrinsically limited scope of the neoclassical formulation which, even in its most general versions, presents an unsatisfactory description of entrepreneurship, ignoring the risk-taking, profit-seeking side of the production process.

Therefore, we have chosen to stick to the best established features of this theory and, most especially, to those that can be accommodated within the framework of general equilibrium theory with the help of the mathematical tools that have been used in this book up to now.

10.2.1. The production set

Consider the commodity space $\mathbb{R}^\ell$. A production, also called an activity, is described by some vector $y = (y^1, \ldots, y^\ell) \in \mathbb{R}^\ell$, where the following sign convention gives two possible meanings to the coordinate y^j:

$y^j > 0$ represents a quantity actually produced, an output;
$y^j < 0$ represents a production factor, an input.

Starting from a bounded amount of various inputs, it is evidently impossible to produce arbitrarily large amounts of all the commodities in the universe. Therefore, not all productions are technically feasible, which leads to the following definition.

Definition 10.1. The production set Y_j of producer j is the set of activities that are technically feasible to producer j.

The definition of the production set Y_j is meant to reflect the current state of knowledge in science and technology and involves no consideration of any economic nature at all. Since techniques of production do satisfy general properties that translate into mathematical assumptions about the production sets, we are entitled to introduce the following set of axioms.

Axiom 10.2. *The production set Y_j satisfies the following properties*:

(1) Y_j *is closed,*
(2) $0 \in Y_j$,
(3) *For $y \in Y_j$ and $z \leq y$, we have $z \in Y_j$.*

The hypothesis (1) is purely mathematical in nature. It is justified for evident reasons of convenience while its relevance raises no problem. The assumption (2) states that zero production is always technically feasible. In other words, any firm is free to stop production. The assumption (3) is but a reformulation of the following idea: If more is feasible, then less also is.

10.2.2. Profit

Let $p \in S$ be a price vector. The profit resulting from activity $y \in Y_j$ is simply equal to the inner product $p \cdot y$, given the sign convention describing inputs and outputs.

10.2.3. The equilibrium of the producer

In a moment we shall define the producer as an economic agent who maximizes his profit subject to the technical production constraints. Adequate within the framework of the universal market (doesn't this amount to maximizing long-run profit?), the relevance of this behavioral rule does not impose itself as readily in the case of actual markets that are much more restricted in scope than the hypothetical universal market. Up to now, economic theory has not proposed totally satisfactory solutions to this problem. Therefore, like most other authors, I shall maintain the hypothesis of profit maximization for the market under consideration despite its shortcomings.

Definition 10.3. The equilibrium of the producer is an activity $y_j \in Y_j$ that maximizes the profit $p \cdot y_j$.

The nature and the properties of the solutions to this problem depend evidently on the geometry of the production set Y_j. Maximizing profit may have no solution, or the solutions may exist but not be determined, etc. We investigate this problem under a set of simplifying assumptions. In fact, we are led to focus on a quite remarkable subset of the production set Y_j, the properties of which are going to play a decisive role.

Definition 10.4. A production $y \in Y_j$ is efficient if the intersection set $(y + \mathbb{R}_{++}^{\ell}) \cap Y_j$ is empty.

Let $Y_{j,\text{eff}}$ denote the set of efficient productions. What makes the concept of efficient production appealing is that it cannot be dominated (in the sense of the inequality $\leq$ taken coordinatewise) by any other feasible production. One notices that a producer equilibrium is necessarily an efficient production. We now propose two simplifying assumptions that are not independent since, as we shall see, 10.6 implies 10.5

Axiom 10.5. *For every price vector $p \in S$ the set $\{y_j \in Y_j | p \cdot y_j \geq 0\}$ is compact.*

The mathematical interest of such an axiom is obvious. Indeed 10.5 entails existence of at least one solution to the problem of profit maximization. Indeed, profit is a continuous function defined on the compact set $\{y \in Y_j | p \cdot y \geq 0\}$ which is non-empty, the zero activity belonging to this set by (2).

The economic interpretation of this condition is not really difficult: it conveys a rather weak form of the "decreasing return" property. In fact, 10.5 means that it is not possible to increase production beyond bounds without diminishing profit — which ends up by being negative.

The following axiom, a technical refinement of 10.5, develops the idea of decreasing returns by imposing convexity of the production set. Furthermore, smoothness is now introduced into the picture. Finally, for the sake of simplicity, we introduce a boundedness assumption that parallels the one made for indifference surfaces, an assumption which could easily be weakened.

Axiom 10.6.

(4) *The production set Y_j is convex,*
(5) *The relative interior $\overset{\circ}{Y}_{j,\text{eff}}$ of the set of efficient productions is an open smooth surface embedded in $\mathbb{R}^l$ with everywhere non-zero Gaussian curvature,*
(6) *The production set Y_j is bounded from above.*

The convexity assumption (4) merely formalizes the idea of decreasing returns. It is reinforced by (5) that introduces a regularity assumption on the production set Y_j. It corresponds to the regularity assumptions made for the consumers by many authors. The hypothesis (6) is intended to yield a reasonably well-behaved producer equilibrium when prices tend either to zero or to infinity.

It is an easy exercise to check that 10.6 implies 10.5. From now on in this section, we assume that axiom 10.6 is satisfied.

Proposition 10.7. *The equilibrium of producer j exists and is unique under the afore-mentioned assumptions. It is defined by a smooth mapping $g_j : S \to \mathbb{R}^\ell$. Profit, which is equal to the inner product $p \cdot g_j(p)$, is always strictly positive.*

Proof. Routine exercise. □

10.2.4. General equilibrium with production

This model, also called the private ownership economy, describes an economic system where the production process is entirely in private hands. We assume that there exist n producers, each of them being characterized by his production set Y_j with j varying from 1 to n. Consumer i owns the share $\theta_{ij} \geq 0$ of enterprise j. The fact that consumer i owns the fraction θ_{ij} of producer j means that he is entitled to receive the θ_{ij}th part of the profit made by producer j. The relationship $\sum_j \theta_{ij} = 1$ then results from the definition. This leads to the mathematical formulation of a private ownership equilibrium with production.

Definition 10.8. The price vector $p \in S$ is an equilibrium price vector of the economy defined by the initial endowments ω_i and the shares θ_{ij} if the following equality is satisfied:

$$\sum_i f_i \left(p, p \cdot \omega_i + \sum_j \theta_{ij} \, p \cdot g_j(p) \right) = \sum_i \omega_i + \sum_j g_j(p).$$

A natural thing to do with this definition would be to investigate for this equilibrium concept the major questions that have been raised in the case of pure exchange economies. Existence of equilibrium, the notion of Pareto efficiency, and the welfare theorems relating equilibrium allocations and Pareto efficiency straightforwardly extend to the case of private ownership economies. These themes are developed at full length in Debreu [12], Koopmans [70], and Arrow and Hahn [45], books that the reader should consult prior to any other ones. But this list of topics is far from being exhaustive. For example, the important notion of a fiber (for the equilibrium manifold) does extend easily to the case of production: a fiber consists of the triples $(p, \omega_i, \theta_{ij})$ where p and the θ_{ij}'s are constant, and the equalities,

$$p \cdot \omega_i + \sum_j \theta_{ij} p \cdot g_j(p) = w_i = \text{constant},$$

$$\sum_i \omega_i = \sum_i f_i(p, w_i) - \sum_j g_j(p),$$

are satisfied. The equilibrium $(p, (f_i(p, w_i) - \Sigma_j \theta_{ij} g_j(p))_i, (\theta_{ij})_{ij})$ corresponds to the no-trade equilibrium encountered in pure exchange economies. Most results of the previous chapters do extend to the case of production.

10.3. Taking Uncertainty into Account

Let us now investigate the new problems arising from taking into account uncertainty within the general equilibrium model. Debreu's [12] concept of a contingent commodity embodies in its definition the state of nature, the realization of which is necessary and sufficient for the contingent commodity to actually be delivered. Debreu's assumption is that all commodities can in principle be indexed by states of nature, an extreme version of the universal market hypothesis extended so as to incorporate states of nature. We begin by stating the main assumptions and definitions of the theory of contingent commodities.

10.3.1. General equilibrium with contingent commodities

For the sake of simplicity, let us consider a finite set N to denote the states of nature. Uncertainties about the realization of one of these states translates into a probability distribution on the set N. A commodity is contingent to the state of nature $\nu \in N$ if, besides its physical and space–time characterization, its delivery also depends on the realization of the state ν. Therefore, a contract implying commodity j contingent on the state ν is a *sure* contract. Uncertainty has been transferred to the actual consequences of the contract.

We denote by $x^{(j,\nu)}$ a quantity of the commodity j contingent on the state ν. Let $p_j(\nu)$ denote the price of commodity (j, ν). This price is sure, being associated with sure contracts. Note that if it turns out that the actual state is the state ν' different from the state ν, then no quantity of commodity j (contingent on state ν) is delivered despite the fact that the value $p_j(\nu)x^{(j,\nu)}$ has been paid by the buyer to the seller.

This readily implies that in order to get the *sure* quantity x^j, i.e., independently of the states of nature, there must be at least as many contracts as there are states of nature. The sure value of x^j then becomes equal to

$$\sum_{\nu \in N} p_j(\nu)x^j = x^j \sum_{\nu \in N} p_j(\nu).$$

With p_j denoting the price of commodity j for sure delivery, we therefore obtain the relationship,

$$p_j = \sum_{\nu \in N} p_j(\nu).$$

Having contingent commodities is by no means inconsistent with consumers characterized through preference preorderings defined on commodity spaces, here contingent commodity spaces. Therefore, the formalism consisting of preordering maximization subject to budget constraints remains unchanged. To the extent that the axioms of Chapter 4 can still be regarded as adequate in this setting (in fact, they will get reinforced later on to take advantage of the stronger structure resulting from introducing the states of nature), every consumer is endowed with a demand function. This enables us to define in the usual way an equilibrium price vector by the equality of aggregate supply and demand of every (contingent) commodity. The general equilibrium model with contingent commodities is therefore formally identical to the general equilibrium model under certainty, the validity of the results of Chapters 4–9 extending to this framework.

10.3.2. The notion of extrinsic uncertainty

We have already mentioned the fact that states of nature bring more mathematical structure to the commodity space. Although the axioms of Chapter 4 remain valid to a large extent in this framework incorporating uncertainty, it becomes more than likely that preferences can be defined to satisfy additional properties, the formulation of which necessitates this extended framework. This is how extrinsic uncertainty comes into the picture: this property of preferences appears very naturally when one investigates the relationship existing between the states of nature on one hand and the final allocation of resources on the other. There is some arbitrariness in the ways that states of nature are defined. For example, it is always possible to decompose a state of nature into two new states by simply introducing a further source of uncertainty, for example, as the one that would be the outcome of throwing a coin. One of the new states corresponds to the conjunction of the former state and of getting heads as an outcome; the other state corresponds to obtaining tails. Hence the following problem: with the definition of the states of nature being arbitrary to the extent it is possible to multiply these states up to infinity, how does the allocation of resources depend on this arbitrariness intrinsically associated with the set of contingent commodities? In this setting, one would clearly expect some sort of invariance principle of the allocation of resources. To study the relationship between states of nature and final allocations, we have to relate the preferences defined on the contingent commodity space to the way states of nature are defined. Before dealing with the general case, let us consider a simple example.

Take two states of nature, namely rain and sun, assumed to be both equally likely, and let us consider the two contingent commodities consisting of an umbrella associated with each of these two states. The services provided by these two contingent commodities are very different from each other, therefore implying noticeable differences in terms of preferences between these two commodities. In other words preference preorderings defined on the contingent commodity space take into account not only the physical and economic content of the commodity or service but also the combination of the (objective or subjective) probability and of the state of nature, sun not being the same thing as rain, as everyone knows.

Let us go back to the umbrella example. But this time define the states of nature as the head and tail outcomes of throwing a coin. Now, it is obvious that there is no significant difference in terms of preferences between an umbrella contingent on the head side of a coin and an umbrella contingent on the tail side. We extend this indifference relation by saying there is extrinsic uncertainty when the contingent commodity is related to the state of nature only through its probability. It is hard to imagine how states of nature can be multiplied in an arbitrary way up to infinity without satisfying the extrinsic uncertainty property, at least when starting with an already large list of states that would contain all those that really count. This leads us to conjecture the following invariance principle: equilibrium allocations are independent of states of nature when preferences satisfy the assumption of extrinsic uncertainty and when individual resources do not depend on states of nature. In fact, we are going to show in a moment that a stronger version of the invariance principle holds true in the general equilibrium model: it suffices that the total resources (not necessarily the individual ones) are independent of the states of nature.

10.3.3. Mathematical formulation of extrinsic uncertainty

For the sake of simplicity, from now on, we represent preferences by utility functions. Let ℓ denote the number of physical goods. We introduce uncertainty through a finite set of states of nature N. Let $\nu \in N$. We denote by $x(\nu) \in \mathbb{R}^\ell$ the commodity bundle that is delivered if state ν is obtained. Let n be the finite number of elements in N. The contingent commodity space can be identified with $\mathbb{R}^{\ell n}$ and consists of the n-tuples $(x(\nu_1), x(\nu_2), \dots, x(\nu_n))$. We find it convenient to identify this n-tuple of contingent commodities with the mapping $x : N \rightarrow \mathbb{R}^\ell$ taking the value $x(\nu_i)$ at $\nu_i \in N$. The contingent commodity space then becomes the set of mappings from N into $\mathbb{R}^\ell$, and is denoted by $(\mathbb{R}^\ell)^N$. The definition of extrinsic uncertainty involves varying the set of states of nature according to well-prescribed rules. Let us consider two sets (of states of nature) N and N'. We say that N' is finer than N if the set N can be identified with a partition of N'. We then associate with the partition N of N' an equivalence relation on N' denoted by $\sim$, the classes of which are precisely the subsets defining the partition N. Consumer i is endowed with preferences or utility functions defined on the two commodity spaces $(\mathbb{R}^\ell)^N$ and $(\mathbb{R}^\ell)^{N'}$. These utility functions are evidently related through some types of consistency we now formalize. First note that the contingent commodity space $(\mathbb{R}^\ell)^N$ is naturally embedded in the contingent commodity space $(\mathbb{R}^\ell)^{N'}$: the mapping $x : N \rightarrow \mathbb{R}^\ell$ defines a mapping from N' to $\mathbb{R}^\ell$ by associating with the element $\nu \in N'$ the image $x(\bar{\nu})$ where $\bar{\nu}$ is the equivalence class of ν for the relation $\sim$. The following axiom (known as the axiom of composed events) relates the values taken by u_i, on the contingent commodity spaces $(\mathbb{R}^\ell)^N$ and $(\mathbb{R}^\ell)^{N'}$.

Axiom 10.9 (of composed events). *Let N and N' be two sets of states of nature such that N' is finer than N. Then, the following diagram defined by the natural embedding from $(\mathbb{R}^\ell)^N$ into $(\mathbb{R}^\ell)^{N'}$ commutes:*

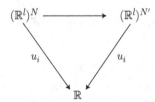

The significance of this axiom is obvious given the former developments. It illustrates the arbitrariness involved in extending a set of states of nature by having finer sets.

Now let N be a finite set of equiprobable states. Let $\sigma : N \to N$ be a permutation, i.e., a bijection. This mapping σ operates on the set of mappings $(\mathbb{R}^\ell)^N$ as follows: the image of the mapping $x : N \to \mathbb{R}^\ell$ by the action of σ is denoted x^σ and defined as the composition $x \circ \sigma : N \to \mathbb{R}^\ell$.

Axiom 10.10 (symmetry of equiprobable events). *For any permutation $\sigma : N \to N$, and any $x \in (\mathbb{R}^\ell)^N$, we have*

$$u_i(x^\sigma) = u_i(x).$$

This axiom can be reformulated as saying that the diagram

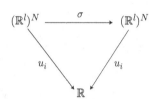

commutes.

For example, in the case $N = \{1, 2\}$, axiom (10.10) implies

$$u_i(x(1), x(2)) = u_i(x(2), x(1)),$$

for any $x(1)$ and $x(2)$ in $\mathbb{R}^\ell$. Therefore, consumer i is indifferent between the ways states of nature are labeled, provided they are equiprobable.

We now deal with non-equiprobable states of nature. Assume for a while that the probability ρ_j of event ν_j is a rational number $\rho_j = \alpha_j / \beta$ where α_j and β are integers, β being the same integer for all states of nature. We decompose state ν_j into α_j equiprobable events each having probability $1/\beta$ by simply considering the event defined by the combination of ν_j and a lottery defined by drawing at random a specified integer chosen between 1 and α_j from the set of integers from 1 to α_j. This construction defines a set of equiprobable states of nature N' which is finer than N. Therefore, it plays a crucial role by enabling us to use Axiom 10.10 in combination with Axiom 10.9 in the case of non-equiprobable states. Nevertheless, this construction is feasible only when the probabilities $\rho = (\rho_j)$ are rational numbers, these being then reduced to the same denominator β.

A continuity assumption is necessary to consider irrational probabilities. Let R denote the closed positive simplex of $\mathbb{R}^n$, i.e.,

$$R = \left\{ \rho = (\rho_j) \in \mathbb{R}^n \,\middle|\, \sum \rho_j = 1; \; \rho_j \geq 0 \right\}.$$

To make things easier, we consider only smooth utilities, and we equip the set of smooth mappings from $(\mathbb{R}^\ell)^N$ into $\mathbb{R}$ with the C^∞-Whitney topology. Note that, up to now, we considered the probability distributions $\rho = (\rho_j)$ as data, not as parameters. From now on in this section, we shall assume that utility functions defined on $(\mathbb{R}^\ell)^N$ are parameterized by $\rho \in R$.

Axiom 10.11 (continuity with respect to probabilities). *The utility function $u_i(\cdot, \rho) : (\mathbb{R}^\ell)^N \to \mathbb{R}$ depends continuously on $\rho \in R$.*

This axiom will enable us to use the density of rational numbers in the set of real numbers in conjunction with Axioms 10.9 and 10.10.

10.3.4. The result on extrinsic uncertainty

We consider a pure exchange economy with m consumers, ℓ physical commodities and a set N of states of nature. Furthermore, we assume that every consumer satisfies Axioms 10.9–10.11 for any set of states N' finer than N. We then have the following:

Proposition 10.12. *Besides having extrinsic uncertainty for every consumer, assume that total resources do not depend on the states of nature (i.e., $r(\nu_1) = r(\nu_2) = \cdots = r(\nu_n)$). Then, Pareto optimal allocations are independent of the states of nature (i.e., if $x = (x_1, x_2, \cdots, x_m)$ denote the Pareto optimal allocation, we have $x_i(\nu_1) = x_i(\nu_2) = \cdots = x_i(\nu_n)$ for $i = 1, 2, \ldots, m$.)*

This proposition states that the set of Pareto optima exhibits a remarkably simple structure invariant with respect to the states of nature. One notices that, in the statement of the proposition, initial endowments appear only after having been added together. In other words, the distribution of these resources is allowed to vary significantly among the agents as a function of the states of nature provided their sum remains constant. We shall come back in a moment to an interpretation of these assumptions and their consequences.

Proof. [Proof of Proposition 10.12] We are going to show that the Pareto optimal allocation does not change if one permutes the states of nature. We start with the equiprobable case where 10.10 enables us to establish the invariance of the Pareto optimal allocation, a result that then extends to rational probabilities by 10.9 and eventually to arbitrary probabilities by 10.11.

Step 1. We begin by considering a set N of n equiprobable states. Consequently, we have $\rho = (1/n, 1/n, \ldots, 1/n)$. Let the allocation $x = (x_1, x_2, \ldots, x_m)$ be Pareto optimal. Now, let σ be some permutation of the set N of states of nature. Let $x^\sigma = (x_1^\sigma, x_2^\sigma, \ldots, x_m^\sigma)$. From $\Sigma x_i = r$, we get $\Sigma x_i^\sigma = r^\sigma = r$, which implies that x^σ is feasible, too. By (10.10), the equality $u_i(x_i^\sigma) = u_i(x_i)$ follows for every i. This implies the equality $x^\sigma = x$ for, otherwise, the allocation $(x + x^\sigma)/2$ would strictly dominate x, contradicting the Pareto optimality of x. The relation $x^\sigma = x$ for every permutation σ of N readily means that the allocation x is invariant with respect to all states of nature belonging to N. This proves the theorem for the equiprobable case.

Step 2. Consider now the case where the probability ρ_j of state ν_j, is a rational number for every j. Using the construction that has been already described based on considering independent lotteries, we can define a set of equiprobable events N' finer than N. The natural embedding described in (10.9) associates with the allocation $x = (x_1, x_2, \ldots, x_m)$ defined for the set N another allocation still denoted by $x = (x_1, x_2, \ldots, x_m)$ but defined this time on the set N'. Let us show that if x is Pareto optimal with respect to the set of states of nature N, then it is also Pareto optimal with respect to the set N'. Let us assume the contrary. Then, there exists $x' = (x_1', x_2', \ldots, x_m') \in (\mathbb{R}^\ell)^{N'} \times (\mathbb{R}^\ell)^{N'} \times \cdots \times (\mathbb{R}^\ell)^{N'}$ that Pareto dominates $x = (x_1, x_2, \ldots, x_m)$ considered as an element of $(\mathbb{R}^\ell)^{N'} \times (\mathbb{R}^\ell)^{N'} \times \cdots \times (\mathbb{R}^\ell)^{N'}$ through the natural embedding described above.

Now define G as the set of permutations of N' that leave the partition N invariant. This means that if ν is a state in N', then $\sigma(\nu)$ and ν belong to the same subset of the partition N of N' (i.e., $\sigma(\nu) \sim \nu$ for the equivalence relation associated with N and N'.) Furthermore, G consists of more than one element as soon as N contains events having unequal probabilities. Let us apply these considerations to x and x'. Axiom (10.10) implies $u_i(x_i'^{\sigma}) = u_i(x_i')$. Assume there exists a permutation $\sigma \in G$ for which $x_i'^{\sigma}$ is different from x_i'. Since G contains at least two elements, the allocation,

$$\frac{1}{\#G} \sum_{\sigma \in G} x'^{\sigma}$$

is strictly Pareto superior to x'. By construction, this allocation is readily seen to be invariant through the action of every permutation $\sigma \in G$. Therefore, this allocation actually belongs to $(\mathbb{R}^{\ell})^N \times \cdots \times (\mathbb{R}^{\ell})^N$ through the natural embedding and is therefore Pareto superior to x with respect to the set of states N, a contradiction. This proves that the allocation x is Pareto optimal when the set of states is N'. Then, Step 1 implies that the allocation x is invariant through every permutation of N', which therefore implies the proposition in the case of rational probabilities.

Step 3. Let us now assume that probabilities can be irrational numbers. Take an allocation x (not necessarily a Pareto optimum). We define the set $K(x, \rho)$ through the relation,

$$K(x, \rho) = \left\{ y \in (\mathbb{R}^{\ell})^N \times \cdots \times (\mathbb{R}^{\ell})^N \,|\, u_i(y_i) \geq u_i(x_i), \right.$$

$$\left. i = 1, 2, \ldots, m \text{ and } \sum y_i = \sum x_i \right\},$$

the utility functions u_i being obviously defined for the probability distribution ρ. Let $\partial(x, \rho)$ be the diameter of the set $K(x, \rho)$. This is a finite real number because the set $K(x, \rho)$ is compact. Clearly, $\partial(x, \rho)$ is a continuous function of x and ρ. Furthermore, the allocation x is Pareto optimal if and only if we have $\partial(x, \rho) = 0$.

Now let x be a Pareto optimum associated with the set of states N and probability distribution ρ. From $\partial(x, \rho) = 0$, there exists a probability distribution $\rho^k \in R$ with rational coordinates such that $\partial(x, \rho^k)$ is strictly less than $1/k$. The set $K(x, \rho^k)$ contains at least a Pareto optimal allocation. Let x^k denote it. We then have the following:

$$\text{distance } (x, x^k) \leq \partial(x, \rho^k) < \frac{1}{k}.$$

By having k tend to infinity, we construct a sequence x^k that tends to x. Since x^k is Pareto optimal (with respect to the probability distribution ρ^k), we apply Step 2 to x^k, which yields

$$x^k(\nu_1) = x^k(\nu_2) = \cdots = x^k(\nu_n).$$

Going to the limit combined with continuity proves

$$x(\nu_1) = x(\nu_2) = \cdots = x(\nu_n). \qquad \square$$

Corollary 10.13. *If total resources do not depend on the states of nature and if preferences satisfy the extrinsic uncertainty assumption, then the equilibrium allocations in the general equilibrium model with a finite number of agents and goods do not depend on the states of nature.*

Proof. Since an equilibrium allocation is necessarily a Pareto optimum, this readily follows from 10.12. $\qquad \square$

Recall that $p_k(\nu_j)$ denotes the price of commodity k contingent on the state ν_j. We now are going to establish a relationship between the equilibrium price $p_k(\nu_j)$ and the probability $p(\nu_j)$ of state ν_j. In order to do this, we rely on the concept of the price p_k of the *sure* commodity k, the price to be paid in order to get a unit of commodity k independently of the states of nature. With this definition, we have already seen:

$$p_k = \sum_j p_k(\nu_j).$$

Corollary 10.14. *The price $p_k(\nu_j)$ satisfies the relationship*

$$p_k(\nu_j) = \rho(\nu_j) p_k.$$

Proof. Let us begin with the equiprobable case. Let us show that for any consumer i, the vector grad $u_i(x_i)$ does not depend on the states of nature.

It results from the definition of a gradient vector that, for any permutation σ of N and given (10.10), we have

$$[\text{grad } u_i(x_i)]^\sigma = \text{grad } u_i(x_i^\sigma).$$

But, we already know that x_i^σ is equal to x_i. Therefore, we get

$$[\text{grad } u_i(x_i)]^\sigma = \text{grad } u_i(x_i).$$

In the equiprobable case, this proves that we have $p_k(\nu_j) = p_k(\nu_{j'})$ at any Pareto optimum, which implies

$$p_k = n p_k(\nu_j),$$

hence,

$$p_k(\nu_j) = \frac{1}{n} p_k = \rho(\nu_j) p_k.$$

This relationship readily extends to rational probabilities, and through a continuity argument to arbitrary probabilities.   □

10.3.5. Application to insurance contracts for individual risks

Proposition 10.12 and its Corollary 10.14 can be given an alternative economic interpretation independent of any invariance concept. Indeed, having individual resources that vary along the states of nature while total resources are constant can be interpreted as the formalization "to the limit" of the concept of individual risk compared to the notion of collective risk. Intuitively, a risk can be regarded as individual to the extent that, though it may be a large one at the consumer's level, it is a small one for the community taken as a whole.

The market that is being considered in this section becomes accordingly an insurance mechanism against the various uncertainties that may be observed in the individual allocation of resources.

Corollary 10.13 can then be read as the complete elimination of individual risks through this insurance market.

Remark 1. Under this interpretation, Corollary 10.14 provides a pricing rule for insurance contracts that sustains Pareto optimality.

Remark 2. Von Neumann and Morgenstern [93] have devised a set of axioms for preferences defined on contingent commodity spaces that enables one to derive the utility of a commodity bundle as the expected value of a utility function associated with sure consumption. One readily sees that these axioms imply the extrinsic uncertainty assumption if the subjective probabilities of the various states of nature are the same ones among all economic agents.

10.4. Time Within the General Equilibrium Model

The possibility of embedding the date of delivery among the characteristics of a commodity is as old as general equilibrium theory. Its combination with the universal market hypothesis leads to mathematical models that are naturally equipped with an infinite number of (dated) commodities and of agents even when the latter have finite lives. The mathematical properties of these models are far from obvious, so that the possibility clearly exists of being led to arduous mathematical developments which are neither compensated nor justified on sufficient economic grounds.

A way of avoiding most mathematical difficulties consists in postulating a finite horizon as in Debreu [12]. Cannot this be justified by the finite span of time of our universe and by the finite number of commodities available on every real market? Despite its appealing features, this approach (which contradicts the universal market assumption) is not fully satisfactory because it does not convey the important fact that the horizon is likely to be located very far in the future. And infinity remains the simplest way of approximating large figures, especially a longtime horizon. Furthermore, one notices that the current modeling exercise is cast within a purely deterministic framework in which having the horizon infinite is the only alternative that does not betray the huge uncertainty bearing on the actual limit of the horizon. Bearing in mind these restrictions about the possible conflicts between mathematical analysis and economic relevance, we begin here the study of the general equilibrium model with an infinite time horizon. Our mathematical and economic hypotheses are aimed at getting a model that requires only the most elementary mathematical treatment given the economic setting. From this perspective, the best model that is currently available is the overlapping-generations model.

10.4.1. The overlapping-generations model

The version we describe is a highly simplified one in order to avoid cumbersome notation. It retains, however, the most essential features related to an infinite horizon. For each period $t = 0, 1, 2, \ldots$, we assume that there exists a finite constant number ℓ of perishable goods, i.e., goods that are available only through the period. There are no durable goods in this simple version.

The life span of every consumer is finite. For the sake of modeling, it is taken equal to two periods. Furthermore, and still for the sake of simplicity, each generation is assumed to consist of only one consumer, whom we can therefore represent by his date of birth. We denote by $x_t^{s,j}$ the consumption of commodity j during period s by consumer t. For the sake of simplicity, we consider only strictly positive consumptions (and initial endowments when we come to them). The utility level of consumer t depends on the commodity bundle x_t, where we have

$$x_0 = x_0^1 = \left(x_0^{1,1}, \ldots, x_0^{1,\ell}\right) \in \mathbb{R}_{++}^\ell$$

and

$$x_t = \left(x_t^t, x_t^{t+1}\right) = \left(x_t^{t,1}, \ldots, x_t^{t,\ell}, x_t^{t+1,1}, \ldots, x_t^{t+1,\ell}\right) \in \mathbb{R}_{++}^{2\ell},$$

whenever t is ≥ 1. When convenient, we also denote by x_0 and $x_t(t \geq 1)$ the sequences $x_0 = (x_0^1, 0, \ldots, 0, \ldots)$ and $x_t = (0, \ldots, 0, x_t^t, x_t^{t+1}, 0, \ldots)$. The initial endowments are denoted by $\omega_0 = \omega_0^1 = (\omega_0^{1,1}, \ldots, \omega_0^{1,\ell}) \in \mathbb{R}_{++}^\ell$ (for $t = 0$) and $\omega_t = (\omega_t^t, \omega_t^{t+1}) = (\omega_t^{t,1}, \ldots, \omega_t^{t,\ell}, \omega_t^{t+1,1}, \ldots, \omega_t^{t+1,\ell}) \in \mathbb{R}_{++}^{2\ell}$ (for $t \geq 1$).

We define $\mathfrak{D}$ to be the infinite-dimensional space, the elements of which are the sequences $(x_0, x_1, \ldots, x_t, \ldots)$, where x_0 belongs to $\mathbb{R}^{\ell}_{++}$ and x_t to $\mathbb{R}^{2\ell}_{++}$ when t is ≥ 1. The space $\mathfrak{D}$ plays the same role in the infinite model as Ω in the finite case. We now introduce prices and incomes. Let $p^{t,j}$ be the price of commodity j ($j = 1, 2, \ldots, \ell$) during the time period t ($t = 1, 2, \ldots$). Then p^t denotes the vector $(p^{t,1}, \ldots, p^{t,\ell}) \in \mathbb{R}^{\ell}_{++}$ and p the sequence $(p^1, p^2, \ldots)$. We adopt the normalization convention $p^{1,1} = 1$ which gives the set of normalized prices,

$$\mathcal{S} = \{p = (p^t) \mid p^{1,1} = 1\}.$$

We denote by $\mathcal{W}$ the set of sequences $w = (w_0, w_1, \ldots, w_t, \ldots)$ with $w_t \in \mathbb{R}_{++}$. Preferences differ slightly from those considered in Chapter 4 for the reason that, although defined on the infinite-dimensional commodity space, only their restriction to the actual consumption set is relevant. More precisely, let u_t be a utility function of consumer t. It is assumed to depend only on x^t_t and x^{t+1}_t (provided $t \geq 1$; if $t = 0$, then u_0 depends only on x^1_0), and to satisfy all the assumptions made in Chapter 4 with respect to these arguments.

Then, each agent is assumed to maximize his utility subject to a budget constraint. This leads us to the two following problems, namely,

$$\begin{cases} \text{maximize } u_0(x^1_0) \\ p^1 \cdot x^1_0 = w_0 \end{cases} \quad \text{for consumer } t = 0;$$

$$\begin{cases} \text{maximize } u_t(x^t_t, x^{t+1}_t) \\ p^t \cdot x^t_t + p^{t+1} \cdot x^{t+1}_t = w_t \end{cases} \quad \text{for consumer } t \geq 1.$$

Solving these problems yields demand functions $f_0 : \mathcal{S} \times \mathbb{R}_{++} \to \mathbb{R}^{\ell}_{++}$ and $f_t : \mathcal{S} \times \mathbb{R}_{++} \to \mathbb{R}^{2\ell}_{++}$ for $t \geq 1$. The same notation f_0 and f_t, is used for the mappings defined by the same formula but considered this time as being defined on $\mathcal{S} \times \mathcal{W}$ and taking their values in $\mathfrak{D}$.

Definition 10.15. The price vector $p \in \mathcal{S}$ is an equilibrium price vector for the economy $w \in \mathfrak{D}$ if the following equality is satisfied:

$$(7) \qquad \sum_t f_t(p, p \cdot w_t) = \sum_t w_t.$$

This definition is a simple extension to the infinite framework of the equality between supply and demand at equilibrium. At first sight, the summations involved are infinite. Nevertheless, there is only a finite number of terms with a given coordinate that is not equal to zero; therefore, the summation always makes sense. Similarly, the inner product $p \cdot \omega_t$ is meaningful since only a finite number of coordinates of ω_t are non-zero. Consequently, the assumption of finite lives avoids all mathematical problems of convergence that otherwise would have been inescapable.

Proposition 10.16. *There always exists an equilibrium price vector $p \in S$ associated with any economy $\omega \in \mathfrak{D}$.*

Proof. We define first the concept of t-equilibrium $p \in S$ associated with the economy $\omega \in \mathfrak{D}$ for $t \geq 1$. It satisfies the equation system,

$$f_0^1(p^1, p^1 \cdot \omega_0^1) + f_1^1(p^1, p^2, p^1 \cdot \omega_1^1 + p^2 \cdot \omega_1^2) = \omega_0^1 + \omega_1^1,$$

$$f_1^2(p^1, p^2, p^1 \cdot \omega_1^1 + p^2 \cdot \omega_1^2)$$
$$+ f_2^2(p^2, p^3, p^2 \cdot \omega_2^2 + p^3 \cdot \omega_2^3) \qquad = \omega_1^2 + \omega_2^2,$$

$$\cdots \qquad\qquad = \quad \cdots$$

$$f_{t-1}^t(p^{t-1}, p^t, p^{t-1} \cdot \omega_{t-1}^{t-1} + p^t \cdot \omega_{t-1}^t)$$
$$+ f_t^t(p^t, p^{t+1}, p^t \cdot \omega_t^t + p^{t+1} \cdot \omega_t^{t+1}) \qquad = \omega_{t-1}^t + \omega_t^t.$$

It is clear from this definition that p remains a t-equilibrium when one changes the coordinates p^{t+2}, p^{t+3}, etc. We now show that there exist bounds α^s and β^s independent of t defined for all $s \leq t$ such that the following inequalities are satisfied for every t-equilibrium p:

$$0 < \alpha^s \leq p^s \leq \beta^s < +\infty, \quad s = 1, 2, \ldots, t;$$

(these bounds are vectors; these inequalities are to be taken coordinatewise).

Let us consider the normalized gradient of consumer 0, namely,

$$\mathrm{grad}_n u_0(x_0) = \frac{\mathrm{grad}\, u_0(x_0)}{\partial u_0(x_0)/\partial x^{1,1}}.$$

At equilibrium, consumer 0's consumption belongs to the compact set,

$$\{x_0 \in \mathbb{R}^{\ell}_{++} | u_0(x_0) \geq u_0(\omega_0) \quad \text{and} \quad x_0 \leq \omega_0^1 + \omega_1^1 < +\infty\}.$$

The image of this compact set by the continuous mapping $x_0 \to \text{grad}_n u_0(x_0)$ is a compact subset of the strictly positive orthant of $\mathbb{R}^{\ell}_{++}$. Therefore, bounds α^1 and β^1 exist in $\mathbb{R}^{\ell}_{++}$ satisfying the inequalities,

$$0 < \alpha^1 < \text{grad}_n u_0(x_0) < \beta^1 < +\infty.$$

Now, if p is a t-equilibrium with $t \geq 1$, we necessarily have $p^1 = \text{grad}_n u_0(x_0)$, which leads to the desired inequality for $s = 1$.

We now assume that the property has been established up to s. We define the normalized gradient,

$$\text{grad}_n u_s(x_s) = \frac{\text{grad } u_s(x_s^s, x_s^{s+1})}{\partial u_s/\partial x^{s,1}},$$

which implies that we have at a t-equilibrium,

$$\text{grad}_n u_s(x_s) = \frac{1}{p^{s,1}}(p^s, p^{s+1}),$$

which belongs to $\mathbb{R}^{2\ell}_{++}$. At equilibrium, consumers' demand belongs to the compact set,

$$\{x_s \in \mathbb{R}^{\ell}_{++} \times \mathbb{R}^{\ell}_{++} | u_s(x_s) \geq u_s(\omega_s) \text{ and}$$
$$x_s \leq \left(\omega_{s-1}^s + \omega_s^s, \omega_s^{s+1} + \omega_{s+1}^{s+1}\right)\}.$$

Using the same line of proof as above, it follows that if p is a t-equilibrium with $s + 1 \leq t$, the vector,

$$(1/p^{s,1})(p^{s+1}) \in \mathbb{R}^{\ell}_{++},$$

in fact, belongs to a compact subset of $\mathbb{R}^{\ell}_{++}$. By the induction assumption, there exist $\alpha^{s,1}$ and $\beta^{s,1}$ satisfying $0 < \alpha^{s,1} \leq \beta^{s,1} < +\infty$. Therefore, there exist α^{s+1} and β^{s+1} with

$$0 < \alpha^{s+1} \leq p^{s+1} \leq \beta^{s+1} < +\infty.$$

This proves the existence of the bounds α^s and β^s for t-equilibria, provided we have $s \leq t$. These bounds α^s and β^s do not depend on t and are defined for every $s \geq 1$.

Let us introduce the set $\mathcal{S}^*$, a subset of $\mathcal{S}$, the elements of which satisfy the inequalities,

$$0 < \alpha^s \leq p^s \leq \beta^s < +\infty,$$

for every $s \geq 1$. Then, let $W(t)$ be the set of t-equilibria belonging to $\mathcal{S}^*$. The sequence of sets $W(t)$ is decreasing, every $(t+1)$-equilibrium being a t-equilibrium. Let us show that $W(t)$ is a non-empty compact set when $\mathcal{S}^*$ is equipped with the product topology. To prove the non-emptiness of $W(t)$, let us add to the equation system defining a t-equilibrium the equation,

$$(8) \qquad f_t^{t+1}(p^t, p^{t+1}, p^t \cdot \omega_t^t + p^{t+1} \cdot \omega_t^{t+1}) = \omega_t^{t+1}.$$

This new system can be interpreted as describing a pure exchange economy with $t + 1$ consumers. In this economy, preferences do not satisfy, rigorously speaking, the hypothesis in Chapter 4 since not every commodity is an argument of the utility functions. Consequently, one cannot apply the existence theorem established in Chapter 6 to this type of equations. It is however possible to use the technique that consists of approximating the utility functions used here by utility functions defined on the "commodity space" $\mathbb{R}_{++}^\ell \times \cdots \times \mathbb{R}_{++}^\ell$ (t times) while satisfying the assumptions of Chapter 4; one then establishes the existence of a solution to the equilibrium system considered above by going to the limit. An alternative approach would be to use the standard existence theorems in Debreu [12] or in Arrow and Hahn [45] or, going back to the source, using a fixed-point argument à la Brouwer. This entitles us to assume the existence of a solution to this system of equations, which amounts to the non-emptiness of $W(t)$, once one notices that a t-equilibrium solution satisfies the first $(t+1)$ inequalities defining $\mathcal{S}^*$, and it therefore suffices to choose arbitrarily the vectors $p^{t+2}, p^{t+3}, \ldots$ provided they satisfy the inequalities defining $\mathcal{S}^*$.

By definition, the set $\mathcal{S}^*$ can be identified with the (infinite) product of the compact sets $\{p^s \in \mathbb{R}^\ell | \alpha^s \leq p^s \leq \beta^s\}$ for

$s = 1, 2, \ldots$ From Tychonoff's theorem (see Bourbaki [54], I, Section 9.5, Theorem 3, for example), $\mathcal{S}^*$ is compact for the product topology. The set $W(t)$ being closed in $\mathcal{S}^*$ is therefore compact.

To conclude the proof of (10.16), it suffices to note that the vector $p \in \mathcal{S}$ is an equilibrium price vector associated with $\omega \in \mathfrak{D}$ if and only if p belongs to the intersection $\bigcap_t W(t)$. This intersection is non-empty as the intersection of a decreasing sequence (in the set-theoretic sense) of non-empty compact sets (cf. Bourbaki [54], I, Section 9.1). □

Remark. The hypotheses surrounding Proposition (10.16) are evidently needlessly strong. For an existence result established in a more general framework, see the Balasko–Cass–Shell [52] article.

10.4.2. Optimum concepts in infinite horizon

There exist at least two extensions of the concept of Pareto optimality or efficiency to the case of infinite dimensions, more precisely of an infinite number of agents. The more straightforward extension is the following one:

Definition 10.17. The allocation $x = (x_0, x_1, \ldots, x_t, \ldots) \in \mathfrak{D}$ is Pareto optimal if there exists no allocation $y = (y_0, y_1, \ldots, y_t, \ldots) \in \mathfrak{D}$ satisfying the following properties:

$$\sum_t y_t = \sum_t x_t,$$

$u_t(y_t) \geq u_t(x_t), \quad t = 0, 1, \ldots, \quad$ with at least one strict inequality.

This extension of the concept of Pareto optima may not be the more interesting one for a variety of reasons. It is indeed implicit in this definition that if the allocation $x \in \mathfrak{D}$ is not Pareto optimal, then the resources can be reallocated among a possibly infinite set of agents, the outcome being an increase in the utility levels of every agent. The feasibility of reallocating an infinite number of times the allocations of an infinite number of agents may turn out to be a real problem, creating difficulties about interpreting this efficiency concept. Furthermore, another reason for not being quite enthusiastic about this concept is that the classical remarkable relationship between equilibrium allocations and Pareto optima does not work with this definition of Pareto efficiency. This justifies introducing a weaker concept of Pareto efficiency, although probably a more interesting one.

Definition 10.18. The allocation $x = (x_0, x_1, \ldots, x_t, \ldots) \in \mathfrak{D}$ is weakly Pareto optimal if no allocation $y = (y_0, y_1, \ldots, y_t, \ldots) \in \mathfrak{D}$ satisfying the following properties exists:

$$\sum y_t = \sum x_t,$$

$u_t(y_t) \geq u_t(x_t), \quad t = 0, 1, \ldots,$ with at least one strict inequality,

$\qquad y_t = x_t$ except for a finite set of t's.

A Pareto optimal allocation is clearly weakly Pareto optimal. The converse is not true. It is possible under the right circumstances to improve a weakly Pareto optimal allocation by modifying the allocation of an infinite number of these agents. The next result extends the classical welfare theorems.

Proposition 10.19. *The allocation $x \in \mathfrak{D}$ is an equilibrium allocation (for some economy) if and only if the allocation $x \in \mathfrak{D}$ is weakly Pareto optimal.*

Proof. The notion of a supporting price vector readily extends to the infinite horizon and to weak Pareto optima. If $p \in \mathcal{S}$ supports $x \in \mathfrak{D}$, it is clear that x is also the equilibrium allocation associated with the resources (or initial endowments) $x \in \mathfrak{D}$ and the price vector $p \in \mathcal{S}$. Therefore, to establish (10.19), it suffices to show that if x is weakly Pareto optimal, then there exists a price vector $p \in \mathcal{S}$ supporting x, and conversely.

Assume first that x is supported by the price vector $p \in \mathcal{S}$. Let us reproduce the proof made in the finite case. We have by definition

$$x_t = f_t(p, p \cdot x_t).$$

Suppose that x is not weakly Pareto optimal. There exists

$$y = (y_0, y_1, \ldots, y_t, \ldots) \in \mathfrak{D},$$

where y_t and x_t coincide for t large enough, i.e., for $t \geq t'$ for some t', and where

$$\sum y_t = \sum x_t,$$

$u_t(y_t) \geq u_t(x_t), \quad t = 0, 1, \ldots$ with at least one strict inequality;

are also satisfied. This readily implies the inequality $p \cdot y_t \geq p \cdot x_t$, the inequality being a strict one if $u_t(y_t)$ is strictly larger than $u_t(x_t)$. By adding up all these inequalities up to $t = t' - 1$, we get

$$p \cdot \sum_{t=0}^{t=t'-1} y_t > p \cdot \sum_{t=0}^{t=t'-1} x_t,$$

which contradicts the assumptions $\Sigma_t y_t = \Sigma_t x_t$ and $y_t = x_t$, for $t \geq t'$. Conversely, let us show that a weakly Pareto optimal allocation $x \in \mathfrak{D}$ is supported by a unique price vector $p \in \mathcal{S}$. Consider the truncated economy consisting of the $(t + 1)$ first consumers, for t arbitrarily chosen. It is then clear that the allocation $(x_0, x_1, \ldots, x_t)$ is Pareto optimal for the truncated economy. This defines a unique supporting price vector $(p^1(t), p^2(t), \ldots, p^t(t))$. Let t vary. We then have $p^s(t) = p^s(t')$ for every $s \leq t$ and $s \leq t'$. Let $p^s = p^s(t)$ for $s \leq t$. The price vector $p = (p^s) \in \mathcal{S}$ supports the allocation $x \in \mathfrak{D}$.

$\square$

We have been able to relate in Chapter 7 the set of Pareto optima and the set of price income equilibria. A similar relationship holds within the framework provided by the overlapping-generations model. More precisely, let r denote the fixed vector of total resources, i.e.,

$$r^t = \omega_t^t + \omega_{t-1}^t, \quad t = 1, 2, \ldots.$$

Let $\mathfrak{P}(r)$ be the set of weak Pareto optima associated with the vector r representing total resources. We now define the analog of the set of price–income equilibria. More precisely,

Definition 10.20. The pair $(p, w) \in \mathcal{S} \times \mathcal{W}$ is an extended price–income equilibrium given the total resources r if the equality,

$$\sum_t f_t(p, w_t) = r,$$

is satisfied. We denote by $\mathfrak{B}(r)$ this set of extended price–income equilibria.

We endow $\mathcal{S} \times \mathcal{W}$ with the product topology. We then have the following:

Proposition 10.21. *The spaces $\mathfrak{B}(r)$ and $\mathfrak{P}(r)$ are homeomorphic.*

Proof. This follows readily from (10.19), with the supporting-price defining, after inner multiplication with the individual resources, a price–income equilibrium just as in Chapter 7. □

This result relates the topological properties of $\mathfrak{B}(r)$ and $\mathfrak{P}(r)$. In this direction, we just mention that $\mathfrak{P}(r)$, hence $\mathfrak{B}(r)$, is connected; for a proof, see Balasko and Shell [51].

Remark. Mathematically speaking, the overlapping-generations model is the simplest extension that accommodates an infinite horizon in the general equilibrium model. Nonetheless, its limits and shortcomings are far from negligible. Interpreting its properties is not always an easy task as it turns out. For example, the mathematical differences between the definitions of a weak and of a strong Pareto optimum are absolutely clear; nevertheless, the economic interpretation of these differences is by no means straightforward.

Parenthetically, strong Pareto optimal allocations can be characterized in the simple model we are considering using the supporting price vector. Let x be supported by $p = (p^t)$. Then x is a strong Pareto optimum if the series $\Sigma_t 1/\|p^t\|$ of the inverses of the norms of the vectors p^t diverges. For a proof of this condition, we refer for example to Balasko and Shell [50]. This result yields the following straightforward application: if the norms $\|p^t\|$ are bounded from above, then x is a strong Pareto optimum (hint: the inverses $1/\|p^t\|$ are bounded from below; therefore, the series $\Sigma 1/\|p^t\|$ diverges).

10.4.3. Money in the overlapping-generations model

Walras attempted incorporating money within the general equilibrium framework. In this direction, he went much further than his immediate contemporaries or followers such as Jevons, Pareto or Edgeworth. Nevertheless, Walras' analysis remained far from providing a satisfactory formal treatment of important functions of money.

The approach we present here was first developed by Samuelson. In fact, he designed a version of the overlapping-generations model with the purpose of relating money to general equilibrium theory. Despite several shortcomings, the model enables one to focus on the function of money as a store of value.

Three major roles are traditionally attributed to money. Namely, they are:

(1) To serve as a yardstick to express the prices of the other commodities;
(2) To facilitate the exchange process by being a convenient intermediary commodity;
(3) To serve as a store of value through short or long periods of time.

The first function has already been taken care of by numeraire. Therefore, only the second and third functions are specific to money. The second one only expresses the idea that money greatly decreases the transaction costs by being an intermediary, intermediation being made possible only by the capabilities of money as a store of value, at least in the short run. This feature of money is basically well-understood. It is therefore the long-run role as a store of value that deserves to be explored, a goal which fits especially well with the overlapping-generations model.

10.4.4. The price of money

Let us assume that money is simply the only durable commodity in a model with dated commodities. At this stage, an infinite horizon is not even a necessary condition, although we shall see very soon that the equilibrium price of money has different properties depending on whether the horizon is finite or infinite.

Let us show first that the equilibrium price of money, if it exists, is constant through time, i.e., from one period to the next. Assume the contrary, for example, that the price in period two is larger than the price in period one. An economic agent buying a unit of money in period one and selling it in period two makes a strictly positive profit. By changing the amount of money, this profit turns out to be unbounded, so that this economic agent practically faces no budget constraint at all, which is excluded by assumption. Consequently, if there is a price equilibrium including money, the price of money must be constant.

Let us now check that the equilibrium price of money must be zero if there is only a finite number of time periods. Consider the last period. The store-of-value function of money becomes useless because there is no point in keeping money for a next period. Therefore, no economic agent wants to keep money during this last period, and its only equilibrium price during this period can only be equal to zero. Combined with the constancy of the equilibrium price of money, this implies that in a finite horizon model, money cannot have an equilibrium price different from zero. In this regard, the infinite model differs from the finite one.

10.4.5. Monetary equilibrium

We assume that money has no direct utility for the consumers, which means that the utility functions do not depend on money. The only effect of money on utility levels is therefore indirect through the budget constraints. Let μ_t, denote the quantity of money available to agent t during his lifetime. Let p_m be the equilibrium price of money. Then, consumer t's wealth is equal to

$$p \cdot \omega_t + p_m \, \mu_t$$

and his demand of physical commodities becomes equal to

$$f_t(p, p \cdot \omega_t + p_m \, \mu_t).$$

We therefore define

Definition 10.22. The pair $(p, p_m) \in \mathcal{S} \times \mathbb{R}_+$ is an equilibrium if the equality,

$$\sum_t f_t(p, p \cdot \omega_t + p_m \mu_t) = \sum_t \omega_t,$$

is satisfied. We call it a monetary equilibrium if p_m is strictly positive.

This definition clearly illustrates the opportunities of intergenerational transfers opened up by money. For $p_m = 0$, one simply gets the standard equilibrium (with no money) of the overlapping-generations model.

The remaining part of this section is devoted to the study of these monetary equilibria. Let $\mathfrak{M}$ denote the set of monetary policies $\mu = (\mu_0, \mu_1, \ldots, \mu_t, \ldots)$. An interesting problem would be to characterize the monetary policies μ for which there exists an economy $\omega \in \mathfrak{D}$ and a monetary equilibrium (p, p_m) (i.e., $p_m > 0$) associated with $\omega \in \mathfrak{D}$ and the monetary policy $\mu \in \mathfrak{M}$. Since it is evidently impossible to consider separately the monetary policy $\mu = (\mu_0, \mu_1, \ldots, \mu_t, \ldots)$ and the economy $\omega \in \mathfrak{D}$, we therefore say:

Definition 10.23. The monetary policy $\mu \in \mathfrak{M}$ is bona fide for the economy $\omega \in \mathfrak{D}$ if there exists a monetary equilibrium $(p, p_m) \in \mathcal{S} \times \mathbb{R}_{++}$ (i.e., with $p_m > 0$) associated with the pair $(\omega, \mu) \in \mathfrak{D} \times \mathfrak{M}$.

One readily sees that if μ is *bona fide*, then any scalar multiple of μ, i.e., $\lambda \mu = (\lambda \mu_0, \lambda \mu_1, \ldots, \lambda \mu_t, \ldots)$ is also bona fide for ω, the pair $(p, p_m/\lambda)$ being the monetary equilibrium associated with $(\omega, \lambda \mu)$. It is then possible to renormalize the *bona fide* monetary policies by considering only those for which the pair $(p, 1) \in \mathcal{S} \times \mathbb{R}_+$ is a monetary equilibrium.

Let $\mathfrak{M}_B(\omega)$ be the set of these normalized *bona fide* monetary policies. Recall that we denote $\mathfrak{B}(r) = \{\mathcal{S} \times \mathcal{W} \in \mathfrak{G} \times \mathfrak{M} | \Sigma_t f_t(p, w_t) = r\}$, the set of price–income equilibria (associated with the total resources r). We then have the following,

Proposition 10.24. *The set* $\mathfrak{M}_B(\omega)$ *is the image of* $\mathfrak{B}(r)$ *through the mapping* $\alpha: \mathcal{S} \times \mathcal{W} \to \mathfrak{M}$ *defined by the formula,*

$$\alpha(p, w) = (\mu_0 = w_0 - p \cdot \omega_0, \mu_1 = w_1 - p \cdot \omega_1, \ldots, \mu_t, = w_t - p \cdot \omega_t, \ldots).$$

Proof. Obvious, once one notices that $(p, 1)$ is a monetary equilibrium if and only if $\Sigma_t f_t(p, w_t)$ is equal to r, with $w_t = p \cdot \omega_t + \mu_t$, which also means $\mu = \alpha(p, w)$. $\qquad \square$

The mapping α makes it obvious that any price–income equilibrium may be reached through a unique monetary policy. Proposition (10.24) combined with obvious continuity arguments implies, for example, that $\mathfrak{M}_B(\omega)$ is connected as the image of the connected set $\mathfrak{B}(r)$. One also notices that the zero vector belongs to $\mathfrak{M}_B(\omega)$.

Remark. It may be worth noting that the classical balanced budged condition $\Sigma_t\,\mu_t = 0$ is neither necessary (contrary to many standard ideas) nor sufficient for a monetary policy to be bona fide. For more details on this issue, see in particular Balasko and Shell [51].

10.5. Conclusion

This chapter has been devoted to several different trends of economic theory. For example, we have dealt with production for the reason that it is hard to imagine a book in economic theory that would not make any mention of production. But our treatment of production is far from being the most advanced one. Indeed, the most remarkable developments in this area have been devoted to getting rid of smoothness and convexity assumptions, in contrast to the approach we have followed here. This explains why our presentation of production avoids the main technical difficulties. As a consequence, extending to this simple model the major results of Chapters 5–9 is mostly a routine exercise we have not pursued. In fact, progress in the modeling of the production process has to be achieved to justify sophisticated analysis of any general equilibrium model incorporating production. Though important features such as monopolistic competition, the relationships between the short and the long run, or indivisibility effects have already been modeled, they have not yet been incorporated in a reasonably simple general equilibrium model worthy of a general presentation.

Embedding time and uncertainty into general equilibrium corresponds to a completely different trend of economic theory. First, the relevance of how these concepts are modeled is hardly questionable, which is one thing. Furthermore, the added structure put on the commodity space as a consequence of having time or uncertainty in the model readily leads to invariance properties of the utmost importance, provided they are formulated in the right context. The result on extrinsic uncertainty provides such an example which can be compared to the much older though related concept of a stationary solution one finds in dynamic models. These invariant solution concepts are known to bifurcate under the proper circumstances into solution concepts with "broken symmetries," the best examples of which are the cycles in intertemporal models and the "sunspot" equilibria introduced by Cass and Shell [56] for uncertainty. These direct expansions of general equilibrium theory are going to play an increasingly decisive role in economic theory.

Mathematical Appendix

The proofs presented in the text often require mathematical notions which are not usually covered in undergraduate curricula. We also need, in the most technical parts of the proofs, various concepts and results for which suitable references are quite dispersed. Therefore, we have tried to put together in this appendix a collection of mathematical statements we use again and again. We shall try to illuminate some of them by comments. Proofs are even given in a few cases. Otherwise, suitable references enable the reader to find proofs when only results are stated. Familiarity with the mathematics taught during the first two years in college combined with knowledge of the material covered in this appendix is in principle sufficient to follow most of the arguments developed in the body of the book.

1.1. Smooth Manifolds

1.1.1. Analysis in several variables

Let $U \subset \mathbb{R}^k$ and $V \subset \mathbb{R}^n$ be two open sets. Let $x = (x_i, \ldots, x_k) \in U$. Let $f : U \to V$ be a mapping, the coordinate functions of which are $(f_1, \ldots, f_n)$.

One says that f is *smooth* or of class C^∞ or, more simply, C^∞ if every partial derivative,

$$\frac{\partial^h f_i}{\partial x_1^{\alpha_1} \ldots \partial x_k^{\alpha_k}} \quad \text{with} \quad \alpha_1 + \cdots + \alpha_k = h$$

exists and is continuous for every $h \geq 1$.

The Jacobian matrix J of f at x is the $n \times k$ matrix where the coefficient of row i and column j is equal to $\partial f_i / \partial x_j$, i.e.,

$$J = \left(\frac{\partial f_i}{\partial x_j} \right)_{\substack{1 \le i \le n \\ 1 \le j \le k}}.$$

Let $X \subset \mathbb{R}^k$ and $Y \subset \mathbb{R}^n$ be two *arbitrary* subsets. One says that $f : X \to Y$ is *smooth* if, for every $x \in X$, there exists an open set $U \subset \mathbb{R}^k$ containing x and a smooth mapping $F : U \to \mathbb{R}^n$ such that its restriction to $U \cap X$ coincides with f. A mapping $f : X \to Y$ is a diffeomorphism if f is a bijection and if both f and f^{-1} are smooth.

1.1.2. Analysis in several variables: The implicit function theorem

(Math 1.1) *Let (f_i) be a collection of n real-valued functions defined in a neighborhood $U \times V$ of the point $(a_1, \dots, a_k, b_1, \dots, b_n)$ in $\mathbb{R}^k \times \mathbb{R}^n$. Suppose that the functions f_i are smooth, $f_i(a_1, \dots, a_k, b_1, \dots, b_n) = 0$ for $1 \le i \le n$, and the Jacobian determinant $(\partial f_i / \partial y_j)_{1 \le i, j \le n}$ is different from zero at $(x, y) = (x_1, \dots, x_k, y_1, \dots, y_n) = (a_1, \dots, a_k, b_1, \dots, b_n)$.*

Then, there exists an open neighborhood $W_0 \subset U$ of $(a_1, \dots, a_k)$ such that, for every open, connected neighborhood $W \subset W_0$ of $(a_1, \dots, a_k)$, there exists a unique system consisting of n real-valued functions g_i defined on W, continuous, and such that $g_i(a_1, \dots, a_k) = b_i$ for $1 \le i \le n$, and

$$f_i(x_1, \dots, x_k, g_1(x_1, \dots, x_k), \dots, g_n(x_1, \dots, x_k)) = 0,$$

for $1 \le i \le n$ and every $(x_1, \dots, x_k) \in W$. Furthermore, the mappings g_i are smooth in W, and the Jacobian matrix $(\partial g_i / \partial x_j)_{1 \le i \le n, 1 \le j \le k}$ is equal to $-B^{-1} \cdot A$, where A (resp. B) is obtained by substituting $g_i(x_1, \dots, x_k)$ for y_i ($1 \le i \le n$) in the Jacobian matrix $(\partial f_i / \partial x_j)$(resp. $(\partial f_i / \partial y_j)$).

Remark. The implicit function theorem holds true if the assumption f_i smooth is replaced by f_i r-times continuously differentiable, $r \ge 1$, or also by f_i analytic.

One of the most important consequences of the implicit function theorem (Math 1.1) is the inverse function theorem, namely:

(Math 1.2) *Let $f = (f_1, \ldots, f_n)$ be a smooth mapping from a neighborhood V of $x_0 \in \mathbb{R}^n$ into $\mathbb{R}^n$. If the Jacobian determinant $(\partial f_i / \partial x_j)_{1 \leq i,j \leq n}$ is different from zero at x_0, then there exists an open neighborhood $U \subset V$ of x_0 such that the restriction of f to U is a diffeomorphism between U and an open neighborhood of $y_0 = f(x_0) \in \mathbb{R}^n$.*

Note that the condition $\det(\partial f_i / \partial x_j)_{1 \leq i,j \leq n} \neq 0$ at x_0 amounts to saying that the derivative f' of f at x_0 is an isomorphism (of linear spaces).

1.1.3. Smooth manifolds: Definition

A subset $X \subset \mathbb{R}^k$ is a *smooth manifold* of dimension n if every $x \in X$ possesses a neighborhood $W \cap X$ which is diffeomorphic to an open set U of the Euclidean space $\mathbb{R}^n$. Any diffeomorphism $g : U \to W \cap X$ is called a parameterization of the domain $W \cap X$. The inverse diffeomorphism $g^{-1} : W \cap X \to U$ is a local coordinate system for $W \cap X$.

It is also possible to define manifolds of class C^r by requiring the parameterization mappings to be of class C^r. Unless the contrary is explicitly stated, we consider only smooth manifolds. Therefore, we use the word manifold to mean smooth manifold.

If X and Z are two manifolds embedded in $\mathbb{R}^N$ and satisfying $Z \subset X$, then Z is a *submanifold* of X. As a special case, the manifold X is itself a submanifold of $\mathbb{R}^N$. Every open subset of X is a submanifold of X. If Z is a submanifold of X, the codimension of Z in X is, by definition, equal to $\dim(X) - \dim(Z)$.

1.1.4. Tangent spaces, tangent mappings

Let $X \subset \mathbb{R}^k$ be a manifold. It is then possible to give sense to the notion of tangent vector to X at x (see the references below), which enables one to define for every $x \in X$ the *tangent space* to X at x, denoted $T_x X$. If n is the dimension of the manifold X, then dim $T_x X$, the dimension of the tangent space, is also equal to n.

If X is an open subset of $\mathbb{R}^k$, the tangent space $T_x X$ can be identified with $\mathbb{R}^k$.

Let $X \subset \mathbb{R}^k$ and $Y \subset \mathbb{R}^n$ be two smooth manifolds. Consider the smooth mapping $f : X \to Y$ with $y = f(x)$. One can then define a linear mapping,

$$T_x f : T_x X \to T_y Y,$$

called the linear tangent mapping to f at x. If X and Y are open subsets of $\mathbb{R}^k$ and $\mathbb{R}^n$, respectively, the matrix of the linear tangent mapping $T_x f : \mathbb{R}^k \to \mathbb{R}^n$ is simply the Jacobian matrix of f at x.

Let $f : X \to Y$ and $g : Y \to Z$ be smooth mappings between smooth manifolds, then we have

$$T_x(g \circ f) = T_{f(x)}(g) \circ T_x f.$$

1.1.5. The inverse function theorem: Global version

Let X and Y be smooth manifolds. We say that f is a *local diffeomorphism* at $x \in X$ if there exists a neighborhood of x diffeomorphic by f to a neighborhood of $y = f(x)$.

(Math 1.3) (Inverse function theorem for manifolds) *Let $f : X \to Y$ be a smooth mapping between smooth manifolds such that the linear tangent mapping $T_x f$ at x is an isomorphism. Then f is a local diffeomorphism at x.*

Using local coordinate systems for X and Y, (Math 1.3) becomes clearly equivalent to (Math 1.2).

1.1.6. Immersions, embeddings, submersions, etc.

We say that $f : X \to Y$ is an *immersion* at x if $T_x f : T_x X \to T_y Y$ is an injection (i.e., is one-to-one). If f is an immersion at every point of X, we simply say that f is an *immersion*.

(Math 1.4) *Let $f : X \to Y$ be an immersion at x and let $y = f(x)$. There exist local coordinate systems in X and Y for which one can* *write*

$$f(x_1, \ldots, x_k) = (x_1, \ldots, x_k, 0, \ldots, 0).$$

An *embedding* $f : X \to Y$ is an immersion which is both injective and proper, (i.e., such that the inverse image of every compact set is compact).

Note also that an embedding $f : X \to Y$ is also an immersion that simultaneously defines a homeomorphism between X and the image $f(X)$.

(Math 1.5) *The image $f(X)$ of the embedding $f : X \to Y$ is a submanifold of Y diffeomorphic to X by f.*

Remark. This property is a very convenient way of proving that the subset $f(X)$ of the manifold Y is actually a smooth submanifold of Y diffeomorphic to X. We use this property in Chapter 5 when studying the structure of the equilibrium manifold.

We say that $f : X \to Y$ is a *submersion* at x if $T_x f : T_x X \to T_y Y$ is a surjection (i.e., is onto). If f is a submersion at every point of X, we simply say that f is a *submersion*.

1.1.7. Singularities of smooth mappings

We say that $x \in X$ is a *critical point* of $f : X \to Y$ if $T_x f$ is not onto, i.e., if f is not a submersion at x. The image $f(x)$ is called a *singular value*.

We say that $y \in Y$ is a regular value of $f : X \to Y$ if y is not the image of a critical point. In other words, the mapping $T_x f : T_x X \to T_y Y$ is onto at every point $x \in X$ such that $f(x) = y$, if y is a regular value.

(Math 1.6) **(Regular value theorem)** *If y is a regular value of $f : X \to Y$, then the inverse image $f^{-1}(y)$ is a submanifold of X, with $\dim f^{-1}(y) = \dim X - \dim Y$.*

(Math 1.7) **(Sard's theorem)** *The set of singular values $f : X \to Y$ has measure zero.*

Corollary. *The set of regular values of $f : X \to Y$ is dense in Y.*

Suppose now that X and Y are smooth manifolds of the same dimension.

1.1.8. Transversality

Let $f : X \to Y$ be a smooth mapping where X and Y are manifolds. Let Z be a submanifold of Y. We say that f is *transverse* to Z if the relationship,

$$\text{Im}(T_x f) + T_y Z = T_y Y,$$

where $y = f(x)$, is satisfied for every x in the inverse image $f^{-1}(Z)$.

(Math 1.8) *Let $f : X \to Y$ be transverse to the submanifold $Z \subset Y$. The inverse image $f^{-1}(X)$ is a submanifold of X. The codimension of $f^{-1}(Z)$ in X is equal to the codimension of Z in Y.*

If $Z = \{y\}$, to say that f is transverse to $\{y\}$ means that y is a regular value of f. A special case of transversality, which is easily interpreted geometrically and is important for applications, is obtained when f is an embedding. Therefore, let X and Z be two submanifolds of Y. We say that X and Z are transverse if for every $x \in X \cap Z$, we have $T_x X + T_x Z = T_x Y$, which is denoted by $X \pitchfork Z$.

(Math 1.9) *If X and Z are two transverse submanifolds of Y, then $X \cap Z$ is a submanifold of Y. Furthermore, we have*

$$\text{codim}(X \cap Z) = \text{codim}\, X + \text{codim}\, Z.$$

It should be noted that the transversality concept is in fact a "globalization," i.e., an extension to the setting of manifolds of the notion of regular value.

References. One of the best references for the implicit function theorem that underlies this whole section is to be found in Dieudonné [16, Chapter X]. There exist many good references about manifolds. Milnor's [29] short book could be used in a first approach to the theory. Guillemin and Pollack [19] merely expands on Milnor by providing a few more details. The abstract end of the spectrum is covered by Lang [25] and Dieudonné [17]. The latter reference is also useful for other topics related to manifolds, such as fiber bundles, Grassmannians, and homotopy theory. Enjoyable accounts of singularity and transversality theory can be found in the books by Golubitsky and Guillemin [18], Arnold [44], Arnold, Gusein-Zade and Varchenko [3] and Doubrovine, Novikov and Fomenko [61] and [62]; these latter authors are emphasizing geometrical intuition.

2.1. Degree Theory and Homotopy

2.1.1. Proper mappings and one-point compactifications

Let X and Y be locally compact topological spaces. A continuous mapping $f : X \to Y$ is proper if the inverse image of every compact set is compact. If X is compact, then all mappings $f : X \to Y$ are proper. In fact, properness retains most properties associated with compactness. This can be seen rigorously by using one-point, or Alexandroff, compactifications: $\tilde{X}$ and $\tilde{Y}$ are derived from X and Y by adding in a suitable way a point at infinity; one often writes $\tilde{X} = X \cup \{\infty_x\}$ and $\tilde{Y} = Y \cup \{\infty_y\}$. These spaces are naturally equipped with a topology that makes them compact. For a reference on these compactification techniques, see, e.g., Bourbaki [54].

(**Math 2.1**) *The continuous mapping $f : X \to Y$ is proper if and only if f can be extended by continuity to a mapping $\tilde{f} : \tilde{X} \to \tilde{Y}$ where $\tilde{f}(\infty_x) = \infty_y$.*

Another useful implication of properness is the following property: The image of any closed set by a proper mapping is closed. Degree theory deals with proper mappings and homotopy, hence the next section.

2.1.2. Homotopy, smooth homotopy and proper homotopy

Let X and Y be two topological spaces. Let f and g be two continuous mappings from X into Y. We say that f and g are homotopic if there exists a continuous mapping $F : X \times [0,1] \to Y$ with $F(x,0) = f(x)$

and $F(x, 1) = g(x)$ for every $x \in X$. The mapping F is called a homotopy between f and g.

Let X and Y be two smooth manifolds and let f and g be two smooth mappings from X into Y. We say that f and g are smoothly homotopic if there exists a smooth mapping $F : X \times [0, 1] \to Y$ with $F(x, 0) = f(x)$ and $F(x, 1) = g(x)$ for every $x \in X$. We call F a smooth homotopy between f and g. Homotopy and smooth homotopy are closely related equivalence relations.

(Math 2.2) *Let X and Y be two smooth manifolds, with X compact. Let $f : X \to Y$ continuous. If d is a distance defining the topology on Y, there exists $\epsilon > 0$ such that every continuous mapping $g : X \to Y$ satisfying $d(f(x), g(x)) \le \epsilon$ for every $x \in X$ is homotopic to f. Furthermore, if f and g are both smooth, then f and g are smoothly homotopic.*

This formulates the idea that two mappings that are close enough are homotopic. Combined with the following approximation theorem which is interesting for its own sake, we are going to see that homotopy can be safely restricted to smooth homotopy (when X is compact).

(Math 2.3) *Let X and Y be two smooth manifolds with X compact. Let $f : X \to Y$ be a continuous mapping. For any distance d defining the topology of Y and any $\epsilon > 0$, there exists a smooth mapping $g : X \to Y$ with $d(f(x), g(x)) \le \epsilon$ for every $x \in X$.*

This approximation property has to be combined with:

(Math 2.4) *Let X and Y be two smooth manifolds, with X compact. Let f and g be two smooth mappings from X into Y. If f and g are (continuously) homotopic, then they are smoothly homotopic.*

Since we are mostly interested in non-compact X, we extend properness to homotopy:

(Math 2.5) *Let X and Y be two smooth manifolds. Let f and g be two smooth proper mappings from X into Y. We say that f and g are (smoothly) properly homotopic if there exists a smooth proper mapping $F : X \times [0, 1] \to Y$ with $F(x, 0) = f(x)$ and $F(x, 1) = g(x)$*

for every $x \in X$. *We call* F *a* (*smooth*) *proper homotopy between* f *and* g.

Like homotopy and smooth homotopy, smooth proper homotopy is an equivalence relation.

2.1.3. The modulo 2 degree

(**Math 2.6**) *Let* X *and* Y *be smooth manifolds of equal dimension. Let* $f : X \to Y$ *be a smooth proper mapping and* $y \in Y$ *a regular value of* f. *Then* $f^{-\ell}(y)$ *is a finite set.*

Proof. The set $f^{-1}(y)$ is compact as the inverse image of the compact set $\{y\}$ by the proper mapping f. By the regular value theorem (Math 1.6), $f^{-1}(y)$ is a dimension 0 submanifold of X, i.e., a discrete set (every point of X is an open set). Therefore, $f^{-1}(y)$ is a discrete and compact set. Its elements define an open covering of the set $f^{-1}(y)$, which therefore admits a finite subcovering, hence $f^{-1}(y)$ is finite. □

(**Math 2.7**) *Let* X *and* Y *be smooth manifolds with the same dimension. Let* $f : X \to Y$ *be a smooth proper mapping. Assume also that* Y *is connected. Then, if* y *and* z *are two regular values of* f, *we have*

$$\#f^{-1}(y) \equiv \#f^{-1}(z) \quad \text{modulo 2}.$$

The congruence class $\deg_2(f)$ associated with the mapping f is, by definition, the modulo 2 degree of f. This enables one to associate with every smooth proper mapping $f : X \to Y$ the congruence class $\deg_2(f)$ that is known as the modulo 2 degree of f.

2.1.4. The Brouwer degree

We define first the orientation of $\mathbb{R}^n$. We say that two bases $(b_1, \ldots, b_n)$ and $(b', \ldots, b'_n)$ of $\mathbb{R}^n$ have the same *orientation* if the matrix of $(b'_1, \ldots, b'_n)$ expressed in the basis $(b_1, \ldots, b_n)$ has a positive determinant. If this determinant is negative, these bases have opposite orientations.

Every vector space possesses two orientations. The natural orientation of $\mathbb{R}^n$ is the one defined by the base $(1, 0, \ldots, 0)$, $(0, 1, 0, \ldots, 0), \ldots, (0, \ldots, 0, 1)$. An *oriented* manifold is a smooth manifold X equipped with the choice of an orientation for each tangent space $T_x X$.

(Math 2.8) *If the manifold X is connected and orientable, then X has exactly two possible orientations.*

Let X and Y be oriented manifolds. Let $f : X \to Y$ be smooth and proper. Let $x \in X$ be a regular point of f. Then $T_x f : T_x X \to T_{f(x)} Y$ is a linear isomorphism between oriented vector spaces. The sign of $T_x f$ is by definition equal to $+1$ or to -1 depending on the fact that $T_x f$ conserves or changes the orientation.

For every regular value $y \in Y$, we define

$$\deg(f, y) = \sum_{x \in f^{-1}(y)} \operatorname{sign} T_x f.$$

(Math 2.9) *Let X and Y be smooth manifolds with the same dimension. Let $f : X \to Y$ be a smooth proper mapping. Assume also that Y is connected. Then, if y and z are regular values of f, we have*

$$\deg(f, y) = \deg(f, z).$$

This integer does not depend on the choice of the regular value y. We denote it by $\deg(f)$ and call it the Brouwer degree or more simply the degree of f.

2.1.5. A sufficient condition for surjectivity

(Math 2.10) *Let X and Y be smooth manifolds with the same dimension and where Y is connected. Let $f : X \to Y$ be a smooth proper mapping. Then either condition is sufficient for f to be onto:*

$$\deg_2(f) \neq 0,$$
$$\deg(f) \neq 0.$$

Proof. Assume the contrary, i.e., there exists $y \in Y$ with $y \notin f(X)$. Then y cannot be the image of a critical point, hence it is not a singular value, and consequently it is a regular value. Since $f^{-1}(y)$ is the empty set by assumption, this implies $\deg_2(f) = 0$ and $\deg(f) = 0$. $\qquad\square$

Remark. One easily checks that $\deg_2(f) \neq 0$ implies $\deg(f) \neq 0$. The converse statement is not necessarily true.

The degree as an invariant of the homotopy class

The following statements show that the modulo 2 degree and the Brouwer degree depend only on the proper homotopy class of a mapping defined on a non-compact manifold.

(Math 2.11) *Let f and g be two properly homotopic (smooth) mappings from X into Y, with $\dim X = \dim Y$. Then we have*

$$\deg_2(f) = \deg_2(g).$$

(Math 2.12) *Under the same assumptions as in (Math 2.11), but X and Y being oriented, we have $\deg(f) = \deg(g)$.*

The two concepts of degree have their origin in attempts at counting the number of solutions of the equation $f(x) = y$. Consider, for example, polynomial equations defined on the set of complex numbers. The number of solutions is equal to the degree of the polynomial, and therefore is invariant if the coefficients of the polynomial are varied, with the degree remaining constant. The degree concepts are the remnants of this invariance property.

Therefore, the degree concepts can be viewed as crude measures of the number of solutions of the equation $f(x) = y$. Their invariance is precious because it enables one to compute their value by reducing the study of the equation $f(x) = y$ to a simpler equation, $g(x) = y$, provided g is homotopic to f. Also note that the invariance property combined with (Math 2.2) and (Math 2.3) enables one to define degree concepts for mappings that are merely continuous (and of course proper if X is non-compact).

References. Milnor [29] is one of the best references for the degree concepts. Although formulated for a compact manifold X, his definitions and proofs carry over straightforwardly to a non-compact smooth manifold X provided the mappings are proper. For homotopy and approximations, we find Dieudonné [17] truly valuable. See especially his Chapter 16, Sections 25 and 26.

3.1. Fibrations and Coverings

3.1.1. Fibrations

A fibration is a triple (X, B, p) where X and B are smooth manifolds, p is a smooth mapping from X into B that is *onto* and satisfies the following condition known as *local triviality*:

For every $b \in B$, there exists an open neighborhood U of b in B, a smooth manifold F and a diffeomorphism $\phi : U \times F \to p^{-1}(U)$ which satisfies the relation,

$$p(\phi(y, t)) = y \quad \text{for every } y \in U \quad \text{and} \quad t \in F.$$

We say that X is the fiber space, B its base, p the projection. For every $b \in B$, the set $p^{-1}(b) = X_b$ is a *closed submanifold* of X called the fiber of b. There exists a neighborhood U of b such that $X_{b'}$ is diffeomorphic to X_b for every $b' \in U$.

Let (X, B, π) and (X', B', π') be two fibrations. A morphism between these two fibrations is a pair (f, g) where $f : B \to B', g : X \to X'$ are smooth mappings that satisfy the relation,

$$\pi' \circ g = f \circ \pi.$$

Let B and F be two smooth manifolds, let pr_1 be the projection $B \times F \to B$. Then, the triple $(B \times F, B, \mathrm{pr}_1)$ is a fibration, called the *trivial fibration*. Every fiber is then diffeomorphic to F. We say that a fibration $\lambda = (X, B, p)$ is *trivializable* if there exists an isomorphism between λ and some trivial fibration $(B \times F, B, \mathrm{pr}_1)$. Such an isomorphism is called a *trivialization* of λ.

The condition for being locally trivial in the definition of a fibration means that every $b \in B$ has an open neighborhood U of

B such that the fibration induced by λ on U is trivializable. One also says that λ is trivializable over U.

3.1.2. Coverings

A covering of B is a fiber bundle X with base B such that the fibers are discrete. The projection $\pi : X \to B$ is then a local diffeomorphism (which is onto).

(Math 3.1) *The triple* (X, B, π) *is a covering of the manifold B if X is a manifold and π a smooth surjective mapping satisfying the following condition:*

For every $b \in B$, *there exists an open neighborhood U of b in B such that $\pi^{-1}(U)$ is the union of the sequence (finite or infinite) (V_n) of pairwise disjoint open subsets of X such that the restriction $\pi_n : V_n \to U$ of π to each V_n is a diffeomorphism with U.*

A covering where every fiber is finite and made of n elements is called an n-sheet covering.

(Math 3.2) *A sufficient condition for the triple* (X, B, π) *to be a covering of B with finite fibers is that the projection $\pi : X \to B$ is a proper local diffeomorphism.*

If B is connected, the number of elements in a fiber is then constant, which implies:

(Math 3.3) *Every covering of a connected and simply connected manifold is a product bundle.*

This implies that if X is a covering of B with n sheets, there are at most n connected components for X.

3.1.3. Vector bundles

Let $\lambda = (E, B, \pi)$ be a fiber bundle such that, for every $b \in B$, the fiber $E_b = \pi^{-1}(b)$ is equipped with the structure of a real finite dimension vector space. We say that $\lambda = (E, B, \pi)$ is a real vector bundle if it satisfies the following condition:

For every $b \in B$, there exists an open neighborhood U of b in B, a real vector space F with finite dimension, and a diffeomorphism,

$$\phi : U \times F \to \pi^{-1}(U),$$

where $\pi(\phi(y, t)) = y$ for every $y \in U$ and every $t \in F$, the mapping,

$$\phi(y, \cdot) : F \to E_y,$$

from F into the fiber E_y being an isomorphism (for the vector space structure of F and E_y).

Let $\lambda = (E, B, \pi)$ and $\lambda' = (E', B', \pi')$ be two real vector bundles. A morphism from λ into λ' is a morphism (f, g) such that, for every $b \in B$, the restriction g_b of g to E_b is a linear mapping from E_b into $E'_{f(b)}$.

3.1.4. Tangent bundle to a manifold

The disjoint union $TX = \bigcup_{x \in X} T_x X$ of the tangent spaces to the manifold X is naturally equipped with the structure of a smooth manifold. The manifold TX is often called the tangent bundle to the manifold X. It defines a vector bundle with the following features:

— the projection $\pi : TX \to X$ associates with the "tangent" vector ξ to x the point $\pi(\xi)$ where this vector is tangent to X;
— let $i(x)$ denote the zero vector of $T_x X$. This defines a cross-section $i : X \to TX$ called the null section;
— the fibers of (TX, X, p) are simply the tangent spaces $T_x X$ where x varies in the manifold X, the base of the bundle.

Let $f : X \to Y$ be a smooth mapping. This mapping defines a linear mapping $T_x f : T_x X \to T_{f(x)} Y$. Let x vary in X. This formula defines a smooth mapping,

$$Tf : TX \to TY,$$

hence a mapping denoted f_* from the tangent bundle to X into the tangent bundle to Y. This mapping sends a fiber of TX into a fiber of TY.

References. The concepts of fiber spaces and coverings play major roles in non-linear mathematics. We mention for references Dieudonné [17, Chapter 16, Sections 12–19]. Steenrod [87] and Husemoller [68] are appropriate for further readings. Doubrovine, Novikov and Fomenko [62] can also be recommended.

4.1. More About Manifolds

4.1.1. Grassmann manifolds

We often have to consider families of linear subspaces in a vector space. This justifies our interest for the concept of Grassmann manifold.

We denote by $G_{n.p}$ the set of vector subspaces of dimension p in the vector space $\mathbb{R}^n$. One shows that there exists a unique structure of a smooth manifold on $G_{n,p}$ on which the orthogonal group $0(n, \mathbb{R})$ operates smoothly. Equipped with this structure, one says that $G_{n,p}$ is the (real) Grassmann manifold of indices n, p. Thus, for $p = 1, G_{n,1}$ is identical to $\mathbb{P}_{n-1}$, the real projective space of dimension $n - 1$. The manifold $G_{n,p}$ can also be considered as the set of spheres of center 0 and dimension $p - 1$ contained in the sphere S_{n-1}, these spheres being in continuous bijection with the dimension p vector subspaces of $\mathbb{R}^n$.

(Math 4.1) *The Grassmann manifold $G_{n,p}$ is diffeomorphic to the quotient space* $0(n, \mathbb{R})/0(p, \mathbb{R}) \times 0(n - p, \mathbb{R})$.

(Math 4.2) *The Grassmann manifold $G_{n,p}$ is a compact connected manifold whenever $n \geq 1$ and $1 \leq p \leq n$. Its dimension is equal to* $p(n - p)$.

Reference. Dieudonné [17, Chapter 16, Section 11].

4.1.2. Properly embedded manifolds relative to a family of linear manifolds

Let X be a dimension s submanifold of $\mathbb{R}^{s+t}$. This manifold may not be compact, which usually complicates the study of the intersection of X with the submanifolds of $\mathbb{R}^{s+t}$. Nevertheless, it is possible to retain most properties resulting from compactness by formulating them as properties of a suitable mapping. Then, one can often substitute properness of this mapping for the compactness of X. This is the line we follow in the use we make in this book of intersection theory.

In the Euclidean space $\mathbb{R}^{s+t}$, we consider the set $\mathcal{A}$ of linear submanifolds of $\mathbb{R}^{s+t}$ having dimension t and not perpendicular to $\mathbb{R}^s \times (0)$. The set $\mathcal{A}$ is open dense in the set $\mathcal{A}^t$, the elements of which are the dimension t linear submanifolds of $\mathbb{R}^{s+t}$, a set which can be identified with an open dense subset of the Grassmann manifold $G_{s+t+1,t+1}$.

Let $\mathcal{X}$ be the submanifold of $X \times \mathcal{A}$ consisting of the pairs $(x, A) \in X \times \mathcal{A}$ and satisfying the relationship $x \in A$. We denote by $\pi : \mathcal{X} \times \mathcal{A}$ the restriction of the natural projection $(x, A) \to A$ to the submanifold $\mathcal{X}$ of $X \times \mathcal{A}$. We say that the manifold X is properly embedded in $\mathbb{R}^{s+t}$ relative to $\mathcal{A}$ if the mapping $\pi : \mathcal{X} \to \mathcal{A}$ is proper.

(Math 4.3) *Let X and X' be two dimension s submanifolds properly embedded in $\mathbb{R}^{s+t}$ relative to $\mathcal{A}$ (as just defined) and not contained in an element of $\mathcal{A}$. If, for every $A \in \mathcal{A}$, the number of intersection points $\#(X \cap A)$ and $\#(X' \cap A)$ are equal, then the manifolds X and X' are identical.*

References. Balasko [49], appendix; for special cases of this statement, see Sulanke [89] and Steinhaus [88].

4.1.3. The Whitney topology

It is not always possible to consider only finite dimensional spaces which have the advantage, from a topological point of view, of having equivalent norms. For spaces of smooth mappings between manifolds, one often uses the C^∞-Whitney topology. Note that for $X = \mathbb{R}^p$, and more generally for X, a non-compact manifold, the topology of uniform convergence or of uniform convergence on every compact subset, which have been somewhat popular, are not really convenient for the reason that the behavior at infinity of the limit of a sequence of functions is not kept well-enough under control by the behavior at infinity of the mappings belonging to the sequence under consideration.

One starts by defining the C^k-topology for any finite integer k. We say that the sequence $f_n : \mathbb{R}^p \to \mathbb{R}^q$ tends to f for the C^k-topology if

— outside a compact set $K \subset \mathbb{R}^p$ and for n large enough, all the f_n are equal (and equal to f);
— on K, all the partial derivatives of f_n up to the order k uniformly converge to the corresponding derivatives of f.

The Whitney C^∞-topology on $C^\infty(\mathbb{R}^p, \mathbb{R}^q)$ (the set of smooth mappings from $\mathbb{R}^p$ into $\mathbb{R}^q$) is the topology generated by all the C^k-topologies. This definition of the Whitney C^∞-topology for mappings from $\mathbb{R}^p$ into $\mathbb{R}^q$ suffices for our purposes. Note, however, that this definition easily extends to sets of smooth mappings defined on an arbitrary smooth manifold X and taking their values in a arbitrary smooth manifold Y.

The Whitney C^∞-topology is indeed an extremely "fine" topology (this means that many sets are open for this topology) because of the exceptionally strong assumptions on convergence at infinity. It is therefore quite remarkable that, despite its fineness, the set $C^\infty(\mathbb{R}^p, \mathbb{R}^q)$ equipped with this topology is a *Baire space*, i.e., a topological space that satisfies the property that the countable intersection of open dense sets is still dense (but, of course, not necessarily open). Such intersection sets are called residual. In other words, residual sets are dense in Baire spaces. Intuitively, they provide one of the most convenient topological formulations of the notion of a "large" or "big" subset.

The next properties of the Whitney C^∞-topology are used in one form or another in this book.

(Math 4.4) *The product $C^\infty(\mathbb{R}^p, \mathbb{R}^q) \times C^\infty(\mathbb{R}^p, \mathbb{R}^r)$ is homeomorphic to $C^\infty(\mathbb{R}^p, \mathbb{R}^q \times \mathbb{R}^r)$ through the canonical identification $(f, g) \to f \times g$ where $(f \times g)(x) = (f(x), g(x))$.*

(Math 4.5) *The composition* $(f, g) \rightarrow g \circ f$ *defines a mapping from* $C^{\infty}(\mathbb{R}^p, \mathbb{R}^q) \times C^{\infty}(\mathbb{R}^q, \mathbb{R}^r)$ *into* $C^{\infty}(\mathbb{R}^p, \mathbb{R}^r)$, *which is continuous at* (f^*, g^*) *if the mapping* f^* *is proper. The mapping* $f \rightarrow g^* \circ f$ *is continuous for every* g^* *and the mapping* $g \rightarrow g \circ f^*$ *is continuous if* f^* *is proper.*

(Math 4.6) *The set* $\mathrm{Diff}(\mathbb{R}^p)$ *of diffeomorphisms of* $\mathbb{R}^p$ *is a topological group for the composition of mappings. As a consequence, the mappings* $a \rightarrow a^{-1}$ *where* $a \in \mathrm{Diff}(\mathbb{R}^p)$ *is continuous. Furthermore,* $\mathrm{Diff}(\mathbb{R}^p)$ *is open in* $C^{\infty}(R^p, \mathbb{R}^q)$.

These properties evidently extend to arbitrary manifolds X, Y and Z.

References. Golubitsky and Guillemin [18, Chapter 2, Section 3]. See Mather [78] for interesting complements.

5.1. Envelope Theory

We use the same notation as in Chapter 8. Consider the family of submanifolds $V(b)$ of $\Omega(r)$ parameterized by $b \in H(r)$. The graph of this correspondence which associates $V(b)$ with b is denoted by G.

The graph G is a submanifold of $H(r) \times \Omega(r)$. The restriction $\Phi : G \rightarrow H(r)$ of the projection $H(r) \times \Omega(r) \rightarrow H(r)$ is a submersion.

Let $\bar{E}(r) = \Phi^{-1}(B(r))$ be the inverse image by Φ of the set of parameters $B(r)$, a subset of $H(r)$. The *source envelope* of the family $\mathfrak{F}$ parameterized by $B(r)$ is the set of critical points of the mapping $\bar{\pi} : \bar{E}(r) \rightarrow \Omega(r)$ defined as the restriction of the projection $H(r) \times \Omega(r)$ to $\bar{E}(r)$. The *envelope* is the set of singular values of this same mapping $\bar{\pi}$.

The point $x \in V(b)$ is said to be *characteristic* if $(b, x) \in \bar{E}(r)$ is a critical point of the mapping $\bar{\pi}$.

The *envelope* is by definition a geometric envelope if, according to Thom, the following two conditions are satisfied:

— the subset consisting of $b \in H(r)$ such that $V(b)$ possesses a characteristic point is open in $B(r)$;
— at every regular point of the envelope, the manifold $V(b)$ is not transverse to the tangent space.

Let dim $\Omega(r) = \alpha$, dim $V(b) = \beta$, codim $V(b) = \alpha - \beta = \gamma$, dim $B(r) = \delta$. Then, we have the following:

(Math 5.1) *The envelope is a geometric envelope if and only if the following inequalities are satisfied:*

$$\gamma - \beta + 1 \le \delta \le \gamma + \beta - 1.$$

Remark. Let us apply these conditions to the setting of Chapter 8: $\alpha = \ell(m-1)$; $\beta = (\ell-1)(m-1)$; $\gamma = m-1$; $\delta = m-1$. They become $(m-1) - [(\ell-1)(m-1) - 1] \le m-1 \le m-1 + [(\ell-1)(m-1) - 1]$. These inequalities are clearly satisfied for $l \ge 2$ and $m \ge 2$.

For the special case of envelopes of projective lines in the plane, one gets:

(Math 5.2) *Given a generic one-parameter family of projective lines in the plane, every line of the family has a unique characteristic point (there is no stationary line). The only singularities of the envelope curve (or envelope) are ordinary cusps and double intersections with distinct tangents. At every regular point, the envelope curve is locally convex. Furthermore, the envelope is connected.*

References. For the abstract general theory of envelopes, the most exhaustive reference remains Thom [91] despite serious shortcomings. For a more elementary (but partial) approach to envelope theory using singularity theory (i.e., from the modern point of view), see Bruce and Giblin [55]. For complements on the global properties of envelopes in a relatively traditional setting, see, e.g., Sasaki [84].

6.1. Convexity and Differentiability: Applications to Strictly Quasi-Concave Utility Functions

Convexity theory is primarily concerned with convex sets, convex and concave functions, quasi-convex and quasi-concave functions. Properties associated with convexity play a crucial role in optimization problems. Very often, some form of convexity can advantageously be substituted for differentiability in the study of maxima and minima. This is also true of general equilibrium theory where the problem of the existence of equilibria can be solved and their efficiency property established, without the need for differentiability assumptions, provided there is enough convexity (see, e.g., Debreu [12]). Rockaffellar's [82] book offers a fairly extensive coverage of high-brow convex analysis. But this mathematically advanced theory is not necessary when convexity is mixed up with differentiability. The differentiability assumption considerably simplifies the analysis of maxima and minima in the presence of convexity. This topic, which is usually dealt with in courses on non-linear programming, is usually neglected in pure mathematics courses. Therefore, to simplify the task of readers without any background in non-linear programming, I have included in this section the proofs of all the results that are needed in order to follow the developments of consumer theory made in Chapter 4.

References. Mangasarian [73] is highly recommendable for the mathematical aspects of non-linear programming. The appendices in Hicks [64] and Samuelson [83] relate the above material to consumer theory.

6.1.1. Convex and strictly convex sets

A subset X of $\mathbb{R}^n$ is *convex* if for every pair of points a and b in X, the segment $[a, b] = \{(1 - t)a + tb \mid t \in [0, 1]\}$ is contained in X.

The linear manifold $L(X)$ generated by the convex set X is the smallest linear submanifold of $\mathbb{R}^n$ that contains X. The dimension of a convex set X is the dimension of the linear manifold $L(X)$. The *relative interior* $\overset{\circ}{X}$ of the convex set X is the interior of X for the topology of $L(X)$.

The convex set X is *strictly convex* if for every pair of points a and b in X, the interior of the segment $[a, b]$ is contained in the relative interior $\overset{\circ}{X}$ of the convex set X.

Remark. Convexity enters consumer theory with the assumption that the set $\{x \in \mathbb{R}^\ell \mid u_i(x) \geq u_i^*\}$ is (strictly) convex for every $u_i^* \in \mathbb{R}$. This can be described as a property of the utility function u_i but this requires extending the concepts of convexity to functions.

6.1.2. Convex, concave, quasi-convex, ..., functions

Let $X \subset \mathbb{R}^n$ be convex. The function $u : X \to \mathbb{R}$ is *convex* if the inequality,

$$u((1-t)x + ty) \leq (1-t)u(x) + tu(y),$$

is true for every x and y in X and $t \in [0,1]$. In fact, u is convex if and only if the set

$$X_u = \{(x, \alpha) | u(x) \leq \alpha \text{ and } x \in X\},$$

is a convex subset of $\mathbb{R}^n \times \mathbb{R}$. The real-valued function u is *strictly convex* if the inequality

$$u((1-t)x + ty) < (1-t)u(x) + tu(y),$$

is true for every x and every y belonging to X and for every t belonging to the open interval $(0, 1)$. In fact, u is strictly convex if and only if X_u is a strictly convex subset of $\mathbb{R}^n \times \mathbb{R}$.

The function u is quasi-convex (resp. strictly quasi-convex) if the set $X_u(\alpha) = \{x \in X | u(x) \leq \alpha\}$ is convex (resp. strictly convex) for every $\alpha \in \mathbb{R}$.

The function u is concave (resp. strictly concave, quasi-concave, strictly quasi-concave) if the function $-u$ is convex (resp. strictly convex, quasi-convex, strictly quasi-convex).

6.1.3. Strict quasi-concavity and differentiability

Because we are mostly interested in strictly quasi-concave utility functions, the following results will be aimed only at this case. They evidently could be extended to more general settings.

Therefore, from now on, we consider a twice continuously differentiable function,

$$u : \mathbb{R}^n \to \mathbb{R}.$$

Furthermore, we assume that u has no critical point.

Let us consider the set $Y_u(\alpha) = \{x \in \mathbb{R}^n | \alpha \leq u(x)\}$. The interior of $Y_u(a)$ is the set

$$\overset{\circ}{Y}_u(\alpha) = \{x \in X | \alpha < u(x)\};$$

the boundary $\partial Y_u(\alpha)$ is the hypersurface $\{x \in \mathbb{R}^n | \alpha = u(x)\}$.

Recall that the function u is strictly quasi-concave if, by definition, the set $Y_u(\alpha)$ is strictly convex for every $\alpha \in \mathbb{R}$.

(Math 6.1) *The function $u : \mathbb{R}^n \to \mathbb{R}$ is strictly quasi-concave if and only if for any x_1 and $x_2 \in \mathbb{R}^n$, $x_1 \neq x_2$, $u(x_1) \leq u(x_2)$ and $t \in (0,1)$, one has*

$$u(x_1) < u[(1-t)x_1 + tx_2].$$

Proof. Necessary condition. Assume that u is strictly quasi-concave. Take $x_1, x_2 \in \mathbb{R}^n$, $x_1 \neq x_2$, $u(x_1) \leq u(x_2)$, and let $t \in (0,1)$. Define $\alpha = u(x_1)$. The set $Y_u(\alpha) = \{x \in \mathbb{R}^n | \alpha \leq u(x)\}$ contains x_1 and x_2. Its strict convexity implies

$$(1-t)x_1 + tx_2 \in Y_u(\alpha);$$

therefore, we have

$$\alpha = u(x_1) < u[(1-t)x_1 + tx_2].$$

Sufficient condition. We have to establish that the set $Y_u(\alpha)$ is strictly convex for every $\alpha \in \mathbb{R}$. Take x_1 and x_2 in $Y_u(\alpha), x_1 \neq x_2$. We can assume, without loss of generality, that we have

$$\alpha \leq u(x_1) \leq u(x_2).$$

For $t \in (0,1)$, this implies

$$\alpha \leq u(x_1) < u[(1-t)x_1 + tx_2],$$

which means that $(1-t)x_1 + tx_2$ belongs to the interior $\overset{\circ}{Y}_u(\alpha)$ of the set $Y_u(\alpha)$, which is therefore strictly convex.   □

(Math 6.2) *The function $u : \mathbb{R}^n \to \mathbb{R}$ is strictly quasi-concave if and only if for any x_1 and $x_2 \in \mathbb{R}^n$, $x_1 \neq x_2$, $u(x_1) \leq u(x_2)$, one has*

$$Du(x_1) \cdot (x_2 - x_1) > 0.$$

Proof. Necessary condition. Define $h = x_2 - x_1$, and consider the function of $t \in [0, 1]$ defined by the formula,

$$u((1-t)x_1 + tx_2)) = u(x_1 + th).$$

By (Math 6.1.1), we have

(Math 6.2.2) $\qquad u(x_1) < u(x_1 + th), \quad 0 < t < 1.$

$\square$

(Math 6.3) *Let* $u: \mathbb{R}^n \to \mathbb{R}$ *be quasi-concave. The restriction of the quadratic form* ${}^t h \cdot D^2 u(x) \cdot h$ *to the hyperplane* $Du(x) \cdot h = 0$ *is negative semi-definite for every* $x \in \mathbb{R}^n$.

We recall that $D^2 u(x)$ denotes the Hessian matrix of u. Then, the vector $h \in \mathbb{R}^n$ is identified and written as a column vector.

Proof. The assumption $Du(x) \cdot th = 0$ combined with (Math 6.2) implies that, necessarily, we have $u(x + th) < u(x), t \neq 0$. Therefore, the function of t defined by $u(x + th)$ has an absolute maximum at $t = 0$. This implies that its second derivative is negative, or, equivalently, ${}^t h \cdot D^2 u(x) \cdot h \leq 0$.

$\square$

We conclude with the following statements:

(Math 6.4) *Let* $u: \mathbb{R}^n \to \mathbb{R}$. *If the restriction of the quadratic form* ${}^t h \cdot D^2 u(x) \cdot h$ *to the hyperplane* $Du(x) \cdot h = 0$ *is negative definite for every* $x \in \mathbb{R}^n$, *then* u *is strictly quasi-concave.*

(Math 6.5) *Under the assumption of* (Math 6.4), *the bordered Hessian matrix*

$$\begin{bmatrix} \dfrac{\partial^2 u(x)}{\partial x^j \partial x^k} & \dfrac{\partial u(x)}{\partial x^j} \\ \dfrac{\partial u(x)}{\partial x^k} & 0 \end{bmatrix},$$

has a non-zero determinant.

This is, in fact, a property of linear algebra about the characterization of the (negative) definiteness of quadratic forms restricted to specified linear subspaces. For an elementary proof of this statements, see, e.g., Hicks [64]. A more general treatment in the linear algebra framework is offered by Mann [74].

Remark. The condition for the restriction of the quadratic form defined by the bordered Hessian matrix to the tangent plane to the indifference surface to be *negative-definite* can be interpreted from a geometric point of view as the non-vanishing of the Gaussian curvature of the indifference surface at this point. For a proof in the context of indifference surfaces, see Debreu [14].

Bibliography

1. R. Abraham and J. Robin. *Transversal Mappings and Flows*. Benjamin, New York, 1967.
2. V. Arnold. *Catastrophe Theory*. 3rd edition, Springer, Heidelberg, 1992.
3. V. Arnold, S. Gusein-Zade and A. Varchenko. *Singularities of Differentiable Maps*, Vol. I. Birkhäuser, Boston, 1985.
4. K. Arrow and G. Debreu. Existence of an equilibrium for a competitive economy. *Econometrica*, 22:265–290, 1954.
5. R. Auspitz and R. Lieben. *Untersuchung über die Theorie des Preises*. Duncker und Humblot, Leipzig, 1889.
6. R. Auspitz and R. Lieben. Die mehrfachen Schnittpunkte zwischen der Angebots- und der Nachfragekurve. *Zeitschrift für Volkswirtschaft, Sozialpolitik und Verwaltung*, 17:607–616, 1908.
7. Y. Balasko. The graph of the Walras correspondence. *Econometrica*, 43:907–912, 1975.
8. Y. Balasko. Some results on uniqueness and on stability of equilibrium in general equilibrium theory. *Journal of Mathematical Economics*, 2:95–118, 1975.
9. Y. Balasko. Connectedness of the set of stable equilibria. *SIAM Journal of Applied Mathematics*, 35:722–728, 1978.
10. Y. Balasko. Wealth concerns and equilibrium. *Journal of Mathematical Economics*, 59:92–101, 2015.
11. A. Bowley. *The Mathematical Groundwork of Economics*. Augustus M. Kelley, New York, 1965.
12. G. Debreu. *Theory of Value*. Wiley, New York, 1959.
13. G. Debreu. Economies with a finite set of equilibria. *Econometrica*, 38:387–392, 1970.
14. G. Debreu. Smooth preferences. *Econometrica*, 40:603–615, 1972.
15. F. Delbaen. *Lower and upper hemi-continuity of the Walras correspondence*. PhD Thesis, Free University of Brussels, 1971.

16. J. Dieudonné. *Foundations of Modern Analysis*. Academic Press, New York, 1960.

17. J. Dieudonné. *Treatise on Analysis*, Vol. 3. Academic Press, New York, 1973.

18. M. Golubitsky and V. Guillemin. *Stable Mappings and their Singularities*. Springer-Verlag, New York, 1973.

19. V. Guillemin and A. Pollack. *Differential Topology*. Prentice-Hall, Englewood Cliffs, 1974.

20. M. Hirsch. *Differential Topology*. Springer-Verlag, New York, 1976.

21. R. Horn and C. Johnson. *Matrix Analysis*. Cambridge University Press, Cambridge, 1985.

22. H. Houthakker. Revealed preference and the utility function. *Economica*, 17:159–174, 1950.

23. W. Jaffe (ed.). *Correspondence of Léon Walras and Related Papers*, Vol. 3. North-Holland, Amsterdam, 1965.

24. W. Jevons. *The Theory of Political Economy*. Macmillan, London, 1871.

25. S. Lang. *An introduction to Differentiable Manifolds*. Interscience, New York, 1962.

26. L. McKenzie. On equilibrium in Graham's model of world trade and other competitive systems. *Econometrica*, 22:147–161, 1954.

27. G. Meigniez. Submersions, fibrations and bundles. *Transactions of the American Mathematical Society*, 354:3771–3787, 2002.

28. J. Milnor. *Morse Theory*. Princeton University Press, Princeton, 1963.

29. J. Milnor. *Topology from the Differentiable Viewpoint*. 2nd edition, Princeton University Press, Princeton, 1997.

30. L. Narens. *Abstract Measurement Theory*. MIT Press, Cambridge, MA., 1985.

31. V. Pareto. *Manuale di Economia Politica con una Introduzione alla scienza sociale*. Societa Editrice Libraria, Milano, 1906.

32. W. Rudin. *Real and Complex Analysis*. McGraw-Hill, New York, 1966.

33. J. Schumpeter. *History of Economic Analysis*. Allen and Unwin, London, 1954.

34. A. Smith. *An Inquiry into the Nature and Causes of the Wealth of Nations*. W. Strahan and T. Cadell, London, 1776.

35. M. Spivak. *Calculus on Manifolds*. Benjamin, New York, 1965.

36. R. Thom. *Stabilité Structurelle et Morphogénèse*. Benjamin, Reading, MA., 1972.

37. R. Thom. *Structural Stability and Morphogenesis*. Benjamin, Reading, MA., 1975.

38. H. Uzawa. Preference and rational choice in the theory of consumption. In K. Arrow, S. Karlin, and P. Suppes, editors, *Mathematical Methods in the Social Sciences*, Chapter 9, pp. 129–148. Stanford University Press, Stanford, 1960.

39. A. Wald. Über einige gleichungssysteme der mathematischen ökonomie. *Zeitschrift für Nationalökonomie*, 7:637–670, 1936.

40. A. Wald. On some systems of equations of mathematical economics. *Econometrica*, 19:368–403, 1951.

41. L. Walras. *Eléments d'Economie Politique Pure.* 1st edition, Corbaz, Lausanne, 1874.
42. G. B. Antonelli, On the mathematical theory of political economy. (English translation from the original Italian version). In J. S. Chipman, L. Hurwicz, M. K. Richter and M. F. Sonnenschein (eds.), (1971), *Preferences, Utility, and Demand. A Minnesota Symposium.* pp. 333–360, Harcourt Brace Jovanovich, New York, 1886.
43. V. Arnold. *Ordinary Differential Equations.* M.I.T. Press, Cambridge, 1973.
44. V. Arnold. *Catastrophe Theory*, Springer, New York, 1983.
45. K. J. Arrow and F. J. Hahn. *General Competitive Analysis.* Holden Day, San Francisco, 1971.
46. R. J. Aumann. Markets with a continuum of traders. *Econometrica*, 32:39–50, 1964.
47. R. J. Aumann. Existence of competitive equilibria in markets with a continuum of traders. *Econometrica*, 34:1–17, 1966.
48. Y. Balasko. Budget constrained Pareto efficient allocations. *Journal of Economic Theory*, 21:359–379, 1979.
49. Y. Balasko. Number and definiteness of economic equilibria. *Journal of Mathematical Economics*, 7:215–225, 1980.
50. Y. Balasko and K. Shell. The overlapping generations model I: The case of pure exchange without money. *Journal of Economic Theory*, 23:281–306, 1980.
51. Y. Balasko and K. Shell. The overlapping generations model II: The case of pure exchange with money. *Journal of Economic Theory*, 24:112–142, 1981.
52. Y. Balasko, D. Cass and K. Shell. A note on the existence of competitive equilibrium in the overlapping-generations model. *Journal of Economic Theory*, 23:307–322, 1980.
53. E. Barone. The ministry of production in the collectivist state. (English translation from the original Italian version) in F. A. von Hayek, 1935. *Collectivist Economic Planning.* Routledge, London, 1908.
54. N. Bourbaki. *General Topology.* Addison-Wesley, Reading, 1966.
55. J. W. Bruce and P. J. Giblin. *Curves and Singularities.* Cambridge University Press, Cambridge, 1984.
56. D. Cass and K. Shell. Do sunspots matter? *Journal of Political Economy*, 91:193–227, 1983.
57. G. Debreu. Excess demand functions. *Journal of Mathematical Economics*, 1:15–21, 1974.
58. G. Debreu. Economic theory in the mathematical mode. *American Economic Review*, 74:267–278, 1984.
59. G. Debreu and G. Scarf. A limit theorem on the core of an economy. *International Economic Review*, 4:235–246, 1963.
60. E. Dierker. *Topological Methods in Walrasian Economics.* Lecture Notes on Economics and Mathematical Sciences, Vol. 92. Springer, Berlin, 1974.
61. B. Doubrovine, S. Novikov and A. Fomenko. *Modern Geometry. Methods and Applications*, Vol. 1. Springer, New York, 1984.

62. B. Doubrovine, S. Novikov and A. Fomenko. *Modern Geometry. Methods and Applications*, Vol. 2. Springer: New York, 1986.
63. F. R. Grantmacher. *Theory of Matrices*, Vols. 1, 2. Chelsea, New York, 1959.
64. J. R. Hicks. *Value and Capital.* Clarendon Press, Oxford, 1939.
65. N. J. Hicks. *Notes on Differential Geometry.* Van Nostrand, London, 1965.
66. W. Hildenbrand. *Core and Equilibria of a Large Economy.* Princeton University Press, Princeton, 1974.
67. M. Hirsch and S. Smale. *Differential Equations, Dynamical Systems, and Linear Algebra.* Academic Press, New York, 1974.
68. D. Husemoller. *Fibre Bundles.* McGraw Hill, New York, 1966.
69. H. Keiding, Existence of budget constrained Pareto efficient allocations. *Journal of Economic Theory*, 24:393–397, 1981.
70. T. Koopmans. *Three Essays on the State of Economic Science.* McGraw Hill, New York, 1957.
71. O. Lange. The foundations of welfare economics. *Econometrica*, 10:215–228, 1942.
72. L. H. Loomis and S. Sternberg. *Advanced Calculus.* Addison-Wesley, Reading, 1968.
73. O. Mangasarian. *Nonlinear Programming.* McGraw-Hill, New York, 1969.
74. H. B. Mann. Quadratic forms with linear constraints. *American Mathematical Monthly*, 50:430–433, 1943.
75. R. R. Mantel. On the characterization of aggregate excess demands. *Journal of Economic Theory*, 7:348–353, 1974.
76. A. Mas-Colell. Continuous and smooth consumers: Approximation theorems. *Journal of Economic Theory*, 8:305–336, 1974.
77. A. Mas-Colell. *The Theory of General Economic Equilibrium. A Differential Approach.* Cambridge University Press, London, 1985.
78. J. N. Mather. Stability of C^∞-mappings II: Infinitesimal stability implies stability. *Annals of Mathematics*, 89:254–291, 1969.
79. J. N. Mather. Stability of C^∞-mappings VI: The nice dimensions. in *Proceedings of Liverpool Singularities Symposium I*, Lecture Notes in Mathematics, Vol. 192. Springer, Berlin, 1971.
80. V. Pareto. *Manuel d'Economie Politique.* Reprinted in (1966) by Droz, Geneva, 1909.
81. M. Polanyi. *The Great Transformation.* Reprinted in (1957) by Beacon Press, Boston, 1944.
82. R. Rockaffellar. *Convex Analysis.* Princeton University Press, Princeton, 1970.
83. P. A. Samuelson. *Foundations of Economic Analysis.* Harvard University Press, Cambridge, 1947.
84. S. Sasaki. The minimum number of points of inflexion of closed curves in the projective plane. *Tohoku Mathematical Journal*, 9:11–17, 1957.
85. E. Slutsky. Sulla teoria del bilancio del consumatore. *Giornale degli Economisti*, 51:19–23, 1915.

86. H. Sonnenschein. Do Walras identity and continuity characterize the class of community excess demand functions?. *Journal of Economic Theory*, 6:345–354, 1973.

87. N. Steenrod. *The Topology of Fibre Bundles*. Princeton University Press, Princeton, 1951.

88. H. Steinhaus. Length, shape and area. *Colloquium Mathematicum*, III, 1:1–13, 1954.

89. R. Sulanke. Integralgeometrie ebener Kurvennetze. *Acta Mathematica Academiae Scientarium Hungaricae*, 17:233–261, 1966.

90. L. G. Svensson, The existence of budget constrained Pareto-efficient allocations. *Journal of Economic Theory*, 32:346–350, 1984.

91. R. Thom. Sur la théorie des enveloppes. *Journal de Mathématiques Pures et Appliuqées*, 41:177–192, 1962.

92. K. Vind. Edgeworth-allocations in an exchange economy with many traders. *International Economic Review*, 5:165–177, 1964.

93. J. Von Neumann and O. Morgenstern. *Theory of Games and Economic Behavior*. Princeton University Press, Princeton, 1944.

94. L. Walras. *Eléments d'Economie Politique Pure*. Corbaz, Lausanne. English translation of the definitive edition. *Elements of Pure Economics*. Allen and Unwin, London, 1954.

Index

Printed in the United States
By Bookmasters